Conservation and Planning

Conserving historic buildings continues to excite and inflame opinion. The means of protecting such buildings and areas are well established but frequently suffer a lack of wider understanding. *Conservation and Planning* takes a detailed look at the way these processes have evolved and their use today by policy-makers and local decision-makers.

The rise of the urban renaissance agenda, the crystallisation of sustainable development and the ascendancy of regional governance are all significant factors which have influenced the policy and practice of conserving historic buildings. The interpretation of value in the built environment is also significant, with a consideration of buildings as independent artefacts often overshadowing their value in an environmental and cultural context.

Few studies have examined the underlying values used to justify the policies and actions undertaken in the name of conservation. This book presents original research into how national and local decision-makers construct and implement conservation of the built environment. The findings in this book challenge many of the assumptions supporting conservation. They suggest that conservation is marginalised in planning, through professional attitudes, procedural emphases and a lack of strategic support for conservation's added value. The aspirations and attitudes of conservation organisations at a national policy level were surveyed and contrasted with the practical application of conservation policy in two local planning authorities in England. These two case studies were used to examine not only how national policy was interpreted, subject to local considerations, but also how abstract conservation values and concepts fared in their real life application.

Edward Hobson's research interests include the quality of the built environment, public space and urban design, conservation and planning and while at the University of Sheffield he taught on the history and operation of the statutory planning system.

Other titles available from Spon Press and Routledge

Conservation and the City
Peter Larkham

Policy and Law in Heritage Conservation
Edited by Robert Pickard

Management of Historic Centres
Edited by Robert Pickard

Tourists in Historic Towns
Aylin Orbasli

Industrial Buildings:
Conservation and regeneration
Edited by Michael Stratton

For further information and to order from our online catalogue visit our website
at www.sponpress.com

Conservation and Planning

Changing values in policy and practice

Edward Hobson

Spon Press
Taylor & Francis Group

LONDON AND NEW YORK

First published 2004 by Spon Press
11 New Fetter Lane, London EC4P 4EE

Simultaneously published in the USA and Canada
by Spon Press
29 West 35th Street, New York, NY 10001

Spon Press is an imprint of the Taylor & Francis Group

© 2004 Edward Hobson

Typeset in Times and Frutiger by
Florence Production Ltd, Stoodleigh, Devon
Printed and bound in Great Britain by
The Cromwell Press, Trowbridge, Wiltshire

British Library Cataloguing in Publication Data
A catalogue record for this book is available from the British Library

Library of Congress Cataloging in Publication Data
A catalog record for this book has been requested

ISBN 0–415–27818–X (hbk)
ISBN 0–415–27819–8 (pbk)

Contents

List of illustrations   viii
Preface   ix
Acknowledgements   x
List of abbreviations   xi

Part I   **The context of conservation**   **1**

Chapter 1   **Contributions and contradictions**   **2**

Introduction   *3*
Conservation planning   *7*
Specific criticisms of conservation   *11*
A challenging context   *14*
Restating the case for conservation   *21*
The need to examine conservation values   *25*

Chapter 2   **The ascendance of conservation**   **26**

Introduction   *27*
A hundred years of continuity and change   *28*
Towards contemporary issues affecting conservation   *41*
Emerging relationships   *53*

Chapter 3   **A thematic framework**   **56**

Introduction   *57*
*The relationship between conservation and
   statutory planning*   *59*
The spatial focus of conservation controls   *61*
The extent of acceptable change   *63*
The basis of conservation's support and legitimacy   *64*
The interpretation of features' interest   *66*
The hierarchy of significance   *68*
*The influence and variety of knowledge and
   experience*   *70*

Contents

Aspects of heritage valuation   *72*
Economic pressures and their impact on conservation   *74*
The influence of political agendas   *75*
Research issues   *77*

Part II   **Conservation values in practice**   **79**

Chapter 4   **Survey of national conservation organisations**   **80**

Introduction   *81*
Conservation planning: an inherent specialism   *84*
Geographical and spatial priorities   *89*
Shaking off preservationism   *91*
Commentary on the scope and focus of conservation
  controls in relation to broader land-use control
  issues   *95*
Special interest   *98*
'National' interest   *101*
Public and professional paradigms   *104*
Heritage and culture   *107*
Commentary on the interpretation and articulation
  of value in features attracting conservation interest   *109*
The economic imperative   *112*
The politics of conservation   *114*
To what extent do economic and political pressures
  affect conservation?   *117*
Concluding observations on the national survey   *118*

Chapter 5   **Conservation in a post-industrial mill town**   **124**

Introduction to the local planning authority
  case studies   *125*
An illustrative background   *128*
Current structure, operation and priorities   *130*
Development cases   *136*
The Lodge   *137*
The Yard   *144*
The Square   *152*
The Mount   *158*
Concluding observations from the case study   *160*

Chapter 6   **Conservation in a historic market town**   **170**

Introduction   *171*
An illustrative background   *171*

	Structure, operation and priorities	173
	Development cases	180
	The Terrace	180
	The Bank	186
	The Annexe	194
	The Gardens	201
	Concluding observations from the case study	204

Part III   **Challenges to conservation**   **215**

Chapter 7   **Making the connections**   **216**

	Introduction	217
	The relationship between conservation and statutory planning	217
	The spatial focus of conservation controls	220
	The extent of acceptable change	222
	The basis of conservation's support and legitimacy	225
	The interpretation features' interest	227
	The hierarchy of significance	230
	The influence and variety of knowledge and experience	232
	Aspects of heritage valuation	235
	Economic pressures and their impact on conservation	238
	The influence of political agendas	241
	Concluding reflections	244

Chapter 8   **Conclusions**   **246**

	Introduction	247
	The nature of conservation planning: integration or marginalisation?	248
	The interpretation of value in the built environment: value in features, value from context	254
	The influence of external pressures: threats or opportunities?	260
	Summary and implications for research and practice	263
	Conclusion	267

Postscript		**269**
References		**273**
Index		**283**

Illustrations

Figures

5.1   Structure in 1999 of the council planning service of the first
      town studied (a post-industrial town in the north of England)   131
6.1   Structure in 1999 of the council planning service of the second
      town studied (a market town in the Midlands)   174

Tables

3.1   Tensions in conservation   58
3.2   The thematic framework   77
4.1   National conservation bodies interviewed   82
5.1   Criteria used to identify suitable local authority case studies   126
5.2   Respondents interviewed in both local authorities   126
5.3   Criteria used to select the development case studies   127
5.4   An outline of development cases' attributes (first case study)   136
6.1   An outline of development cases' attributes (second case study)   179

Preface

The focus of conservation planning is the physical remnants of previous generations' building and development. It is therefore appropriate that a study of its practices and policies should also involve looking at the accumulation of justifications and assumptions forming its core values.

This book considers what these values are and how they are applied in practice. It is largely based on original research undertaken for a PhD thesis on this subject. While the empirical work was conducted prior to many of the recent significant changes to the planning system, it is arguable that the statutory and policy framework for conservation planning has changed less markedly over that time. Indeed, attitudes and values can sometimes lead policy, but conversely they can be also more deeply entrenched. The consequence is that often alterations to the nuances of policy can take time to fully percolate the range and depth of values held throughout conservation practice. It is this ongoing evolution of value and interpretation which provides the interest and context to this work.

The richness provided by a qualitative approach is a major strength of this work, allowing a much-needed depth of analysis. Inevitably the study also represents a snapshot in time. Much has changed in the landscape around conservation; for instance, the rise of the urban renaissance agenda, the crystallisation of sustainable development and the ascendance of regional governance have all been significant and influential factors over recent years. These trends are all acknowledged, and if the subjects of the study are revisited, then perhaps a different picture might emerge. The depiction presented here remains important for the contrast and continuity revealed in the values underpinning conservation.

Acknowledgements

I would like to thank all respondents who graciously devoted their time and effort to contribute to this study. To all those people who helped me complete this book and the thesis preceding it, a heartfelt thank you.

Abbreviations

BPO	building preservation order
BCSC	British Council of Shopping Centres
C&D	Conservation and Design
CABE	Commission for Architecture and the Built Environment
CAPS	Conservation Area Partnership Scheme
CBA	Council for British Archaeology
CBH	cultural built heritage
CIC	Construction Industry Council
COI	Central Office of Information
CVM	contingent valuation method
DC	Development Control
DCMS	Department of Culture, Media and Sport
DEFRA	Department for Environment, Food and Rural Affairs
DETR	Department of the Environment, Transport and the Regions
DNH	Department of National Heritage
DTLR	Department of Transport, Local Government and the Regions
DoE	Department of the Environment
EH	English Heritage
EHTF	English Historic Towns Forum
ESRC	Economic and Social Research Council
ETC	English Tourist Council
GPDO	General Permitted Development Order
HEI	Heritage, Environment and Implementation
HERS	Heritage Economic Regeneration Scheme
HLF	Heritage Lottery Fund
ICOMOS	International Council on Monuments and Sites
MHLG	Ministry of Housing and Local Government
MORI	Market and Opinion Research International
MTCP	Ministry of Town and Country Planning
NAS	national amenity societies
NGO	non-governmental organisation
ODPM	Office of the Deputy Prime Minister
PFI	Private Finance Initiative

Abbreviations

PPG15	Planning Policy Guidance Note 15: *Planning and the Historic Environment*
PSI	Policy Studies Institute
RCHME	Royal Commission on the Historic Monuments of England
RDA	Regional Development Agency
RTPI	Royal Town Planning Institute
SPAB	Society for the Protection of Ancient Buildings
SRB	Single Regeneration Budget
TCRA	Town Centre Residents' Association
UDP	Unitary Development Plan
UNESCO	United Nations Educational, Scientific and Cultural Organization
UTF	Urban Task Force

PART I

The context of conservation

'To be is to have been.'
(Lowenthal 1985: xxv)

1 Contributions and contradictions

Introduction

The form of towns and cities represents the physical legacy of preceding generations' aspirations, uses and limitations. As each successive wave of society has interpreted and contributed to this collective inheritance, attitudes towards such historic buildings have not been characterised by any consistency. Over time the treatment of historic relics has encompassed a curious mix of reverence and sanctity, abrogation and destruction.

It is significant to remember that conservation merely represents one way of dealing with historic structures. It is largely a culturally determined attitude of our time that old buildings should be protected. While conservation is a framework of policies and controls, more fundamentally it is also a reflection of deeper cultural attitudes to the past.

Although a conservation urge has exercised the 'civilised' conscience over thousands of years, in most western countries the state's involvement is little more than a century old. Even during that short time, attitudes towards the past have changed beyond recognition, reflecting broader cultural shifts. For instance, two hundred years ago outmoded timber-frame buildings were refaced with stone or render to keep abreast of fashionable Georgian architecture. While the motivation was aesthetic it was also a purposeful display of the building owner's finances and ability to match the dynamism of the growing town or city. In contrast, performing such an act on a historic building today would be decried as wanton vandalism by perhaps those similar property-owning sections of society. A display of wealth now would be the financial ability to step outside the pace of change and, ironically, protect the old – that 'original' eighteenth-century period property.

Just as attitudes towards the past are not static, nor is the physical environment in which conservation operates. While the layering of historical residue in the urban fabric contributes to the intensity and appeal of towns and cities, the built environment is in a perpetual state of flux. A cycle of obsolescence and decay dictates when buildings have outlived their economic life and replacing old structures with vibrant contemporary buildings is vital. The sight of cranes marching across a city skyline, far from intruding on a historical scene, is an inexorable symbol of progress and success.

For conservation to intervene in this process of renewal, it must do so on a firm foundation. However, conservation is not a single entity, nor does it comprise just one approach: arguably there is still no one definitive purpose or conservation ethic (Worskett 1982; Larkham 1996). The cumulative range of policy

Avebury stone circle: the inspiration behind Sir John Lubbock's lobbying for the introduction of the first protection legislation
© Kevin Schafer/CORBIS

justifications for conservation is incredibly diverse, reflecting the growth of practice. Antiquarian concerns with preserving the fabric of isolated artefacts for their didactic interest is certainly far removed from land regeneration pressures to reinvent the role and uses of ageing buildings.

These justifications do allow conservation to perform a variety of roles but they inevitably create a wealth of contradictory positions. It is this confusion at the heart of conservation which has led to criticisms of its burgeoning scope and potential restrictions.

This book examines these contradictions by exploring the perceived values and justifications underlying conservation planning in the UK from the strategic level down to the detail of real buildings. It takes a novel approach in highlighting the relationship between the ideals supporting policy and what is actually built (or not) in the name of conservation.

Part I examines the development of conservation planning in the UK, and by exploring essential themes provides a framework for understanding the various tensions in conservation practice. By way of introduction, this opening chapter outlines the mechanics of conservation planning and the challenges it faces – specifically, in the criticisms levelled at conservation practice over the years, and generally, in the context of the urban renaissance agenda. Chapter 2 reviews the establishment of conservation planning from its early origins rooted in antiquarianism through to the present day, taking in statutory landmarks as seminal periods in this process. This review reveals a wealth of embedded values as professional practice has periodically responded to various threats and opportunities. In moving closer into the planning mainstream, conservation was influenced by planning's prevalent paradigms, but despite this relative proximity, conservation controls were often peripheral to the planning machinery. Chapter 3 pulls together a diversity of strands to develop a unique thematic framework covering the scope and focus of conservation planning, the interpretation of what is considered worth protecting and the influence of pragmatic external issues. This framework provides a robust tool for interpreting the case study material and analysing the emerging themes.

In Part II, the values and issues raised in the preceding chapters are tested by investigating both national and local levels of conservation activity. Chapter 4 presents a qualitative survey of national organisations – those influential bodies contributing to the national operation and direction of conservation policy. The purpose is to address underlying perceptions of what conservation should be doing – its normative standards. In comparison, chapters 5 and 6 address the micro scale of conservation practice using two different local planning authorities as case studies. A metropolitan council in the north of England and a market town in the Midlands present contrasting contexts for the operation of conservation policy. Following an account of the context, organisation and culture of the authorities' conservation activity, eight completed building schemes are examined in detail. These case studies are intended not only to test the correspondence of principle against practice but also to identify and canvas wider opinions from local parties outside the local planning authorities.

In Part III, the themes from these national and local levels are extracted and analysed, and the wider implications of the findings discussed. Chapter 7 compares and contrasts findings in relation to thematic framework developed in chapter 3. The findings challenge many accepted beliefs about the position of conservation within planning and the reasons why it is supported. The conclusions are brought together in chapter 8 by considering the overall picture in relation to broader issues affecting land-use planning, the interpretation of conservation value and the external influence of economic and political agendas. In summary, implications and pointers for future conservation research and practice are highlighted before the final conclusions are presented.

A continually shifting landscape

> The conservation movement creates what it wants to conserve.
>
> (Ashworth 1991: 25)

It has been emphasised that the benefits of conservation are 'self-evident'; indeed, current popular opinion would agree that conserving a historic building is preferable to demolishing it. This has not always been the case; the underlying justifications for conservation have developed in response to direct threats and paradigm shifts in attitudes towards the past. Each successive wave contributes to and influences the existing approach and values, resulting in their gradual coalescence. This residual diversity of values which support conservation can be easily conflated in broad policy statements but offer a range of different approaches in actual decision-making. Such flexibility may be requisite, but in assuming that conservation's contribution is not only self-evident but also operates in the 'public interest', these claims mask the fundamental questions: why conserve, conserve what, and for whose benefit?

Evidently, values will have percolated differentially across the breadth of the conservation system, between national and local levels, and these different levels must be studied in detail. This pursuit is intended to highlight the contemporary relevance of conservation and its contribution to the planning system. But why examine the values underpinning conservation now? There have always been challenges and often vocal criticisms of conservation activity within the statutory planning system.

More recently there has been a notable shift in the wider political context affecting land use development. In the UK, the past five years has seen a greater challenge to conservation's mantle than ever before. Conservation, with its attendant focus on the arts, history and architecture, is no longer the torch-bearer for building aesthetes. Perhaps it never was, but following periods of insensitive urban development in the 1960s and 1970s, the swing towards conservation-oriented planning did offer an alternative to such large-scale, non-contextual design. Conservation planning promoted attempts to prioritise and control aesthetic standards of new development and emphasise once more the quality of locality as a design principle. During this time, conservation certainly had a role to play in planning, but it can no longer claim an exclusive responsibility, or championing role, for these functions today.

The various government and professional initiatives falling under the banner of 'urban renaissance' have rejuvenated the urban design agenda after years of neglect in the 1980s and early 1990s. Urban design has emerged as a potent force influencing new development and regeneration and has perhaps stolen a march on conservation and English Heritage (EH) in directing the debates about urban living, about the quality of 'character', about defining and creating places. Urban design appears popular with the current (Blair) government; conservation *per se* does not.

The question for conservation now is how do its policies, professionals and bodies define conservation? How does it respond to the challenge? Can it contribute greater value within planning or is it facing marginalisation if its star is fading?

There have been significant moves to address these questions at a strategic level. English Heritage is assimilating the language of urban regeneration in its policy documents and emphasising the economic contribution of the heritage to wider socio-economic priorities. But although EH is the lead body for the historic environment, there is only so much influence it can wield over the many operational layers and key players across the country who effect the implementation of conservation policy on the ground.

Consider the statutory planning system: while UK planning and conservation policy has become more centralised, the inherent flexibility of British civil administration ensures that conservation remains as varied as those individuals interpreting it. Contrasts in value perception arise not only through the intrinsic diversity of conservation policy justifications, but also through a system whereby different pressures and agendas impinge on local and/or national decision-making. This is not unique to conservation or planning, but it illustrates that there is an inevitable tension between central control and local autonomy in all modern states' system of governance. Ensuring consistency and coherence is difficult, not least in identifying at which end of the regulatory spectrum any one issue is best placed.

Attempting to embrace new value orientations will be particularly difficult if the starting point for this change is far from clear. Conservation is supported by diverse philosophical strands which do not necessarily complement one another.

Few studies have ever attempted to look at the values underpinning conservation planning policy and practice, to assess their efficacy and to challenge their relevance. There is simply a lack of knowledge.

In addressing this gap, the research presented in this book throws up lessons for policy-makers, practitioners and academics in understanding the cultural, institutional and perceptual barriers to making conservation planning work. Like any other area of government policy, the planning framework is subject to constant revision: investigating the impact of policy is like trying to measure a moving target. The empirical and analytical work for this book was largely conducted prior to the major sea change in attitudes heralded by the Urban Task Force (UTF) and the subsequent impact of *Delivering an Urban Renaissance* (DETR 2000b). However, the policy framework for conservation remains unchanged over this period, which is in itself reflective of the twin-track agendas for urban design and conservation. Indeed, changing policy affects attitudes on a much longer timescale. It is even arguable that government policy has little impact on individuals' own beliefs, which makes this study all the more poignant for the valuable insight gained into the perceptions and cultures of those engaged in conservation planning.

Conservation planning

The processes, principles and practice of 'conservation' occur among a diversity of professional disciplines, from fine art to ecology. In terms of definition and application, the various spheres in which conservation operates occlude, rather than highlight, a common approach.

While each country with a legacy of historic buildings has devised its own individual approach to conservation, each system faces similar pressures and constraints, and the lessons from this study are equally applicable to different contexts. In the UK, conserving the historic environment is performed through statutory land-use planning: generally, through sensitive land-use policies and, specifically, through separate consents relating to listed buildings and conservation areas. In addition to protecting what exists above ground, the planning system carries responsibility for protecting relics below ground. Generally, features of archaeological interest are dealt with according to a separate policy (PPG16; DoE 1990) and legislative framework (the Ancient Monuments and Archaeological Areas Act 1979). Though the distinction between the two systems is far from clear, historical inertia has meant that many important listed buildings are also protected as ancient monuments. However, the consequent definitions of 'special interest' and regulation of controls over archaeological relics are quite distinct from those for listed buildings and conservation areas (Jewkes 1993; Pickard 1996). This study focuses principally on conservation as applied and interpreted through the planning system, listed building and conservation-area controls.

The policy framework of built environment conservation

Planning Policy Guidance Note 15, *Planning and the Historic Environment* (PPG15) (DoE/DNH 1994), sets out the current framework for conservation planning. Published in 1994, it is perhaps now ready for review in the light of changing political priorities around it but its principles remain steadfast. At the outset, the document outlines the justifications for the state's involvement in conservation. Though broad and varied, these justifications receive only a brief exposition:

> It is fundamental to the Government's policies for environmental stewardship that there should be effective protection for all aspects of the historic environment. The physical survivals of our past are to be valued and protected for their own sake, as a central part of our cultural heritage and our sense of national identity. They are an irreplaceable record which contributes, through formal education and in many other ways, to our understanding of both the present and the past. Their presence adds to the quality of our lives, enhancing the familiar and cherished local scene and sustaining the sense of local distinctiveness which is so important an aspect of the character and appearance of towns, villages and countryside. The historic environment is also of immense importance for leisure and recreation.
>
> (DoE/DNH 1994: para. 1.1)

Highlighting these justifications, the document sees conservation as:

- contributing to environmental sustainability;
- helping to maintain relics' physical presence and visual appearance;
- having a didactic role in education and understanding the past;
- contributing to the cultural significance of places' identity and distinctiveness;
- helping to provide orientation and familiarity in the environment; and
- having leisure and recreation uses.

Though a wide range of justifications is appropriate, their variety raises the question of whether they are all of equal importance or whether there are certain imbalances, exclusions or even direct conflicts in their realisation.

PPG15 then moves to explain the relationship between conservation and planning:

> We must ensure that the means are available to identify what is special in the historic environment; to define through the development plan system its capacity for change; and, when proposals for new development come

forward, to assess their impact on the historic environment and give it full
weight alongside other considerations.

(DoE/DNH 1994: para 1.3)

While PPG15 is by no means an old document, it was written at a time when
the government was keen to deliver, or – more cynically – to be seen to implement, a planning system which could carry the principle of sustainability
(Brindley *et al.* 1996). Following the Town and Country Planning Act 1990
and the Planning and Compensation Act 1991, PPG1 (DoE 1987b; revised DETR
1997) emphasises the development plan as the principal planning policy instrument to lead all local authorities' development decision-making. To accompany
this 'plan-led' system, Planning Policy Guidance notes (PPGs), published by
central government, are intended to provide coherence across all local planning
authorities in the way they form and implement the policies contained in their
respective development plans.

In replacing the conservation policy contained in Circular 8/87 (DoE 1987a),
PPG15 responded to this change by stating that conservation ought to be fully
represented at all levels of the development plan (paras 2.1–2.26). This may be
a realisation of conservation's rightful place at the heart of planning (CBA 1966;
Dobby 1975). However, conflict and tension are equally evident between conservation and development interests (Cantell 1975; Mynors 1984). Listed building
consent and conservation area consent are the principal control mechanisms with
which to protect the historic environment, but specific policies for their implementation or elaboration are specifically excluded from local development plans
(PPG15: para 2.4).

Complementary regimes?

On the face of it, conservation would appear well represented in the planning
system. The renewed primacy of development plans had addressed some of the
threat from unalloyed market interests promoting profit over conservation, and
special conservation consent systems protected features of special interest. An
official line had been presented that within the planning framework, the uniform
presence of a single legal system and set of planning powers would provide
consistency and uniformity of operation of planning controls (COI 1993).
To a degree this is true: certainly the separate regimes of listed buildings and
conservation areas utilise the same legislative criterion to define what's worth
conserving – that of 'special architectural or historic interest'. However, while
the systems share this basis, there are intrinsic differences in the regimes' operations which impart different values in the interpretation of 'special interest',
thereby affecting subsequent practice (Shelbourn 1996). Others have looked in
great detail at the mechanics and intricacies of conservation regulation (Mynors

1995; Ross 1995; Pickard 1996; Suddards 1996) but an outline of the basic structure is necessary.

Listed buildings

The listing of buildings is an administrative process whereby structures are
nationally surveyed and evaluated against the criterion of whether or not they
possess sufficient 'special architectural or historic interest' (PPG15: paras 3.3,
6.10). By receiving a grade – I, II* or II – a structure is identified as being of
national interest (PPG15: para 6.16) and requires a 'listed building consent' to
be obtained prior to the execution of any works or alterations to the structure.
Listed status is not an award, or a prohibition of change, merely recognition of
a feature's special interest.

Listing a building is a centralised process, with EH being the principal adviser
to the Department of Culture, Media and Sport (DCMS). Ministerial approval
is required to ensure a fair balancing of the public interest in protecting the
building against the restriction which listed status places on development options
for the owner of a listed property. Though there are different processes of identifying potential candidates for listing – including regional surveys, schematic
surveys by building type or spot-listing for one-off incidents – listing remains a
rigorous process under the administration of civil servants and historic building
experts. This rigour is required in order to guarantee a relatively objective and
neutral evaluation, as outlined in PPG15 section 2. An interesting departure from
this executive function has been the process of public consultation in listing post-
war buildings (Cherry 1996). EH has sought public support and acceptance for
modern buildings which may not immediately strike the public conscience as
being of special interest.

In contrast, the control of changes by listed building consent is predominantly
the responsibility of the local planning authority – though there are call-in powers
and special provisions regarding consultation and notification (DETR/DCMS
1997) for the respective grades. While the upkeep of listed buildings depends
largely on their owners' co-operation, carrying out works in breach or in the
absence of a listed building consent is a criminal offence.

Conservation areas

Unlike listing, conservation areas operate under the complete discretion of local
planning authorities, which have a duty to 'designate as conservation areas any
"areas of special architectural or historic interest the character or appearance of
which it is desirable to preserve or enhance"' (DoE/DNH 1994: para 4.1).

There are no statutory criteria or processes by which to identify area-based
character, though PPG15 (para 4.4) and EH guidance (EH 1995a) do provide

some direction. The intention behind the original legislation was to encourage planning authorities to recognise the distinctiveness of their own locality free from central government inhibition (Kennet 1972). There is no compulsion to designate conservation areas, simply to consider the potential of an area for protected status; similarly, there is no requirement to implement preservation or enhancement strategies, merely to prepare them following the designation of a conservation area (PPG15: para 4.3).

The regulation of change within a conservation area is much weaker. Following the *Shimizu* decision, the requirement to obtain an additional consent in a conservation area over and above normal planning permission only covers such extensive alterations to a feature that it permits a near-total demolition (Brainsby and Carter 1997). The government has clarified the situation (DETR/DCMS 2001) but conservation area control has been fundamentally undermined. An Article 4 Direction may be approved locally – narrowing or removing permitted development rights within conservation areas – but relatively few have been implemented across the country (Larkham and Chapman 1996).

Specific criticisms of conservation

Despite the success of the conservation system in preventing demolition of buildings and in becoming a component of mainstream planning, it has always attracted criticism. Recently that criticism has appeared more forceful, questioning the scope, processes and justifications of conservation.

The scope of conservation control has increased the number of structures protected, far exceeding the original intentions for its use. In 1967 there were approximately 100,000 listed buildings and it was estimated that a mere 1,250 conservation areas would suffice to protect all the important sites in the country (Larkham 1996). However, recent figures indicate that there are approximately half a million listed buildings and approaching 10,000 conservation areas (ETC/EH 2001). Around 5 per cent of England's total building stock therefore is subject to some form of conservation control. Apart from creating administrative problems not envisaged when these systems were introduced, the sheer scale of responsibilities has raised questions about the desirability of conservation.

Listed buildings

The listing of a building restricts an owner's ability to alter that property, inhibiting private householders and commercial organisations alike from unilaterally modifying and revising their buildings. In relation to domestic owners, it seems that the restrictive application of these controls or the fastidiousness of their detail, for example specifying the correct colour for window frames, has caused a counter-reaction among conservation's traditional middle-class support (Corval 1995; Clark 1999). A listed building is not necessarily an entirely desirable property but may in fact be seen as a liability (Rowland 1997). The mentality persists that an Englishman's home is his castle, over which the state ought to reduce rather than increase its incursions (James 1994).

Before such potentially onerous restrictions are imposed, property-owners may feel that the merits of conservation designation require close scrutiny. The listing of modern buildings has been criticised, as some feel that modern buildings are inappropriate for conservation's attention (Bevan 1996). With buildings such as Park Hill estate in Sheffield being grade II listed in 1998, a significant collision of value interpretation with a stereotypical image of a 'listed building' is precipitated, creating confusion over conservation's purpose and direction. Although EH guidelines accommodate the different uses and issues involved with listing modern buildings (EH 1995b), owners and tenants, particularly in the commercial office sector, have argued that listed status makes the management of a building too inflexible to accommodate their rapidly changing requirements (Harding-Roots 1997; Rees 2002).

Conservation areas

Criticisms of listing pale when compared with the attacks on conservation areas over the past 15 years. While the expansion in numbers of listed buildings has been presented as recognising the contribution of under-represented architecture (e.g. vernacular, industrial), the increase in conservation area designations has been portrayed as the profligate indiscretion of local planning authorities. Designation without due consideration of local qualities and characteristics has led to accusations of 'debasing the coinage' from the original intention to protect areas of special architectural or historic interest (Morton 1991; Suddards and Morton 1991). It would appear that local authorities' application and management, rather than the concept or provisions for area-based protection, are at fault. Sadly, a national survey (Jones and Larkham 1993) echoed similar findings to a smaller-scale survey 20 years previously (Gamston 1975). Local planning authorities were criticised for not utilising the available controls and for lacking a strategic framework capable of managing and responding to those local characteristics that defined their conservation responsibilities. *Townscape in Trouble* (EHTF 1992) highlighted the physical results of local authorities' inconsistency and malaise in ensuring sensitive development. Tolerating a high degree of minor changes to the built environment was cumulatively eroding the overall quality and character which conservation area designation was intended to 'preserve'.

Fundamental problems

The specific criticisms of these protection regimes are largely concerned with efficacy and internal conservation practice. Indeed, these procedural questions have largely formed the main considerations in all national policy reviews to date. Delafons (1997b) considers that the lack of substantive reform proposals in the face of tangible development pressures is evidence that conservation has lost its impetus. It is arguable that conservation practice has drifted somewhat from the 'original intentions', but Maguire (1998) argues that current conservation thinking has become too preoccupied with preservationist attitudes which his generation had attempted to reform with the introduction of the conservation area. Reade (1991) argues that the administrative process of conservation creates results which bear little relation to improving environmental quality. The whole process tends to ignore the socio-economic circumstances which create disparities in environmental quality: furthermore, it ignores the socio-economic consequences on communities of its own actions.

The exclusivity of the conservation profession has also been noted, though such critiques are not necessarily new. Eversley (1975) attacked the bias towards favouring the interests of middle-class property owners, not only in terms of ensuring their pleasant amenity through conservation areas but also in the grant regimes which contributed to the costs of repairing their listed buildings. More recent writings have identified a distinction between the professional and general public's awareness and interpretation of conservation value (Townshend and Pendlebury 1999; Larkham 2000). While the profession operates under the auspices of 'public interest', it is possible that the public's conception of conservation is wider than the professionals' relatively academic determination. This diversity also questions the legitimacy of professionals identifying a single conservation value when there is a plurality of competing interpretations which currently may be excluded.

This is of particular concern in the heritage literature, which, in acknowledging the political conflicts which underlie value representation, is more advanced than that of conservation planning. Selecting features for conservation involves a conscious process which, far from being a neutral choice, inflates or rejects particular features as much for their socio-political association as for their architectural quality. Indeed, the criterion of authenticity, a touchstone for conservation, is similarly open to criticism as reflecting not so much the original and pure state of a feature, as its good fortune to have survived and been shaped by circumstances through time (Ashworth 1997). Basing conservation on authenticity does not protect a representative sample of history, as conservation encourages removing these features from the inevitable process of decay and mutation, thereby rendering them less authentic.

It is partly this removal from the natural progression of time which has led

13

some to criticise other manifestations of 'heritage' as detrimental to conservation. Hewison (1987) argues that heritage commodification has prioritised appearance over content; the superficiality of reproduction imagery blunts sensitivity to genuine, objective evidence of the past. That heritage attractions find an enthusiastic audience is portrayed as an obsession with the past, a cultural preoccupation with a retrospective vision (Wright 1985). Some consider it a constraint on being able to review accurately the development of contemporary society (Ascherson 1987).

Perhaps more sinister though is the accusation that the representation of the past in the form of 'national heritage' can be used as a tool of political obfuscation, to present an image of unity and established order, despite a period of significant socio-political changes (Wright 1985; McGuigan 1996). Given that conservation is based on professional values and neutrality, it struggles to answer accusations of a political nature – even where they relate directly to the exercise of conservation control (Graves and Ross 1991).

A challenging context

It is not simply the specific criticisms of conservation which are challenging conservation. While the powers, policies and responsibilities within the conservation framework have not changed greatly over the past five years, the wider context for conservation and planning has changed dramatically. And this may be a cause for concern.

Shortly after Labour won the 1997 general election, the new government pledged to address the deteriorating state of the UK's urban areas. The UTF, under the chairmanship of Richard Rogers, was charged with responsibility for investigating the problem, providing expert guidance and coming up with practical solutions. The problems were easy to identify and still remain with us. Many areas in the UK's towns and cities have suffered such economic underinvestment, neglect, depopulation and social polarisation that they are no longer places where people want to, or indeed are able to, work and live. General economic growth and, to some extent, the planning system have fuelled a pattern of development outside city centres, whereby new housing, public facilities, retailing and the like are built on or beyond the urban fringe on greenfield sites. However, this not a standard pattern across the country: there is a marked disparity of development needs between the North and the South.

The problem of housing development highlights the dilemma. The government estimates that a further 3.8 million new households will be required in the UK over the next 25 years. At then current development rates and densities of greenfield and brownfield sites across the country, the UTF proposed that the government would struggle to meet its target to accommodate 60 per cent of this new development on brownfield sites. Moreover, the way in which land and building assets are managed has contributed to an over-supply in areas where there is low housing need in contrast to areas such as the South-East where there is low supply yet high demand. In order to regenerate urban areas and make them attractive for investment, employers and residents, a comprehensive overhaul of urban policy was required.

The UTF report *Towards an Urban Renaissance* was published in 1999, accompanied by an almost evangelical clamour for change in the way the UK's towns and cities are treated. The key themes emphasised measures to reverse decline and reinvigorate urban areas as attractive, prosperous places:

- to recycle existing buildings and derelict, vacant or under-used sites;
- to improve the quality of urban design, creating more co-ordinated land uses and coherent communities;
- to ensure that the planning system and local authorities can deliver by providing greater autonomy and powers to lead this urban renaissance;
- to secure long-term strategic goals in terms of public investment and cross-cutting government commitment to urban regeneration.

The report sent a clear message about the necessity of accommodating higher densities of new development within towns and cities. Higher-density dwelling, in turn, would be acceptable and successful only if new development conformed to the principles of good urban design, and high quality characterised all new building and public space projects.

The report did not produce the radical overhaul of government urban policy which Lord Rogers *et al.* desired. The government accepted the report in principle but a majority of its recommendations remain unimplemented. With the benefit of hindsight, we can see that the real success of the report was in highlighting the issues facing urban regions' development, moving urban design up the political agenda and, most significantly, changing attitudes to accepting design as a central component in improving the urban realm.

> [W]e have long had a tradition of creating towns and cities of quality and beauty – places that can bind communities together. Many of our best towns and cities retain that quality or are recreating it today. But in other places it is a tradition we have lost. . . . We need to recapture this tradition. In most places this means making the most of our existing urban fabric, maintaining it well and making incremental improvements. In some places nothing short of a complete physical transformation will do.
>
> (DETR 2000b: 41)

In contrast, the report was well received by more progressive-thinking local authorities, particularly in the larger northern cities. These authorities necessarily had to implement regeneration strategies to improve their city centres and now led the way.

While the report and the government's response a year later in the Urban White Paper, *Delivering an Urban Renaissance* (DETR 2000b), have slightly different outlooks, there is a great deal of common ground between the two. While these documents propose wide-ranging reforms, it is worth concentrating on the most important themes affecting conservation planning.

The White Paper firmly prioritises people's needs in a broader context of policies for social and economic, as well as physical, regeneration. The Paper's key themes highlight the vision of an urban renaissance to offer a high quality of life in urban areas through:

- engaging the public in shaping and developing their own communities;
- ensuring better local and regional leadership;
- improving the design and quality of the urban fabric;
- enabling all towns and cities to create and share prosperity;
- providing good-quality services that meet people's needs.

In responding to the specific challenge for accommodating new, particularly residential, development, the White Paper announced a series of measures to counter the problems highlighted above:

- Concentrating new development within the existing urban fabric, utilising brownfield sites and marking a return to more compact cities with key uses and services located in the centre rather than the periphery.
- Building at higher densities, which has influenced subsequent new planning policy such as PPG3 regarding housing (DETR 2000a). Building at higher densities requires a more sensitive and imaginative use of space whereby good design should champion and define urban renaissance.
- Promoting sustainable patterns of development by ensuring co-ordinated mixed-use development. Accommodating residential, commercial, leisure uses and public services together reduces the need to travel and the polarisation of urban areas into single activity zones.
- Emphasising the importance of design as an essential element in creating quality places which ameliorate people's lives.

For a policy framework directed at maximising the potential of the existing urban environment, the anticipation for significant interaction with conservation policies would be high. However, within this broad cross-cutting agenda, the historic environment is but one very small aspect. In the Task Force report, historic buildings were mentioned as a valuable asset, but only in so far as they can be put to good use. The implicit message that may well flow from this statement is that the impetus towards regeneration requires a wider appraisal of what qualities historic buildings and areas offer. The evaluation and perception of historic assets as purely cultural artefacts demanding protection can no longer be politically and economically supported within current land management practices. Harsh decisions about what should continue to be conserved and what can be replaced will have to be taken.

The White Paper is notable too for its omissions about the historic environment. In contrast to its wide range of recommendations and action points regarding other initiatives, there is just one page specifically relating to the historic environment, located in the section 'Looking after the existing environment'. It is notable that conservation is not viewed with a particular reverence – it is simply a means within a process of improving the overall quality of places. The comment simply summarises English Heritage's principal grant programmes contributing to urban regeneration. There are no recommendations other than a reference to EH's own review of its policies, later published as *Power of Place* (EH 2000), suggesting either the government's confidence in conservation bodies to maintain a progressive policy approach or its disregard for conservation as an anachronistic luxury.

Therefore, for its own survival it is essential that conservation planning is responsive and sensitive to the agendas receiving political backing in the Urban White Paper – that is to say, to provide effective local governance, to make the planning system more proactive and to promote quality design in delivering an urban renaissance.

Responsive planning

Despite the intention in the early 1990s to make the planning system more proactive and set clear principles through the primacy of the development plan, it was clear by the time the Task Force reported that these goals had not necessarily been met.

Plan-led planning had not delivered the speed, certainty and direction which was intended. By 2001, 13 per cent of local authorities in England had still not adopted their development plans (DTLR 2001). Their lengthy preparation and a lack of meaningful consultation had, to government at least, made plans appear undemocratic. The government perceived local development plans as lacking integration with a range of broader government initiatives to deliver improvements to the physical and social fabric of towns, such as Community Strategies.

There are important local issues to be balanced in creating a robust development plan but subsequent policy indications from government have arguably represented a move away from championing local and unitary development plans. The Urban White Paper noted new arrangements under PPG12 (DETR 1999) encouraging a speedier adoption process of shorter, more criteria-based plans. The processing of planning applications was to be streamlined and a greater emphasis placed on meeting performance targets. While there has been a constant tension in planning between providing a quick administrative service for (fee-paying) applicants and ensuring a decision is made on the basis of all material considerations, the bias in government policy recently has certainly been moving to emphasise delivering a quality service to the applicant.

This trend (for better or worse) is embodied in the Planning Green Paper (DTLR 2001), which sets out a framework for further modernising the planning system. At the time of writing, the measures contained in this document could only be taken as an indication of the government's intent and so it is difficult to be certain about the definitive future of the planning system. The measures proposed are wide-ranging and it is not the intention here to cover them all. Certain proposals are highly controversial and will be, no doubt, subject to intense public debate and, later, Parliamentary scrutiny, such as the removal of third-party rights of appeal over planning applications. There are many, especially in the environmental lobby, who argue that these proposals sacrifice democratic rights and access to satisfy the commercial needs of land development.

However, it is possible to pick out certain themes in the Green Paper relating to the mechanics of development plans and development control that are likely to be implemented, given continuing political stability and support. These will have a significant effect on the scope and application of conservation policy and controls.

Development plans

Local development plans and structure plans (or unitary plans where relevant) are to be replaced with new Local Development Frameworks. These are to be far punchier, being less concerned with detail but containing a core of essential local policies which will be regularly updated. The aim is to have objective-based policies focused on achieving results. Actions plans for specific locations (such as for conservation areas or the greater use of master-planning areas for regeneration) can be included in the framework but their status is as yet unclear.

Picking up the theme of 'modernising government', greater emphasis is placed on proactive local policy-making in a looser and less prescriptive national framework. While the need to better integrate distinct regional policies is acknowledged, there is also a commitment to review all the Planning Policy Guidance notes. The Paper comments that national policy is over-laden with detail and fails to distinguish between core policies and good practice guidance. PPG3, *Housing* (DETR 2000a), is highlighted as a model framework: a slimmed-down policy document accompanied by supplementary design guides illustrating best practice. PPG1, *General Policies and Principles*, and PPG15, *Planning and the Historic Environment*, are identified as prime candidates for review in the next two years. It will be interesting to see how far the clamour for PPG15's revision is driven by the conservation bodies' and professions' dissatisfaction with its present incarnation.

Development control

The main concern is to make the process of obtaining planning permission more applicant-friendly. Many initiatives are proposed, though two in particular affect conservation. The first is the proposal to have a single consent regime embodying all special consents (such as listed building control). There is a question here over how this arrangement would affect taking conservation issues into account when determining a single permission. The second is the re-appraisal of statutory consultees. Although the Paper states that statutory consultation relating to listed buildings will not be pared down, many conservation area cases are currently also seen by non-statutory consultees – such as other conservation bodies with an interest in protecting certain features. Removing these bodies from the frame could seriously reduce the quality of scrutiny over conservation-related planning applications. Furthermore, it is possible that much advice from conservation bodies may be reduced to merely standing advice rather than guidance tailored according to specific schemes. The gravity of these issues for conservation is magnified when considered against the proposal in the Paper to place more responsibility on applicants to consult with interested parties prior to application. This contrasts with the current arrangement whereby local authorities co-ordinate public consultation and respond according to the views expressed.

Taken together, these revisions to the planning system do not readily support conservation measures or the ethos that conservation is something distinct and special. It remains to be seen whether care of the existing environment can be achieved through other planning policy means such as emphasising the onus on local authorities to demand high standards of design in approving planning applications.

High-quality urban design

One of the most significant consequences of the Urban Task Force is the sea change in attitudes towards the contribution of urban design, not only within the planning system but more generally for all parties involved in the development and regeneration of land.

In the 1980s, design was not a high priority in the planning system: design guidance comprised a meagre appendix in PPG1 (DoE 1987b). Now design is at the heart of the urban renaissance agenda and the message appears to be seeping through government thinking. The establishment of the Commission for Architecture and the Built Environment (CABE) as the nation's design champion signalled a watershed in the active promotion of good-quality design. CABE received a wider role and continued support in the Urban White Paper, and subsequently a close relationship with DETR, DTLR and now the Office of the Deputy Prime Minister (ODPM) has seen the growing emphasis of good design on planning policy. Both PPG1 and PPG3 now have supplementary design guidance to identify and promote best practice in *By Design* (DETR/CABE 2000) and *Better Places to Live* (DETR/CABE 2001) respectively. CABE's own publications continue to influence the agenda, from setting out the accrued benefits of investing in good design (CABE 2000) to cementing its practical application, for instance in developing Design Quality Indicators (CIC 2002).

The wider promulgation of good design is evident. Other agencies are encouraging higher standards of design, for instance by issuing guidance in the form of the *Urban Design Compendium* (English Partnerships/The Housing Corporation 2000). The spirit and language of urban design appear to be filtering into areas where design would once have withered on the vine. For instance, the British Council of Shopping Centres has produced a design guide (BCSC 2001) on raising the quality of new development in town centre retail environments. Considering the proliferation of mediocre shopping centres throughout the UK, it is encouraging that sectors driven by the balance-sheet are responding to the message that investing in design pays dividends.

This buy-in is secured by a persuasive message: skimping on design at the outset will cost more in the long run. Bad design can create wider problems in terms of levels of crime, poor health and social exclusion for the users of poorly designed environments. Good design can create a sense of both personal and community well-being and a greater feeling of ownership over a local environment. The socio-economic advantages of investing in good design place design as a central component to help in realising many of the government's other programmes, such as reducing crime through better-planned environments. Indeed, since the Urban White Paper, central government departments have been encouraged to appoint design champions and produce action plans to direct and encourage high-quality design throughout the process of procuring new public buildings under PFI arrangements to try to avoid these problems.

For conservation, resurgence in urban design, visual awareness and the quality of architecture must be a welcome measure. However, there are tensions between championing the new and protecting the old within the built environment. CABE and EH do have very different remits but they co-exist and provide guidance over the same built environment. Bridges between the two agendas have been built and in practice accommodating new design in sensitive contexts is perfectly achievable, as demonstrated by the schemes in *Building in Context* (EH/CABE 2001).

However, in the larger political arena there are pressures to reposition the conservation agenda. The implicit message underlying the political support for urban design is that creating successful regeneration schemes requires a wider appraisal of the qualities offered by historic buildings and areas. The evaluation and perception of historic assets as purely cultural artefacts, and their management as such, can no longer be politically and economically supported. Harsh decisions about what continues to enjoy protection and what can be replaced will have to be taken.

Arguably, urban design – understanding context, uses and community needs and creating new development within that environment – offers a much broader framework of appreciation than conservation does. From a spatial perspective, conservation of the historic environment may be seen as a subset of urban design. However, from a purely architectural perspective, conservation is quite distinct from urban design and its sphere extends much further into the history and detailing of buildings and areas. There is an impetus for conservation to broaden its view and fit in with the urban design and regeneration agenda. However, some would see this as deserting the essence of architectural conservation. There are few bodies which currently are able to perform this role of protecting and championing conservation. This is a significant tension which EH, as the lead body for the historic environment, must ultimately face.

Restating the case for conservation

Following the Urban White Paper, EH conducted a review of policies relating to the historic environment, culminating in the publication of *Power of Place* (EH 2000). This review was a major opportunity for EH to restate its case and call for measures to benefit the whole historic environment sector. It is worth reviewing EH's wish-list against the government's response later in the year in *A Force for Our Future* (DCMS 2001).

Power of Place was informed by a major consultation exercise across the historic environment sector. It includes a MORI poll commissioned by EH, the largest survey ever of public attitudes towards the historic environment. The results were carefully presented to show the public's deep feeling of connection to their heritage and its contribution to their quality of life. Interestingly, the report's introduction highlighted the fact that the contents were not necessarily EH's own view; though this looked like a disclaimer, it did allow EH the scope to present to government, a more direct statement of its real wishes.

It is clear that EH's main priority was to convince government of the contribution conservation can make to urban regeneration, placing conservation at the heart of regeneration. Admittedly, *A Force for Our Future* only summarised government action (as compared to the wider challenges for local authorities and the heritage sector presented in *Power of Place*), but, to judge by its tenor, arguably the regeneration message was only partially received. The government response prioritised changes within the institutional framework, promising that greater account would be taken of heritage issues across government instead of direct outputs in terms of additional powers, grants or responsibilities to integrate conservation. Furthermore, the recommendations regarding historic environment education, access and participation were greatly expanded in *A Force for Our Future*, perhaps indicating the government's preferred future direction for EH. The role of EH is most likely to be shaped not by the historic environment lobby but by the over-arching priorities of DCMS to deliver the government's agenda, especially on education.

In terms of key hits, the government's response did seem stronger on hype and hyperbole than on promising definite action. With over 120 action points between the two documents, only those points of greater relevance are highlighted. Many priority areas in *Power of Place* were ignored completely in *A Force for Our Future*, such as:

- setting funding targets for EH and local authorities to clear the backlog of repairs to buildings at risk;
- placing a statutory duty of care on owners of listed buildings;
- producing regular surveys on the state of the historic environment;
- using Best Value to encourage local authorities to maintain high-quality historic environment services;
- developing with local authorities an integrated information system for dealing with the historic environment cases;
- giving conservation plans and management agreements statutory force – further work was considered necessary on these points; and
- applying Best Value to local authorities' management of their historic environment.

Perhaps these were unrealistic demands, and maybe even EH did not want these responsibilities without additional resources, but they would have made a significant difference. Other proposals were partially met in the government's response:

- encouraging Regional Development Agencies (RDAs), local authorities and Local Strategic Partnerships to consider (rather than taking full account of) the historic environment in their economic and community partnerships;
- levying a (specially low) 5 per cent VAT rate on repairs just to ecclesiastical buildings (rather than all buildings);
- receiving a commitment to review the case for integrating all consents into a single planning consent in the mid- to long term; and
- raising the skills in local authorities regarding the historic environment by encouraging local authorities to have champions for the historic environment. This is particularly disappointing, stopping well short of requiring comprehensive training for officers and members.

Many proposals were not met explicitly, but arguably this was due to the fact that other initiatives covered similar ground. It is debatable how far these following initiatives will explicitly help the heritage sector:

- Improving the management and maintenance of public spaces and parks is subject to the recommendations in the Urban Green Spaces Task Force (2002).
- Promoting good design throughout local authorities is one of CABE's responsibilities, yet they are not specifically focused on assisting raising standards of design specifically in the heritage sector.
- Encouraging local authorities to make better use of spatial master plans over historic environments has been taken up generally in the Planning Green Paper, as has legislating to remove inconsistencies in processing consents.
- Raising design skills is being promoted as part of 'modernising planning' and is an issue for ODPM (as identified in the Urban Design Skills Working Group (2001)) but one not specifically confined to skills regarding the historic environment.

The government did meet expectations in certain areas, though these measures represent the easier end of implementation as they are largely concerned with making existing systems more efficient and transparent:

- making public bodies more accountable for their historic estates;
- including the historic environment as part of the remit of the 'green Ministers';
- providing better co-ordination within government, involving DCMS, ODPM and the Department for Environment, Food and Rural Affairs (DEFRA) in future discussions on the strategic direction of the lead heritage bodies;
- supporting EH in its role to better co-ordinate research and strategic partnerships across the historic environment sector.

Despite the government's commitment to the principles contained in PPG15, its stated wishes for historic environment management to become more proactive and less concerned with regulation do not appear to be supported in terms of funding and greater responsibilities.

Perhaps a clearer indication of government thinking is given by the first stage report in the Quinquennial Review of EH (DCMS 2002). The review, based on a widespread consultation exercise, broadly supported EH's work and recommended retention of its strategic, regulatory and investment functions. However, a much clearer over-arching framework was required, it said, and while improving relations with government departments was key, the main emphasis was to define EH's role in terms of being the lead body, a regulator, an enabler or a delivery body. These roles had become blurred and EH was seen to lack strategic vision. It can be seen as ironic that while DCMS had been saying that 'EH is now firmly established as a regeneration agency' (DCMS 2001: 48), the review concluded that EH had strayed beyond its original remit and did not necessarily have the skills successfully to perform functions such as enabling regeneration.

Most importantly, the review proposed a significant recasting of EH's relationship with regional and local governance. While EH should concentrate on providing the lead national role and strategic guidance, it should focus its direct influence regionally and actively withdraw from involvement at the local level. In line with 'modernising government', greater autonomy and responsibilities for conservation were to be devolved to the local level. However, EH had become so involved 'at the coalface' because of the lack of skills across many local authorities to deal with conservation issues effectively.

So how does conservation work in local authorities?

The low availability of expertise and resources has been recognised as a longer-term problem for conservation planning. The more recent of two studies commissioned by EH into the state of local authority conservation practice (Baker and Chitty 2002) identifies many policy issues which are as poignant now as when the research for this book was undertaken. While there is an increasing demand for specialist conservation advice – a third of all planning applications involve some historic environment issues – there has been up to an 8 per cent reduction in real terms in conservation funding across local authorities. Concentrating resources on delivering more immediate targets has occluded the strategic role for conservation. A lack of monitoring of the outcomes of planning decisions on conservation assets presents a huge knowledge gap and a barrier to realising best practice. Moreover, conservation staff tend to be drawn from a variety of backgrounds and so possess few core skills.

An earlier study (Grover *et al.* 2000) highlights inconsistencies in local authority conservation practice, for instance in the variety of ways in which PPG15 was applied and the permitted responsibilities of conservation staff within the planning department. There is a balance to be struck between involving conservation officers early on in a planning application to assist with complex historic environment issues and excluding them completely because this would delay the approval process. Rather than PPG15 being at fault, the practical local framework in which the policy is applied is far more influential on the outcome of conservation decisions. Although the study recommends that Best Value guidance be applied to historic environment management, all the problems noted above still persist throughout local practice.

Certainly the framework of local government and its relationship with regional bodies has changed dramatically over recent years. While these are significant revisions to the structure of administration, their bearing on the interpretation of conservation value is not the central focus of this study.

The need to examine conservation values

For all the changes around conservation, there remains a need to look at how national aspirations for conservation policy and local treatment of those principles interact. What is permitted or prevented in the name of conservation can be a world away from the ideals supporting PPG15. It is vital that a study examines in detail just how the levels of decision-making actually shape the nature of the UK's built environment.

The policy framework for conservation is effectively unchanged over the past three years and the attitudes and values underlying conservation practice are characteristically slow to change. The findings of this research retain their relevance despite the significant changes in attitudes towards urban design happening around conservation. There are some distinct questions already emerging:

- How does conservation actually work within statutory land-use planning?
- What is it about conservation that sets it aside from being one of many design issues?
- Are there differences between local and national authorities' perceptions of what conservation means?
- What actually happens in terms of physical development as a result of conservation policy in a local area?

2 The ascendance of conservation

Introduction

Conservation planning may seem a dry subject when viewed merely as a statutory activity. However, understanding how conservation became a part of the planning system and becoming aware of the motivating factors behind that pursuit reveal a story which leads us to question basic assumptions about how we perceive our position in time and space. It may sound fanciful but having an idea about what is worth conserving reveals far more than a preference for a certain architectural period.

Understanding the variety of conceptions that exist in the contemporary realm of conservation requires an examination of its evolution. This may draw accusations of unnecessary historicity, but just as conservation protects the relics of preceding societies, so the ideas prevalent in conservation's own history are equally maintained, protected and reproduced in its current justifications.

In response to threats exposing the inadequacies of the existing conservation controls, creating new values does not sweep aside former ones but merely overlays them with new interpretations. The current system is the cumulative result of these successive responses. Furthermore, there has been ample opportunity for individuals to shape fundamentally its development. Several writers have commented (Hunter 1996) on the influence of key players in the formation of legislation and policy, officially and through successful lobbying, imparting their own personal values and zeal in the process. Hall (1988) notes how the intellectual justifications behind planning ideology were formulated decades prior to their manifestation in practice, shaped often in periods of different socio-economic pressures.

> An understanding of the motivation is needed to explain the origins and nature of the conserved historic city, not least because the sort of motive is a determining influence upon the criteria and thus the selection of what is to be conserved, as well as upon the interpretation of the past to its users.
>
> (Ashworth 1991: 8)

It is not necessary to chart comprehensively the development of the conservation movement, as other works cover this history admirably (Delafons 1997a). All too often, conservation literature has written its own history and chosen to hang its story on convenient pegs of development threat and conservation response – for example, the Adelphi, Euston Arch, Covent Garden, and so on. The formation of the (now statutory) amenity societies throughout the twentieth century is an example of how convenient a narrative this provides. While it is

St Albans Cathedral: restoration of the west face by Sir George Gilbert Scott and Lord Grimthorpe helped polarise Victorian aesthetic sensitivities useful to see this cycle of reaction, an alternative is to look at conservation's history in relation to the issues affecting the policy framework for land-use planning, which shaped attitudes to implementing the nuts and bolts of conservation control. Seminal periods of interaction with planning are given closer attention, illustrating the circumstances and attitudes which have subsequently informed values. Distinguishing particular historical periods is fraught with difficulties, not only in attempting to define causal links between circumstances but, more fundamentally, in artificially isolating issues from their longer development over time, but there are identifiable periods of greater significance:

- antiquarianism confronting early twentieth-century concerns to protect amenity;
- the post-war introduction of listing, complementing modern planning; and
- dissatisfaction in the 1960s with conservation protection in planning.

Such a periodic treatment of more contemporary issues is not appropriate. Instead, these are examined as a variety of themes, following:

- the schismatic effects of Thatcherism;
- regeneration and planning; and
- the influence of heritage on attitudes towards conservation.

In the following review of conservation's development, distinct themes start to emerge; these are taken forward and explored in greater detail in the next chapter.

A hundred years of continuity and change

Wright (1985) has observed that people tend to protect and value things only when those objects are threatened by change. Indeed, it is agents of change which make us aware of the past and, necessarily, of the future. But our perception of change does not remain constant either. We could embrace it or we could be fearful of it, and this affects what we do with those relics of the past which represent something to cherish or, alternatively, dispose of.

To understand a society's valuation of the objects from the past at any particular era, the perceptions of change and relations in time in that society at that time are equally important (Fawcett 1976). Falk (1988) provides a helpful categorisation of these perspectives, characterising a society's relations with its past and future as being either naturalistic, progressive or regressive.

In the naturalistic perception, the past flows into the future through the present. History is perceived as a continuum in which the past possesses the same values as the present. Protecting physical relics is also irrelevant as their decay in the present reflects the natural passing of time. Instead, the emphasis is on applying the knowledge bestowed by antiquity to inspire the present (Lowenthal 1985).

However, following the Enlightenment, historical scholarship tended to identify differences rather than continuity between ages. The implications for the relics of the past were considerable: physical remains were unique and irreplaceable, being genuine artefacts which could assist objective historical knowledge (Plumb 1969). When the past is seen as different from the present, either a progressive or regressive relationship arises.

In the progressive perspective of a society which sees the present as the first step to the future, the past is a defunct realm whose presence can only inhibit this realisation. While Victorian society had a strong belief in its ability to improve on the past (Samuel 1994), modernism shared this trait – change meant progress. The vestiges of the past are shaken off with a confidence in building a better future; protecting such relics is anachronistic.

In contrast, the regressive perspective sees a future of uncertainty and anxiety. The past is resurrected as an alternative, embodying qualities which society finds lacking in the present: stability, continuity and identity. Indeed, Merriman (1991) concludes that people perceive the value of the past as its ability to illustrate the contrast with their everyday lives. Moreover, the 'past' is becoming more recent – the golden age of our times being childhood rather than golden age of Victorian nostalgia residing in medieval romance (Hunter 1981; Wright 1985). Thus the relics of the past gain greater levels of protection as symbols and vehicles for these social sentiments.

Evidently no period was ever defined by an extreme of one or the other perspective, but it is important to bear in mind these broader currents in society's relations with the past when examining the development of conservation measures that specifically protect its remnants.

Antiquarianism and amenity

Establishment protection

In the emerging involvement of the state in land-use planning as a distinct concern from established housing and public health measures, the effects of nineteenth-century antiquarianism were considerable. John Ruskin and later William Morris, for Miele (1996) 'the first conservation militants', left a complex legacy. In practice, their efforts prevented the destructive restoration of medieval churches and other ecclesiastical structures, although their motivations related as much to moral and temporal authenticity as to aesthetic concerns. Of these monuments, Ruskin stated:

> We have no right whatsoever to touch them. They are not ours. They belong partly to those who have built them, and partly to all the generations of mankind who are to follow us. The dead still have their right in them.
>
> (quoted in Binney 1981: 205)

Victorian society was torn between a strident belief in progress – the ability of science and technology to deliver a better future – and a dewy-eyed sentimentality in the arts, looking to a lost social order and grace (Lowenthal 1985). The artistic culture of Victorian Britain was particularly influenced by the values of an elite minority, which in turn appeared to hold sway over much of the middle-class social conscience (Weiner 1981). Indeed, Morris and others, in forming the Society for the Protection of Ancient Buildings (SPAB), set the organisation's agenda by what 'educated, artistic people' would protect on account of its 'artistic, picturesque, historical [or] antique ... merit' (SPAB 1877). Its manifesto remains unchanged to this day.

A fundamental concern, for these aesthetes, was the search for a genuine representation of the spirit of the age. Mass-produced, manufactured goods and artistry were perceived as crude – shallow and banal in comparison with the great achievements of 'antiquity' or medieval craftsmanship (Kennet 1972). Many, like Morris, looked to return to a utopian 'golden age' of medieval rurality where men would once more become craftsmen and not machine operators. However, both Morris and Ruskin, while posthumously critiqued for their obsession with the past, were not interested in the past *per se*. They believed that the separation of art and beauty in industrialised society was a cause of many urban social and environmental problems. Morris in particular sought more radical aspirations for social transformation – the integration of spiritual transcendence through art being as much a social goal as an aesthetic one (Chitty 1998). Indeed, Macmillan (1993) notes that Patrick Geddes' approach of planning the environment as an organic whole echoes these earlier socialist sentiments.

Early monumentalism

Despite the social goals of these pioneers, it is lamentable that their focus remained on the built fabric to the total exclusion of people's needs or desires (Townshend and Pendlebury 1999). Their interest was predominantly in the actual fabric of the relics. Greater historical understanding was in part delivered by the actual physical remnants of relics, and therefore protecting the authenticity of these remains became absolutely sacrosanct. Binney (1981) lampoons Ruskin's influence and passion for 'authenticity' in creating the intellectual straitjacket in which protection measures are now dressed. Prince (1981) characterises this approach as scholastic and paternal, a powerful combination of political interests among the Arts and Crafts movement, SPAB and the National Trust. D. Smith (1974) and, more critically, Reade (1987) identify weaknesses shared with broader socio-political movements such as the emergent Garden Cities movement, collectively comprising varieties of environmental determinism on which much early planning activity was justified. It appeared altruistic but was ultimately naïve.

Early conservation legislation characterised this exclusion of 'life' in the isolated archaeological features it protected. The uninhabited relics first scheduled under the Ancient Monuments Act 1882 were then placed under the responsibility of the Office of Works, a slightly obscure government body of the day. However, tucked away in a quiet recess of Whitehall, this administrative separation allowed early protection measures and attitudes to be exclusively determined by the overriding culture of SPAB's antiquarian and academic preferences (Saint 1996). Any justification for protecting these features in the public interest could be said to be merely paternal and cursory (*Journal of Planning and Environmental Law* 1989). Thus statutory protection at this time was far removed, conceptually and physically, from the pressures felt by rapidly industrialised urban areas (Kennet 1972) and the emerging ideas of planning 'seers', as Hall (1992) terms them.

This is not to say that antiquarianism was wholly removed from socio-political currents at that time. Reade (1987) comments that the middle-class ideas of a better environment supporting the need for early planning measures reveal a distinct similarity to the values of those people championing the protection of ancient monuments – a distinctly anti-urban, anti-metropolitan attitude characterised by longing for the unspoilt countryside. A critical link between the two is that although the problems facing urban areas were recognised as economic and social, planning ideas were solely oriented to providing physical solutions. Simply changing the squalid urban environmental to resemble the more pleasant rural one would not address the significant economic disparities which created such deprivation.

Misguided or otherwise, much of the thinking behind early planning legislation revolved around the 'key concept' of 'amenity' (Cullingworth and Nadin 1994), which dominated state planning until the 1930s (Punter 1986b). As Punter (ibid.) notes, though amenity was sparingly used in planning legislation, it has always been invoked as a material consideration and remains a very useful cover-all. In D. Smith's (1974) analysis, amenity as a planning concept consists of three environmental heads: health (previously accomplished by Victorian public health legislation); 'pleasantness' (implicit in all planning decisions); and preservation, which has been taken as a narrow legislative concern. Foley (1973) too has identified this 'improvement of the environment as an end in itself', i.e. physicalism, as a dominant ideology in planning. Thus because it is intrinsically linked with amenity, Reade (1987) argues that protection is a bastion of this tendency towards physicalism which has traditionally dogged planning.

Early planning schemes

Saint (1996) contends that it was this care for amenity in early planning legislation which secured acceptance for later conservation measures. There was no separation between protecting buildings or areas, merely an all-encompassing desire to see that new development was pursued with regard to the existing qualities of the surroundings. 'Amenity' involved protecting the beauty of the natural and urban environment.

The progress of this early legislation regarding 'town schemes', from 1909 to 1932, is traced in detail by Delafons (1997a). Town schemes were a very early forerunner of a development plan, whereby local councils could start to set out land-use policies for designated areas if they so wished. It is here that the statutory phrase 'special architectural, historic or artistic interest' was first used to define those features which could possibly be identified as worthy of protection under a such a scheme. Significantly, there appeared to be little Parliamentary debate surrounding the introduction of the clause, 'as though there were a mole in the Ministry of Health, an early conservationist perhaps, who contrived . . . covertly to insert these provisions' (Delafons 1994: 511). Cocks (1998) traces this 'mole' to a group of committed civil servants and lawyers who were particularly interested in saving their Oxford *alma mater* from encroaching development.

A series of Acts followed, from the Housing Etc. Act 1923 to the Town and Country Planning Act 1932. These all tinkered with voluntary planning arrangements for local councils. A further bemusing aspect of these early Acts is the narrowing of the statutory phrasing relating to conservation, which changed from having a focus on protecting general amenity to being more focused on protecting specific buildings. Unfortunately, the lack of any guidance and the spectre of financial compensation against local authorities for infringing property owners' rights to develop their land deflected enthusiasm among councils for using town schemes and thinking about conservation.

Positively, town schemes presupposed a relatively broad approach to conservation as an integral tool for planning. More importantly, although town schemes were not widely taken up, national responsibility for them was vested in the then Ministry of Health (the forerunner of later Planning Ministries) rather than the Office of Works (responsible for the state preservation of ancient monuments). A vital aspect of the 1932 Act was the power of local councils to identify and then schedule inhabited buildings of interest. This is in direct contrast to the then scheduled monument arrangements, which applied only to ancient ruined features. In the Parliamentary debates regarding this new power under the 1932 Act,

> some legislators viewed [it] as just a way of tacking historic country houses on to the ancient monuments legislation. But others saw it as a prelude to surveying the whole country, not so much for the historic buildings per se as for everything of amenity and beauty, natural or man-made.
>
> (Saint 1996: 118)

Importantly, for the first time these Acts established that planning and conservation exhibited overlapping spheres of interest. Nevertheless, the statutory phrase defining those features that might be worth protecting, 'special architectural or historic interest', remained an unscrutinised and omnipresent term even though it received singularly little elaboration of its meaning or effect, either prior to enactment or in subsequent policy (Delafons 1997a).

The modern planning system: the introduction of listing

Although planning ideas and practices were changing throughout the 1930s, the destruction and necessary rebuilding after the Second World War provided an opportune catalyst for a radical approach. Hall (1992) notes how the style of planning very much reflected the re-emerging confidence of the age.

The existing planning policy culture was a legacy of Geddes' *'survey–analysis–plan'* approach, whereby comprehensively collecting all information relating to a particular area would enable skilled administrators to produce a 'once and for all' master plan for decisions affecting the development of land. In this mould, there had already been pre-war suggestions of the need for a country-wide survey for historic buildings, and a timescale of two years had been considered adequate to complete this (Delafons 1997a).

> It is clear that there was an idea implicit in much of the legislation that the urban architectural heritage existed in a fixed quantity and that the task of government was to define, locate and preserve it. Practice has shown that this was a misconception.
>
> (Ashworth 1991: 25)

Although the aftermath of the Second World War had a significant impact on planning because of the need to rebuild the country, much of the thinking about how to co-ordinate such a framework for renewal had already been developed. Though the ground-breaking Town and Country Planning Act 1947 established the modern planning system, the earlier 1944 Act of the same name was of greater importance in terms of conservation, as it introduced the concept of listing.

Prior to the 1944 Act there was the potential to incorporate ancient monuments into the prospective planning mainstream by establishing a single Ministry of Works and Planning. However, the impetus to quickly set up a planning system led to the creation of two separate Ministries – the Ministry of Town and Country Planning and the Ministry of Works – in 1943. Unfortunately, this arrangement divorced responsibility for listing, which followed ancient monuments into the Ministry of Works, from the new planning agenda.

People were distressed by the historic destruction caused by bombs. And yet scholars and sentimentalists apart, their distress was less than some might now project back upon them. Many welcomed the prospect of a fresh, post-war recasting of communities. To expedite this, they sought a guide – a list – to what ought be kept and, where necessary, reinstated. In that way, when the experts came to lay their plans they would know without ambiguity or delay what to incorporate or skirt around . . . lists were conceived as a workaday tool which official planners could have by their side as they refined their approach to the urban . . . landscape.

(Saint 1996: 121)

The first drafts of the 1944 Bill, though woefully underdeveloped, offered an opportunity for certain influential members of the Georgian Group to steer the new conservation proposals towards a comprehensive listing system (Stamp 1996). Barely a decade earlier, the Georgian Group had broken away from its parent body, the SPAB. Saint (1996) describes this rift between ideas of the Georgians' modern, metropolitan, 'snobbish but politically astute' membership colliding with the SPAB's 'tweedy' Arts and Crafts traditions of those middle classes obsessed with the rural idyll. Despite a great loss of Georgian buildings during the 1930s to new urban development, the Georgians were more progressive and eager to support listing's incorporation within the emerging planning framework. Acworth, their secretary in 1944, stated: 'preservation in general is only of value when it is co-ordinated and related to a plan of positive development' (Saint 1996: 127). Abercrombie, a member of the Georgian Group, embraced this progressive interest for historic protection *vis-à-vis* area-based planning. Apparently, Parliamentary debates regarding the 1944 Bill centred more on protecting places than on protecting buildings (Saint 1996).

However, the Maclagan Committee, appointed to formulate the terms of reference for listing, displayed distinct preferences towards SPAB-ish antiquarianism and scholarship in its recommendations. Such tendencies were particularly exemplified by its proposal to grade listed buildings, 'not unlike academic degrees' as I, II and III (Saint 1996: 129). The Committee was a distinct contrast from the type of modern planning-oriented approach which had received support in previous Parliamentary debates.

Although listing was intended to serve as a development tool, identifying which features should not be torn down in the reconstruction of bombed neighbourhoods, the lengthy nature of the process of listing buildings was hindering its useful contribution to this process.

Planning and listing were going separate ways again; and little more seems to be heard of the incorporation of lists in to the local development plan. . . . This shaky start to the listing process had major consequences. The whole conception of listing drew gradually away from the urgencies of planning that had brought it to maturity. It became an end, and eventually a little industry, in itself, with its own cultural frame of reference, art-historical criteria and programme.

(Saint 1996: 130)

While protection was recognised as a legitimate concern of government, listing was never integrated into either the development plan or development control: a leading property lawyer at the time consigned listing to the 'Backwaters' section of his book detailing the Act (Megarry 1949)! Listing developed in a narrower vein, whereby providing a proactive guide to local planning authorities conflicted with the artistic concerns of those charged with identifying specific buildings of interest. The general concept of amenity, while 'recognised as one of the main purposes of planning legislation' (MTCP 1951: 138), was not explicitly extended to the protection of historic areas.

The instructions issued to listing inspectors in 1946 reveal a certain breadth in scope yet constraint in practice (Earl 1997). In terms of relating the value of individual buildings and their context, the instructions recognise and highlight the importance of 'character'. However, they presumed that 'the normal exercise of planning control' would be sufficient to protect all other features not of intrinsically listable quality. This advice and the down-grading of grade III status almost immediately after its introduction effectively condemned many buildings of lesser importance, leaving only isolated buildings of exceptional value. Saint (1996: 133) similarly observes that although group value is today recognised under listing policy, it is 'by any standards a poor and insufficient rubric under which to address the architectural and historic problem of place – of the cultural value of total built environments'.

The finite life of finite planning?

For all planning's grand schemes, the system needed to establish itself as a legitimate state activity and also as a new profession distinct from the established ones – architecture, surveying and civil engineering – which fed its ranks (Glass 1973). It did this by several devices which ultimately proved to be fundamental weaknesses.

Planning strove for a comprehensive appropriation of expertise concerning all things relating to the environment (Brindley *et al.* 1996). This 'holistic attitude', as Reade (1987) calls it, pervaded all aspects of the system both substantively and procedurally. It perhaps was most evident in the justification of planning as being in the 'public interest'. This concept has been taken to represent the post-war consensus in the rebirth of Britain. Yet rather than its representing public opinion, Glass (1973), among others, notes that the 'public interest' was more of a political construction drawn up by those elites that wished to legitimate the existence of planning. It was characteristically vague so that even conflicting interests could interpret it favourably, and their support was presented as a resounding consensus in favour of planning (Reade 1987). As planning was the land-use aspect of the welfare state, the public interest was presented as a self-evident truth; criticism would have amounted to heresy in Bevan's 'New Jerusalem'.

Thus rather than clarify the public interest in protection, the influence of planning did precisely the opposite. The ambiguity surrounding the 'public interest', its breadth allowing a variety of interpretations, meant that the scholarly historicist and architectural values held by a paternal minority could pass quite effortlessly to justify this public function, quite irrespective of any consideration of advantage to the public from the protection of such relics. At the time, the National Trust, later under the chairmanship of James Lees Milne, was busy acquiring country houses 'for the nation'. Quite remarkable, then, that in his mission to protect the relics of the aristocracy Milne later commented of the period, 'A whole social system has broken down. What will replace it beyond government by the masses, uncultivated, rancorous, savage, philistine, the enemies of all things beautiful? How I detest democracy' (quoted in Hewison 1987: 61). The continuation of such values in protection could hardly be further removed from the egalitarian aims of the welfare state. Protection remained separate from the functions of planning as the controlling elites were diametrically opposed. Thus while country houses were being saved for the nation through Hugh Dalton's National Memorial Fund, planning was clearing their urban counterparts to make way for the new.

The introduction of conservation areas

Falk's (1988) progressive interpretation of society's views may be identified in the dramatic changes introduced by comprehensive redevelopment, 'slum' clearance and car transport priorities (Tarn 1985). The sentiment of societal progress at the time is well illustrated by the historian J. H. Plumb (1969: 60): '[T]he needs for personal roots in time are so much less strong than they were a mere hundred or even fifty years ago'.

Planning, a creation of modernism, continued to pursue its tenets although sections of society were becoming uneasy over its effects. Its success became increasingly tenuous, as it still concerned itself with the physical aspects of land use, neglecting socio-political problems manifest in the environment (Reade 1987). Its confidence in progress was sweeping away familiar environments and buildings which were conceived as 'old-fashioned' and ripe for replacement (Hewison 1987). This may have been an appropriate tack, but the 1960s clearance policies have been subsequently criticised for destroying the very community essence they were attempting to foster (D. Smith 1974). Comprehensive development created social amnesia, a loss of identity and place – a traumatic experience comparable to bereavement (Marris 1993).

In attempting to maintain a veneer of social responsibility, planners increasingly adopted natural and social science theory to assist planning policy and theory. However, as the planning profession strove for a non-political role, rather than informing and enlightening planning's values the social sciences were used more to furnish greater theoretical technicism and legitimise planning's decision-making processes (Kirk 1980). The substance of planning was further removed from the everyday reality of those for whom planners were planning (Reade 1987). Planning produced such unpopular and adverse effects that its abstract and impenetrable processes required reform. The criticisms bore fruit in the late 1960s, accompanying the general tide in planning towards more social, environmental and participatory planning heralded by the Planning Advisory Group, the Skeffington Report and the reform of development plans in the Town and Country Planning Acts of 1968, 1971 and 1972 (Hall 1992).

The threat to historic towns

Throughout the 1960s, these concerns were highlighting a particular threat to the centres of England's more precious historic towns by unsympathetic and ubiquitously mediocre new development: 'Since the war the machinery for preservation has not been markedly successful. Historic areas have at best been regarded as aggregates of individual buildings' (Smith 1969: 149).

The creation of the Civic Trust in 1957 may be viewed as a reflection of growing unease about the form of new development. The modernist approach prevalent in architecture at the time consciously made little reference to the existing surroundings, an arrogance which Nairn (1955) famously and vehemently rebuked. Listing could only identify particular buildings rather than protect whole areas, which, as the government itself later noted, was becoming essential (MHLG 1967a). Indeed, it could be argued that until the mid-1960s there was a complete lack of any government policy regarding conservation within planning (Delafons 1997a): 'At an official level, historic towns were still regarded as "problems" and preservation was regarded as not merely unremunerative, but positively burdensome on owners' (Andreae 1996: 140).

The encroachment of development and the absence of protection for the urban fabric, street plan, open spaces and lesser features raised widespread concern. Even listed buildings were still vulnerable, as the mechanism for actually protecting them, the building preservation order (BPO), was thoroughly arcane (listed building consent was only introduced as late as 1968!). Wayland (later Lord) Kennet, Parliamentary Secretary for the Ministry of Housing and Local Government, described this system as 'byzantine' and the progress of listing as 'glacier-like'. He was amazed by 'the willingness of Parliament to set up, and the civil service to operate, a system designed to have a certain effect without ever checking whether it was having that effect, or another, or none' (Kennet 1972: 53).

With the displacement, or at least questioning, of end-state master-planning's dominance, the protection lobby caught planning reform on the crest of a wave: its emphasis on planning for people and place reflected a united criticism of the previous destruction of the existing urban fabric. Yet the pressure for protection could be seen in another dimension. Samuel (1994) notes that the introduction of conservation areas was the government's response to placate the property interests of the middle classes who wished to secure their pleasant residential environs. It was associated with a rise in property ownership and a sea change in cultural fashions to 'renovate' rather than 'modernise' property.

Perhaps it was a combination of these sentiments which ensured that the Civic Amenities Act 1967, introduced as a Private Member's Bill by Duncan Sandys (the founder of the Civic Trust), received unanimous support through Parliament. In the concept of the conservation area, planning was relinking specific protection measures with its broader amenity conception. As Delafons (1997a: 97) notes of the mould-breaking policy publication *Historic Towns: Preservation and Change* (MHLG 1967a), it sought 'to integrate conservation into the planning process as had never been done before'.

The concept of area-based conservation

Superficially it would seem logical to unify conservation areas with listed building protection by using the same criteria to identify them both. Thus essentially, conservation areas were directed towards the same values as listing at the time. 'It seems rather odd that the draftsman should have used the terminology of listed buildings to define areas which were clearly not intended to be limited to such buildings' (Delafons 1997a: 96). Thus the phrase 'special architectural or historic interest' defined broader notions of the 'character' and 'appearance' of an area as well. However, just as listing was introduced in a period of planning dominated by architecture, conservation areas were introduced in a period of planning oriented to social science. Public participation was encouraged through the creation of conservation area advisory committees (MHLG 1968: s18–22). Areal conservation was subject to greater societal influences, yet the identification of areas to conserve still relied on mainly architectural criteria through the inertia of legislative drafting. Significantly, the whole process was devolved to local planning authorities to implement and manage. Contrary to quality-control expectations (D. Smith 1974) there was no central intervention, no duty to consult the Ministry and no call-in powers: 'The entire edifice rested on the discretion of individual planning authorities' (Gamston 1975: 1).

There was little explanation at the time regarding the meaning of 'special architectural or historic interest' as it applied to areas, in contrast to the more co-ordinated guidance for defining special architectural or historic interest in the listing process (Kennet 1972). Despite the commissioning of the celebrated but esoteric Four Towns studies (Buchanan and Partners 1968; Burrows 1968; Esher 1968; Insall and Associates 1968), this lack of guidance was a continual glaring omission, since identifying areas ought to take into account a host of societal factors beyond the scope of those appropriate for identifying buildings alone. Circular 53/67 (MHLG 1967b) accompanying the Civic Amenities Act 1967 contained only a brief mention of any criteria:

> Clearly there can be no standard specification for conservation areas . . . [they] will naturally be of many different kinds. . . . It is the character of areas, rather than individual buildings that section 1 of the [Civic Amenities Act 1967] Act seeks to preserve.
>
> (MHLG 1967b: memorandum para. 2)

As D. Smith (1974) noted, wider considerations of 'amenity' were left undefined and implicit in the guise of areas' special architectural or historic interest. Gamston (1975) too noted that national policy was inadequate to guide inexperienced local planning authorities in identifying areas of 'special' interest. Moreover, there was little time to consider the 'special architectural or historic interest' of areas. Government policy emotively stated that designation ought be expedient,

> starting with areas in which conservation measures are most urgently needed because of pressures for redevelopment or because of neglect and deterioration, instead of waiting until they are ready to move on to a broad front. The need is very urgent in many historic towns.
>
> (MHLG 1967b: memorandum para. 2)

Kennet favoured this approach, as he 'wanted the local planning authorities to designate many and large areas, which they probably would if they did so before thinking out what had to be done' (1972: 66). He admitted it was a political move to satisfy public concern for *action* in protecting historic towns and villages. It was anticipated that a body of wisdom would coalesce out of local planning authority experience to guide future practice (D. Smith 1974), though arguably that is only now just emerging (EH 1995a; EHTF 1998). The potential breadth of interpretations of the new provisions would inevitably create differences. At the time, it was considered in many areas of the architectural and planning professions that 'conservation' was to signify a distinctly new approach from the previous ethos of 'preservation'. As Maguire (1998) reflects, it indicated a fresh, creative use of the past, permitting new ways of utilising ageing buildings and incorporating them into a renewed urban fabric. The policy of the day included the message (MHLG 1967b: s4) that conservation areas were to 'represent a shift of emphasis from negative control to creative planning for preservation'.

Although the policy was enthusiastically received, there were no extra resources or financial backing for local authorities to support this rhetoric (Larkham and Jones 1993). Remarkably, this policy was intended as a watershed in revising 'acceptable change', yet it would appear to conflict with the policy ethos introducing listed building consents with the Town and Country Planning Act 1968:

> Circular 61/68 introduced an entirely new doctrine – 'the presumption in favour of preservation'. This doctrine was expounded in the exaggerated terms that came to typify conservation policy as it moved rapidly away from the balanced approach reflected in *Preservation and Change*.
>
> (Delafons 1997a: 101)

However, the consequences of this early policy malaise and lack of definition led to local planning authorities unilaterally identifying special architectural or historic interest on an *ad hoc* basis, often with little justification (Gamston 1975). There was no model policy or good practice guidance. Designations were often made with little analysis or survey of the qualities or interest of the area. Designation was as much an attempt to cling on to a fragment of character against new mediocre development as it was to protect genuinely special areas. Gamston (1975) also found that planners used the conservation area as a flag-waving exercise – an indicator of intent (yet inaction) to satisfy vociferous local conservation groups. Samuel (1994) also notes that many conservation areas came into existence because of the class of people in them and reflected their aspirations rather than any historic quality of the area. Ashworth (1991) poignantly states that conservation areas were designated according to pre-subjective notions of a received image of 'historical' areas clustering around existing listed buildings. Thus the legacy of the preservationist lobby initially narrowed the potential of conservation areas for new revisions of the value of the past.

Government policy, though characteristically vague, later changed when Circular 46/73 (DoE 1973) introduced the idea that conservation areas were applicable to protect the 'familiar and cherished local scene'. Delafons (1997a: 105) comments that conservation 'had now billowed out to embrace the conservation of 'existing communities' and 'the social fabric'. Gamston (1975) notes that this was straying away from strict 'special architectural or historic interest' and admitting broader socio-political factors. Mynors (1984: 145) later reflects that 'the meaning of the critical word "special" in the definition is being inevitably widened – every local scene is "familiar" to many, and most are "cherished" by some'. Such criticisms reveal that conservation areas, originally intended to pursue the same principles as listed buildings, had been contorted to take on board wider societal interests in their definitions of 'special', yet the question of how these were assessed was left unanswered.

Towards contemporary issues affecting conservation

If the amount of published literature on conservation indicated the extent of the public's interest in the subject, then there was an explosion of concern in the 1970s over the destruction wrought by new development in historic towns and cities, polemically illustrated in a variety of emotive tracts: *The Sack of Bath* (Fergusson 1973), *The Rape of Britain* (Amery and Cruickshank 1975) and *Goodbye Britain* (Aldous 1975).

The depressed economic situation of the latter half of the decade perhaps halted the pace of development and also undermined belief in the modernist future. In this depression, necessity required the re-use of resources, and with the gradual rise of the environmental agenda, building conservation took on a new mantle, not as an obstacle to development, but as a renewable alternative to building afresh (Kain 1981; Mageean 1999). Andreae (1996: 149) notes how Dame Jennifer Jenkins' directorship of the Historic Buildings Council in 1975/6 zealously promoted this message to Ministers – 'a clarion call for a change of heart'. Similarly, in *Preservation Pays* (SAVE 1979) and *Preserve and Prosper* (Hanna and Binney 1983) SAVE pushed these economic arguments for protecting existing features. The impetus was so strong that an editor commented that 'conservation was now the received wisdom behind planning' (*Built Environment* 1975). Such an economic justification for protection was unprecedented (Ashworth 1991), although it became used for different ends during the 1980s.

The ideological impact of Thatcherism

Planning under the New Right

The 1980s have become synonymously linked with socio-economic polarities. The influence of Thatcherist monetarian policies directly conflicted with the traditional Keynesian model of land-use planning. Despising the ideological 'muddle' of the welfare state, the administration dismantled the planning apparatus, leaving only its bare essentials in the brave 'New Right' world of economic liberalism (Thornley 1993).

While many have written on the fragmentation of planning (Brindley *et al.* 1996), there is some disagreement as to the effects of these ideological changes (Allmendinger and Thomas 1998). Reade (1987) argues that planning was 'consolidated' during the 1980s – its latent deference to the market was made explicit. Thornley (1993) disagrees, since the nature of planning was changed beyond recognition from a regulative to a facilitative role for the land market. Nevertheless, planning has since become more tightly controlled by central government – a trend which has continued beyond the Conservatives' stay. The discretion afforded to local planning authorities was tolerable only in so far as their policies conformed to the implementation of Thatcher's economic programme (Thornley 1993). Traditional, or 'market critical', planning, as Brindley *et al.* (1996) have termed it, became less feasible as central policy initiatives gained supremacy.

Moreover, the basis on which traditional planning had been justified, the 'public interest', with its socialist overtones, did not accord with free-market principles. Planning was overwhelmed partly because this fundamental justification was founded on such insubstantial knowledge and a false consensus which disguised a multitude of conflicting sectional interests. As Thornley (1993) has commented, the transfer from 'public interest' to 'customer' and 'corporate' interest effectively saw the rejection of social and community values under Thatcherist planning ideology.

The sanctity of conservation?

However, the Omega Report 1982 (quoted in Thornley 1993), the basis of much of the then 'New Right' planning politick, identified the protection of historic buildings as a sphere in which regulative state planning may be advantageous: 'at a time when the Government had for nearly ten years been pursuing de-regulatory policies and seeking ways of simplifying the planning process, a different attitude was taken towards conservation' (Delafons 1997a: 167).

Thornley (1993) identifies a dual planning system in the 1980s. Pursuing a 'market-led' approach (Brindley *et al.* 1996), central government relaxed planning guidance, undermining local planning authorities' power to challenge developers' applications, irrespective of their merit. The imposition of standards, or upholding community objectives, was perceived as creating delays for development; the role of the planner was dramatically altered. Forever a contentious area, aesthetic control suffered particularly badly following the ideological preference towards market creativity (Punter 1986a).

However, deregulation resulted in a backlash from 'middle England' as new development encroached on their pleasant surroundings. Voters in Tory heartlands could not be too antagonised for fear of losing their political support; protecting their amenity was an area in which more regulatory planning might have been appropriate. While it may justify critiques of planning that point to its protecting the amenity of those enjoying the benefits of private property ownership (Foley 1973), arguably the emphasis on amenity favoured the conservation lobby. It is ironic that given prominent concerns over the style of new development (Charles, Prince of Wales 1989), conservation offered planning a solitary haven (RTPI 1990) in the face of such a widespread assault.

During this time, the Conservative government maintained enthusiastic support for the heritage. While Michael Heseltine (then Secretary of State for the Environment) promoted the accelerated resurvey of listed buildings, the government maintained active support for conservation. The creation of English Heritage (EH) in 1983, encompassing the responsibilities of the former Historic Buildings Council, to advise the government over heritage matters, could be seen as a further measure of deregulation and was initially greeted with some scepticism in the profession (Andreae 1996; Larkham and Barrett 1998). A new consolidating circular, Circular 8/87 (DoE 1987a), at the height of the 1980s property boom, retained the all-important presumption in favour of preservation of listed buildings and emphasised the 'overwhelming' public opinion in favour of conservation. While planning was being remoulded, conservation escaped relatively unscathed (Allmendinger and Thomas 1998).

However, in practice, conflicts remained as stricken local authorities were criticised for misapplying conservation in an abortive attempt to control development pressures and exercise some local autonomy over central government policy (Morton 1991). The tighter controls which conservation provided were seen by some to enable local planning authorities to 'plan' rather than 'respond' and to restate their local agenda on developers (Graves and Ross 1991; Thomas 1994). However, conservation has been used to both positive and negative ends. It has proved useful in some urban centres, enabling the councils to control development and create a place image through a closer control of the centre's appearance (Tarn 1985). But Morton (1991) laments that while it offers local councils the opportunity to enhance areas, many merely use it to prevent change. Conservation's misapplication could be criticised for compensating for the shortcomings of a revised planning system and thus straying further from the original justifications for protection.

Partnership in the 1990s

Sustainability and the plan-led system

If planning were ever in need of a white knight following the 1980s, perhaps it arrived in the form of the sustainable development agenda. While arguably this subject was nothing new for planning as a discipline of environmental management (Millichap 1993), the advent of 'plan-led' planning in the 1990s provided fresh impetus for planning activity, though opinions remain split over its practical results. The Town and Country Planning Act 1990, Planning and Compensation Act 1991 and PPG1 (DoE 1987b; revised DETR 1997) signified a strong, inclusionary framework for the production and enforcement of planning policies. By strengthening the status of the development plan, making it *the* material consideration, the framework appeared to show that conservation could benefit from an increasingly close relationship with statutory planning. However, early debates focused on the suitability of incorporating the minutiae of conservation controls, for example in local listing consent policy and conservation area designations in the local plan (Morton and Ayers 1993; Larkham 1994).

Despite the closer policy integration, a new Department of National Heritage (DNH) was created in 1992 with responsibility *inter alia* for conservation and 'heritage', while responsibility for mainstream planning remained in the then Department of the Environment. A new policy flagship emerged in 1994 expounding this joint ethos, PPG15, which, far in advance of its predecessors, emphasised the mutual goals of conservation and planning (DoE/DNH 1994). However, as Delafons (1997a) notes, it is rather difficult to 'square the circle', for planning 'to reconcile the need for economic growth with the need to protect the natural and historic environment' (DoE/DNH 1994: para. 1.2).

Sustainability provided a principle, if not the practice, with which to realise some of this common conservation language. However, the two documents intended to guide planning authorities' formation of regional, structure and local plans (EH 1993, 1996b) were more oriented to natural environment conservation. It is questionable how far this advice broadened the approach to the historic environment beyond the archaeological discipline, which has to date led the interpretation of sustainability in conservation practice. In contrast, a later discussion document about sustainability (EH 1997) appeared to revise the emphasis on conservation: sustainability involved taking a more holistic approach to the built environment, encouraging wider public interest and participation in identifying the meaning and symbolic importance of all elements in the historic environment, not just the efficient use of listed buildings.

Specific issues in conservation practice

There was a marked increase in the features subject to conservation protection throughout the 1980s and 1990s. The abolition of the 30-year rule has drawn post-war modern buildings into listing's frame of reference (EH 1996a). The renaming of The Thirties Society as the Twentieth Century Society reflects the ever-quickening realisation of value in the immediate past (Stamp 1996). Indeed, age could be seen as irrelevant, as even some protagonists of recent modern architecture wish the representations of their movement to be protected before their natural obsolescence calls forth pressures for redevelopment (Cunningham 1998). Such post-war listings were, without precedent, opened to public consultation. EH ran several campaigns to win hearts and minds, to raise public awareness and smooth the path for their listing; without a public understanding of the value of these features, there would be little popular support to justify these listings (Cherry 1996). Despite greater openness, the short-listed candidates were still received with incredulity by many of the broadsheets (Bevan 1996; Mellis 1998). Most of these buildings are now listed despite initial reactions; listing continues to lead public taste rather than react to it.

Although listing has been criticised for a lack of accountability and monitoring (Griffith 1989), conservation areas were also subject to a welter of criticism regarding their management. While listing has retained its legitimacy in pushing out the boundaries of 'special' interest in more diverse features, conservation area designation has suffered accusations of undermining the original intentions of the practice. While local authorities' autonomy to interpret local values and priorities is seen as conservation areas' main strength (Skea 1996), it permits hugely differing standards in practice.

The RTPI study *The Character of Conservation Areas* (Jones and Larkham 1993) worryingly echoes many of the conclusions of Gamston's (1975) much smaller survey, which preceded it by nearly 20 years. A lack of systematic designation, poor awareness and analysis of areas' character, a lack of policies for their enhancement and management, and a negative application of the available controls characterised many local authorities' practice. The study observed that the absence of a clear knowledge base for the value of a conservation area engendered a more preservationist attitude in controlling change in conservation areas. Morton (1991, 1998) indicates that local planning authorities' role of judge and jury allowed them to dictate protection measures without scrutiny, and lambasted their negative, preservationist attitudes. Even the law is uncertain of the positive duty on local planning authorities to improve their conservation areas (Hughes 1995; Larkham 1996). There has been mounting criticism of the ethos surrounding conservation areas: that they stifle modern design and instead harbour some of the worst examples of pastiche reproduction (Fairs 1998; Taylor 1998).

There appears to be simultaneous condemnation of the breadth of conservation's attention yet frustration with the toothlessness of controls to protect these 'special' features (Mynors 1984). The actual conservation area controls available to local authorities have been continually criticised for their weakness (EHTF 1992). Without an Article 4 Direction, small incremental changes, such as the ubiquitous satellite dish and plastic window, slip through conservation area control. (An Article 4 Direction, made by a council under Article 4 of the Town and Country Planning (General Permitted Development) Order 1995, makes it necessary to apply for planning permission to make changes that normally do not need it.) The *Shimizu* case (Brainsby and Carter 1997) which interpreted 'demolition' as 'complete demolition', meant that conservation area consent was rendered inapplicable to most cases concerning destructive 'alterations' in conservation areas. EH and the national amenity societies (NAS) have mooted a revision of conservation area consent (Saunders 1998). Instead of an express consent over demolition, the withdrawal of Permitted Development Rights in conservation areas would allow local authorities greater control over the incremental changes that have assaulted much of the original character which designation was meant to highlight. While this issue has now been clarified (DETR/DCMS 2001), conservation area controls remain weak.

There have always been calls to consolidate the various consent regimes, and Mynors' proposals (1998) to review the whole legislative framework of conservation areas and listed building consents, incorporating them into a single planning permission, are no exception. If we accept that the whole framework has become muddled and creates undue repetition, the proposals would integrate conservation culture into planning, rather than have it remain a marginalised activity (Aldous 1997).

English Heritage – the 'lead body'

Emerging from its formative years and an apparent preoccupation with managing the state's own properties, EH formed strong associations with the conservation movement and may be in the questionable position of acting as an advocate for, rather than an adviser on, conservation matters (Delafons 1997a). However, EH experienced a distinct change following Sir Jocelyn Stevens' appointment as chair in 1992. Stevens' forthright leadership had an immediate impact in the publication of a new agenda (EH 1992). The document indicated a retreat from an all-embracing patronage of conservation to a strategic refocusing of resources on high-priority cases and being an enabling body, with local authorities taking greater responsibility for their conservation assets. While this prompted a violent response from other conservation organisations, it was welcomed in certain respects as the first clear strategic response to the problems of managing such a large number of listed buildings and conservation areas (Delafons 1997a). However, Stephens had his critics too and has been accused of leading the organisation down several dead ends. The new chair, Sir Neil Cossons, appears to be a pragmatic head but faces many challenges from competing agendas, not least in defining EH's own role as a conservation regulator, adviser and provider.

Realising the economic benefits and marketability of re-using historic buildings brought EH into contact with regeneration agencies – English Partnerships in particular – and the general scope of the Single Regeneration Budget. EH needed to revise its sphere of influence and overcome the difficulty of functioning from the margins of the Department of National Heritage. The change of government in May 1997 was to prove decisive, particularly the new administration's support of urban regeneration. Soon after, EH announced

> [a] radical role change . . . to become much more of a planning watchdog as
> well as a 'front-line regeneration agency' in a move away from its traditional
> conservation role. . . . English Heritage can no longer think just of 'conserva-
> tion' but rather must consider 'environment quality'.
>
> (Rogers 1997: 3)

While EH has always been involved in promoting the re-use of buildings, it may
be survival instinct that drives its pursuit of the wider urban regeneration
agenda. The threatened reduction of heritage bodies following the 1998 Comprehensive Spending Review saw English Heritage become the lead body in the
sector, incorporating the functions of the Royal Commission on the Historic
Monuments of England (RCHME). However, the new administration presented
a different playing field for heritage: where once there had been support, there
now appeared to be apathy (Venning 1998). In promoting the modernisation of
public administration, 'heritage' appears anathematic to the Labour government. At one level, changing the Department of 'National Heritage' to the
Department of 'Culture, Media and Sport' may appear superficial. At another,
the terms of reference for the Urban Task Force (UTF 1999) and its recommendations maintained a cursory treatment of the positive contribution of
conservation-based approaches.

EH has actually lost its lead role in providing grant assistance to projects.
Though it is retained as adviser to the Heritage Lottery Fund, a new funding
agenda has replaced EH's previous monopoly. The re-assessment of the short-
lived Conservation Area Partnership Scheme (CAPS) and the creation of the
Heritage Economic Regeneration Scheme (HERS) see priorities and application
criteria change from purely a concern with the historic fabric to equally
promoting investment in jobs and business in more neglected areas (Antram
1999). Meanwhile, the Townscape Heritage Initiative, run by the Heritage Lottery
Fund, would appear to be stalking English Heritage's traditional ground, though
again the emphasis is on economic regeneration (Johnston 1998).

The political shift towards emphasising large-scale urban regeneration at the
expense of contextual conservation was criticised by Dame Jennifer Jenkins as
being as potentially destructive as the comprehensive clearance schemes of the
1960s (Bateson 1998). Other conservation bodies, endorsing this reaction, have
lobbied under the joint auspices of their report *Catalytic Conversion* (SAVE
1998), which stresses the re-use of listed buildings and empty premises to meet
development pressures (Binney 1998). Similarly, two English Heritage reports,
Conservation-Led Regeneration (1998) and *The Heritage Dividend* (1999), also
highlight their successful grant-funding for the progressive re-use of old buildings. The language and presentation, of the latter particularly, reflect the political
preferences for strategies promoting economic regeneration and social inclusion,

environmental quality and sustainability. As the chair noted, 'The role of the built heritage in the regeneration of communities, however, has not always been fully understood' (ibid.: 5). The extent to which the political consensus supporting conservation has been undermined, or at least altered, by this change of priorities remains to be seen.

Professionally, the distinctions between the rhetoric of conservation, urban regeneration and design quality may be disappearing (Worthington *et al.* 1998). Indeed, many in the urban design professions believe that the aims of conservation increasingly should correspond with their own (Stones 1998). Similarly, the conversion of old buildings became a defining architectural expression of the late twentieth century (Brolin 1980; Powell 1999). As part of its remit, the new Commission for Architecture and the Built Environment (CABE) includes not only the promotion of good modern design but also a reciprocal concern about the preservation of modern architecture (Lewis 1999). However, another reason for CABE's role may be the anomalous position of EH commenting on modern design issues while maintaining no professional architectural representation in the upper echelons of the organisation (Bateson 1999).

Irrespective of the relationship of planning, conservation and architecture, there is no denying the ballooning scope of 'value' that conservation identifies in the built environment. The statutory framework for conservation cannot be discussed without reference to this increasing interest in the past and the emergence of 'heritage'.

The rise of 'heritage'

Aside from the burgeoning official heritage in the ever-increasing numbers of listed buildings and conservation areas, the past 25 years has witnessed a dramatic rise in popular interest in the past. Is there any relationship between the two? Should conservation planning be more attentive in widening the scope of what it ought to consider protecting, or are these just passing fads?

The recycling, repackaging or rediscovery of the past is ubiquitous in everyday life: the penchant for period homes, various 'retro' fashions, antique-collecting, 'heritage' attractions and museums, huge increases in National Trust membership, TV costume dramas, family history societies . . . the list is endless (Fowler 1992). It is convenient to label this phenomenon 'heritage', yet

> heritage is a slippery concept. The word alludes to ownership being passed on, but it is perhaps more accurate and useful to recast the heritage idea to stand for things created, maintained and held within a community which it wants to continue to maintain and hold.
>
> (Thomas 1994: 70)

This increased use of the past raises some fundamental questions. Is this rise a reflection of genuine interest in the past or is it an artificial manipulation of circumstances for ulterior purposes? Is this less orthodox and more popular use of the past debasing credible historic interpretation or is it a creative economic phenomenon which makes the past a more vibrant and useful resource? Heritage has most influenced conservation in two inter-related ways: 'commodification' of the past and its political manipulation.

'Commodification'

The conservation of relics has traditionally been justified by their intrinsic historical or artistic value. However, commerce's realisation of a distinct market of heritage consumers exploits the use and interpretation value of features and their environments. Wright (1985) observes that the rise of a heritage enterprise culture in the mid-1980s coincided with the market-oriented heritage programme of the Thatcher administration: encouraging private commerce replaced the reliance on state subsidy to maintain the nation's cultural heritage. Moreover, the social prestige associated with 'old things' made previously unloved relics into profitable assets: for example, the restoration of old buildings for office use lent an immediate image of tradition and status.

The effects attracted criticism, Hewison's (1987) attack on this heritage 'industry' being one of the most acerbic. Perceiving Britain to be a spent industrial force, he lambasts the recycling and reconstructions of the past in museums and 'heritage attractions' the country over. Rather than 'innovate' a way out of socio-economic decline, factory museums preserved outmoded production. The heritage industry, exploitative and voyeuristic, spoon-fed tourists a processed view of the once 'Great' Britain, accompanied by 'authentic' merchandising. While echoing Davis's (1979) exploration of resurgent social and personal nostalgia for the past, he concludes that heritage is a media creation.

However, as Corner and Harvey (1991) note, these critiques were written at a time of industrial economic decline. Arguably, the 1990s witnessed a more creative use of heritage resources. The economic benefits of heritage are well documented in relation to tourism and leisure industries (Urry 1990, 1995; Fowler 1992). Ashworth (1994), among others, notes the potential conflicts created between different heritage markets when the distinctiveness of the local historic environment is marketed according to a homogenising pre-subjective image of an historic attraction. However, the revenue generated by tourism is an important multiplier in the local economy. Commodification occurs at another level, when the historic fabric is used to project an attractive urban image. In the competition for mobile capital and investment, the use value of the heritage may be paramount in local political economic priorities (Strange 1996).

The 'national heritage' and 'national past'

> Who controls the past controls the future; who controls the present
> controls the past.
>
> (Orwell 1989: 37)

The second change was the political or ideological use of the 'national identity'. There is no denying that 'the past' is far from a static and immutable certainty (Wright 1985). The past only exists as the politics and culture of the present construct it through a process of selective representation (Fowler 1992). Thus although temporarily passed, the past is continually rewritten, a product and reflection of contemporary society (Lynch 1972).

The 'national past' and the 'national heritage' were concepts implicitly nurtured by the Conservative Party and arguably exploited by the Thatcher administration to ease society's acceptance of the drastic economic transformation of Britain. Wright (1985) notes that relics from the past – old buildings and monuments – represent a physical and tangible arena to which the abstract 'national past' could attach. The 'national heritage' is politically constructed; events and characters are selected to legitimate the current situation. Such 'national' visions invoke past grandeur and the glory of military and political success (against communism and socialism), of state pomp and aristocratic luxury.

Through selective representation, a dominant, narrow interpretation of Englishness could be used to promote and legitimate Conservative values of tradition and continuity (McGuigan 1996). These values were essential to maintaining the popularity of the Conservatives' mandate as perversely their new economic and social order was destroying regional and class traditions and social customs which lay outside this 'essential' heritage. The superimposed projection of an oligarchic class conception of the past excluded personal and community interpretations of the past. Instead of emphasising plurality, the emphasis lay on the great events in state history.

Displacing history

Antagonists claim that while heritage purports to be educative, it actually 'draws a screen between us and our past' (Hewison 1987: 10). It is sanitised, stripped of its authenticity, and in its pre-processed nature offers no scope for reflective criticism or personal awareness. Popular it may be, but this is no sign of historical quality (Beazley 1981).

Similarly, the success and legitimacy of a 'national heritage' is dependent upon a history which commemorates grand events and characters at the level of state importance. This history is entropic, the story is presented as definitive –

complete and unassailable (Wright 1985). Though the 'national heritage' is dependent on historical fact, its nostalgic and mythical aura 'floats' above objective history. Yet the whole idea of objective history was to emancipate individuals from the mythical and pseudo-religious hold which subservience to the past engendered (Plumb 1969) – though as Wright (1985) and Lowenthal (1985) note, the past cannot be burned away by historical objectivity; it resides in the personal, emotional and localised experiences of individuals.

It is possible to see how the legacy of Enlightenment (and modernist) tendencies to uphold technical rationality as the sole purveyor of reason down-graded the emotive world of everyday experience and the personal and social values therein in historical inquiry and legitimisation (Wright 1985). However, as Samuel (1994) has noted, the rise of 'heritage' has brought new interpretations of the form and content of historical knowledge. Through heritage, the abstract and general nature of history is replaced with a more inter-subjective use of the past according to the specific and emotional way in which people relate to their own past. The 'establishment mode' of history is displaced by the more socially oriented historiographic approach, which offers a more conciliatory relationship with heritage.

Heritage as a broader concept

Critiques of heritage generally follow a consumerist or a structuralist perspective. Yet Samuel (1994) perceives heritage as a field of agency or individual expression. Rather than being a phenomenon emanating from top-level political and commercial interests, heritage is the pluralist representation of interest, perception and use of the past. Arguably, Wright and Hewison were premature in aligning heritage to Thatcherism since the latter's economic liberalism still allowed private property interests to destroy valuable aspects of the built heritage. By setting heritage in a longer time frame and broader context, Samuel argues that the term 'heritage' is no more right-wing than it is left. Heritage is history outside the confines of archival historical study; it is access to the living past and a creative, personal interpretation of it (Macmillan 1993). The value of features emanates from personal assimilation, not one imposed by didactic politics. Such interactive use of the relics of the past can be a powerful tool with which to deconstruct more conservative notions of heritage (Lowenthal 1981).

Lord Clark notes that civilised humankind needs a 'sense of permanence' and 'must feel that he belongs somewhere in time and space' (Cantell 1975: 8). It is this realm in which the separate theses of Lowenthal, Wright and Samuel coalesce: 'The surviving past's most essential and pervasive benefit is to render the present familiar' (Lowenthal 1985: 39). Lowenthal (1985) categorises the benefits of the past's relics as being the familiarity, re-affirmation and validity, identity, guidance, enrichment and escape they provide. The past provides personal, social and spatial identity; such reference points are necessary to live in the 'temporal collage' of the built environment (Lynch 1972). It reaffirms and validates the uncertainties of the present. Wright (1985) has commented that the capitalist economy has created increasing spatial and personal dislocation by demanding a mobile workforce and the development of areas with minimal reference to their existing character. By consciously filling our environments with relics of the past, their presence acts to offset the loss experienced in this change (Hareven and Langenbach 1981); their value lies beyond our human timescale (Lynch 1972). In their possession and use, the search for temporal and spatial roots accounts for the rise of interest in personal and group heritage which Samuel (1994) identifies.

Wright (1985) explains this phenomenon by the concept of 'everyday historical consciousness', which rests on 'the sense of historical existence' and 'not . . . any special knowledge of history or the past but . . . the everyday consciousness of "practically everyone who reflects upon his/her life experience in our world"' (Wright 1985: 143).

Put simply, this means that the past is not defined by history – particular taught knowledge or the state; the past exists within individuals' interpretation of the qualities of age in the environment surrounding them and in the use of those qualities to improve their understanding and enjoyment of the present. Heritage thus potentially rises in everything pre-dating the present moment, but its defining characteristic is the active and creative use of the qualities of that 'relic', not merely its physical preservation *per se* (Macmillan 1993).

Heritage – a new paradigm for conservation?

While 'heritage' has been much discussed in history and cultural studies, it often falls between established protagonist and antagonist positions regarding conservation planning. Those who oppose the politicisation of state protection see heritage as extending the hand of the dead over the living (Ascherson 1987). Innovation and progress are stifled in this dogmatic reverence for the past as society becomes resentful of any change (O'Rourke 1987). Those who support conservation on the traditional criteria of special architectural or historic interest generally view the wider heritage as undermining the status afforded to special features in the built environment for which conservation was originally intended (Mynors 1984).

However, there are very poignant questions raised by 'heritage'. Ashworth (1991, 1994, 1997) perhaps goes furthest in his re-appraisal of conservation. Fully accepting the commodification of features that heritage engenders, he concludes that this new relationship of multiple users or consumers of the past is the most helpful way of redesigning a responsible conservation system.

Arguing that protection has not escaped the preservationist legacy or its origins (despite counter-claims that 'conservation' is a progressive art), he sees the preservationist monopoly as becoming increasingly untenable.

The preservationist paradigm exudes an unquestionable, self-evident belief that the past ought to be preserved in the public interest. Further analysis is deflected through generalised norms which lack any evidential support. In contrast, the heritage paradigm, being more open and pluralist, actively acknowledges the variety of heritage users and their requirements.

The concept of 'authenticity', on which the current criteria for defining special interest rest, is presented as objectively definable and recognisable, given appropriate professional training. However, this creates two fundamental problems. First, it secures the legitimate determination of these features in the hands of an expert minority. Second, the concept of authenticity itself, as Lowenthal notes, is 'a dogma of self-delusion' (quoted in Ashworth 1997: 97). By the time features become considered for protection, they have already become 'sacralized' into potential monuments by surviving the natural processes of erosion and obsolescence. Once selected for protection, they become further 'fossilised' by the halting of the natural processes of decay to which the rest of the environment is subject. 'Selection for preservation is further likely to favour the spectacular over the mundane, the large over the small, the beautiful over the ugly and the unusual over the commonplace' (Ashworth 1997: 97). Since this produces an end state which is neither authentic nor capable of evolution, Ashworth argues that rather than concentrate on the object, the heritage paradigm focuses on the quality and authenticity of experience felt by the user of these features.

Thus heritage emancipates protection so that value is not solely the universal, objective and academic interpretation but allows a flexible and diverse interpretation. Since the preservationist legacy sees value as intrinsic and obvious to the expert, 'the idea that interpretations of the past should play contemporary political or social roles will be denied, or at least distanced as mere propaganda' (Ashworth 1997: 98). A heritage interpretation involves polysemic and continually evolving meanings which allow the relationship with pressures for land-use development to be mediated since it applies throughout the whole environment and not just those bits of it defined as 'special'.

This cultural diversity in the heritage is starting to be acknowledged in EH's literature, but while it is relatively easy to champion diversity in short statements, it is far more difficult to work it into the interpretation of statutory conservation responsibilities.

Emerging relationships

In reviewing salient periods in a hundred years of conservation planning and current influential trends, it is evident that conservation has been used to different ends at different times. The mechanisms which might have been suitable for one context may not have always been the best tools to apply to a further set of new problems which raised their own challenges. However, it is evident that conservation has been remarkably flexible and fleet of foot in its responses; it is debatable whether it continues to be so in its current institutional guises, but that is an issue to be explored later.

Clearly, conservation's justifications have been shaped by its responses to wider social, economic and political circumstances. There remain a great many tensions within these justifications and some do not easily sit alongside each other. The interface of these conflicts provides the most accessible and interesting place to start teasing apart what conservation stands for. These relationships are not between specific processes or objects of conservation concern but pose the following general questions:

- Given the gradual coalescence between planning and conservation practices, how do the mechanics and scale of conservation complement (or otherwise) planning?
- How do various interpretations of what conservation should be protecting change both over time and according to different people's backgrounds and perceptions?
- How far are the experience, use and exploitation of conservation resources influenced by various other national and local interests and agendas?

Though these relationships are still very general, they provide a starting point for mapping out conservation's intricacies in the following chapter.

3   A thematic framework

Introduction

While chapter 2 provides an interesting story about conservation's emergence within statutory land-use planning, it does not in itself provide any tools with which to test the values and justifications which underlie contemporary practice. In fact, few pieces written on conservation do.

What is clear is that conservation has developed many facets, implicit and explicit, with the potential to illuminate or indict the received wisdom about its operation within planning. However, the distribution, use and interpretation of these values are far from uniform, with different systems and levels of conservation pursuing potentially contradictory objectives. There are several significant relationships already identified, but within these are more specific themes with their own inherent tensions that can be used as a framework within which to analyse themes in the empirical evidence gathered.

This thematic framework needs to encompass the 'big picture', embracing all aspects of conservation: principles and policies, processes and practice, personnel, subjects and objects. While any number of existing theoretical perspectives could have been used to illustrate a particular area, for instance a postmodern conceptualisation of values and 'reality', no single theory could provide a comprehensive analytical tool for the whole of this study. Thus rather than draw exclusively on one or two areas, a broader approach to theory is required, especially given the diversity of values highlighted and the lack of a single conservation ethic.

Other writers conclude their studies with a similar thematic dissection and exposition of value relationships in conservation (Larkham 1996; Mageean 1999). Considering their consistency and cogency in highlighting particularly significant issues, an analysis using these self-referencing themes seems particularly appropriate.

The thematic framework necessarily has to be flexible to accommodate a wide range of issues, some of which may not be apparent until the final analysis. It needs to perform a range of functions too throughout the study, providing a credible intellectual basis not only for conducting the research but also for analysing the findings. However, this thematic framework cannot be said to be definitive or universally accurate: it is a construct based on the literature of the field, which in itself may be exclusionary or biased.

The advantage of constructing this bespoke thematic framework is that (conservation plan or character assessment studies aside) there is no existing equivalent framework for conservation research and so it may be seen as a methodological innovation in itself.

The Adelphi, London: the destruction of Adam's terrace was one of many inter-war losses that catalysed the formation of the Georgian Group
© E. O. Hoppé/CORBIS

To recap on the preceding chapter, the main emerging questions are:

- Given the gradual coalescence between planning and conservation practices, how do the mechanics and scale of conservation complement planning?
- How do various interpretations of what conservation should be protecting change both over time and according to different people's backgrounds and perceptions?
- How far are the experience, use and exploitation of conservation resources influenced by various other national and local interests and agendas?

Evidently each question raises many inter-related issues which cannot be considered in isolation. Perhaps it is easiest to conceptualise them not as a tightly knit bundle, but by extrapolating them to create two distinct and opposing viewpoints. Within this spectrum, different positions and arguments can be positioned relative to one another.

The presentation of these polarised issues in table 3.1 is not meant to symbolise two distinct and unified perspectives of conservation. Rather, the headings iden-

Table 3.1 Tensions in conservation

How do the scale and mechanics of conservation complement planning?

Conservation is separate from planning	Conservation is integral to planning
Conservation is structure specific	Conservation is environmental
Conservation is about preservation	Conservation is about conservation
Conservation is a minority interest	Conservation is a popular interest

How do various interpretations of what conservation should be protecting change both over time and according to different people's backgrounds and perceptions?

Conservation is architectural and historic value	Conservation is societal and cultural value
Conservation is of special, national importance	Conservation is of familiar, local interest
Conservation is about expert opinion	Conservation is about lay opinion
Objective historical knowledge	The past as a cultural collage

How far is the experience, use and exploitation of conservation resources influenced by various other national and local interests and agendas?

Conservation is about intrinsic value	Conservation is about commodity value
Conservation enjoys a purity of choice	Conservation is a political tool

tify the extreme ends of a particular interpretation, which affect the various levels and regimes of conservation differentially. For any one issue, somewhere between these poles there will be a point where the two viewpoints collide. Where this happens along the spectrum will depend on different people's perceptions and the particular level or practice of conservation under study. This idea of a spectrum of polarities illustrates tensions quite neatly but it could be judged as over-prescriptive. Instead, these polarities were recast as particular themes within conservation, which offered a more flexible interpretation.

Although these themes' success in providing a relevant and robust framework throughout justifies their definition, they remain heuristic interpretations. It is worth noting that several significant revisions were made to the framework during the study. Some changes were needed to make the framework into a workable tool to accommodate the nature of individuals' responses. Other revisions were caused when the fieldwork threw up new themes which were not apparent in the existing conservation literature.

What is clear, though, is that this approach provides a way of breaking down the messy amalgam of individuals' expressions into ten distinct themes. These are explored below and are used throughout the fieldwork and subsequent analysis.

The relationship between conservation and statutory planning (separate from planning . . . integral to planning)

Emerging from different backgrounds and pressures in the last century, conservation and planning have gradually coalesced. Over this time they have been similarly influenced by the prevailing political, economic and social conditions. Two questions may be asked of their relationship: first, the extent to which these systems benefit by closer integration; second, the extent to which their principles, policies and procedures do fit with one another.

It appears to be the norm to describe the relationship as a cyclical one in terms of development threats and reactionary politics establishing new conservation regimes and values. An ever-closer relationship between planning and conservation has seen planning providing the means and muscle previously lacking to prevent the last late lamented demolition of a valuable historic feature.

While the greater part of the literature presents this as a natural unfolding order, there was 'no implied progression in the sense of either logical inevitability or desirability' in their coalescence (Ashworth 1997: 94). Certain events may have catalysed legislative or other responses, drawing on (or even forming anew) a groundswell of opinion, but this often produced knee-jerk responses rather than a definitive and principled agenda. While this shaped a closer relationship between planning and conservation, there has been little in terms of actual foresight to achieve this. Mynors (1998) concludes that the legal framework that has been created is totally illogical and requires drastic simplification.

In its development, conservation has been influenced by prevailing attitudes towards the concept of land-use planning. The first legislation, the Ancient Monuments Act 1882, was introduced at a time when the absence of any co-ordinated planning system allowed the ethos of protection to develop quite freely from other issues. Early planning legislation from 1900 onwards was mostly concerned with ensuring the amenity of new development.

Although listing was considered a backwater of the 1947 planning system, it was originally intended to be of integral assistance to the formation of strategic plans. The planning culture of the day that espoused finite master plans and 'once and for all' surveys influenced the approach to compiling statutory lists of features of special interest even though the listing process was carried out quite independently (Ashworth 1997). It also reflected the physicalism and comprehensivism dominating the planning profession. However, listing's operational separation continued a distinction between the consideration of a building's development and of a building's artistry.

As planning was criticised for its sloth and inflexibility in reacting to social and economic change, so too listing inadequately protected features as individual morsels while their characteristic surroundings were redeveloped. Despite the introduction of listed building consents in 1968, conservation required a broader concept of area-based protection. Although the early rapid designation of conservation areas was imperative and meant the omission of many recognised planning requirements (Gamston 1975), it gradually came more to resemble planning, with the introduction of tighter consent procedures for alterations and demolitions in conservation areas in 1971 (DoE 1972). Yet at the time, Rock (1974) observed that protection was internally confused over its direction: protection concerned much more than buildings alone, yet planning legislation was lagging behind. From the early 1970s, the conservation area and listed building consent procedures have paralleled the procedural decision-making of general planning permission cases (Ross 1995).

Following Circular 8/87 (DoE 1987a), PPG15 further emphasises that conservation is integral to planning through the development plan. It seems that conservation has fully achieved integration, with such official statements as 'Conservation in the built environment is most emphatically not something separate from mainstream town and country planning' (RTPI 1993: 1) and 'Conservation is moving into the mainstream of national life and planners are helping to put it there' (*Planning* 1998: 15).

Some observers doubt how practical the generalised nature of development plan policy will be for the specific requirements of the management of discrete areas (Larkham 1994). Indeed, continuing calls for local authorities to embrace conservation plans beyond their planning responsibilities (Clark 1998) and the unresolved lack of protection for many locally important unlisted buildings (Boland 1999) indicate that statutory planning is still not as effective for conservation as many would wish to see it. However, the official recognition that conservation is a significant component in planning is welcome (Barrett 1993). It ought be recognised, though, that in pursuing integration, conservation becomes equally susceptible to the political conflicts inherent in planning.

While the following section looks at the focus of conservation controls, it is important to highlight these in relation to the planning framework. Some writers have commented that listing and conservation areas are proof that planners do not have the necessary skill and appreciation to protect the 'historic' environment without its being specifically highlighted (Ayers 1977). Reade (1991) goes further, criticising the administrative segregation of conservation, which reduces the importance of conservation as a general planning principle. Punter (1987) also criticises this two-tier system of conservation since it down-grades the features and areas not on administrative lists: they receive perfunctory standards of design control, thereby eroding the identity of less 'pretty' areas. Proposals to incorporate conservation controls into planning permissions may solve this marginalisation but there still exists a professional distinction between conservation and planning exposed by the creation of the Institute of Historic Building Conservation at a time when the Royal Town Planning Institute (RTPI) was attempting to embrace conservation.

The spatial focus of conservation controls (structure specific . . . environmental)

Conservation has evolved from protecting isolated sites of ancient archaeological interest to encompassing whole sections of the urban environment. Within this huge spatial range, the respective control regimes' strengths and weaknesses reveal the inherent priorities and values in the system.

On one level, the relative strength of controls reflects the political support behind them. Similarly, funding for the various conservation regimes indicates where priorities lie. On another level, the breadth of conservation's focus involves different conceptual and professional approaches. Comparing minute details in a building's construction with the environmental capacity of the historic environment encompasses professional approaches with differing languages and philosophies, from architectural historians to environmental conservationists. Any relative strength of one scale of protection over another is also reflective of the dominant professional values in conservation; the question is the extent to which any potential differences create conflict and tension.

The resilience of private property rights in the face of any state intervention has moulded statutory conservation control, the Ancient Monuments Acts of 1882 and 1913 being classic examples. Contrary to prevailing expectations prior to listing introduction, listing practice has shunned a more holistic view of the protection of places: the professional preference and administrative direction for listing concentrated on individual buildings (Earl 1997). Contextual value was considered more appropriate for general development control, though the influence of private property rights persisted in listed building consent case law, refining the introspective concepts of curtilage, fixtures and fittings: considering the building in isolation rather than in its context (Mynors 1995; Suddards 1996).

The focus on individual features in the environment became more apparent when new development, often dramatically, changed the context of these isolated 'gems'. Introducing area-based conservation heralded a new approach to perceiving the value of features: 'If the townscape or cadastral unit is the object of concern then this has implications for the functioning of such areas which were not so obvious when monuments could be treated as isolated islands' (Ashworth 1991: 21). While the conservation area was a major triumph for lobbyists, its legislative phrasing continues to provoke criticism. First, while broadening the physical scale of protection, it extended concepts of 'value' far wider than could be realistically accommodated within the existing listing criteria of 'special architectural or historic interest'. This will be dealt with in greater detail below (see p. 66).

Second, area-based conservation involved not only buildings of minor interest but also the spatial relationship between built elements. A renewed discipline emerged through the townscape analysis work of Worskett (1969) and Cullen (1971) among others. Although later criticised for its pictorial simplicity (Hubbard 1994), it started to blur the professional distinctions separating conservationists, urban designers and planners. Moreover, in addition to the spatial expansion of value, the 'character' of an area is not definable solely by its buildings. The uses and users of these areas, the social and less tangible cultural dimensions of character, were not represented in conservation guidance, despite the Civic Amenity Act's introduction during a period of planning characterised by a strong public participation agenda. Ironically, to prevent the erosion of areas' character, the strengthening of building-specific controls has been mooted for conservation areas (EHTF 1992).

Third, despite the introduction of conservation area consent in 1972 and its extension in 1974 to cover all demolitions of unlisted buildings in conservation areas (DoE 1974), the controls accompanying designation have remained fairly weak. The lack of clear area-based concepts and the reluctance of central government to direct local authorities' initiatives in this field have not supported conservation area controls. Listing, by contrast, enjoyed an introduction in a period of planning characterised by strong regulatory controls.

The combination of weak area-based concepts and controls, leaving context poorly understood and protected, has created a 'critical cultural gap that remains to be filled' (Saint 1996: 133). The contribution of more intensive urban townscape and morphological analysis has not been fully realised in planning practice (Barrett 1993; Larkham 1996; Mageean 1999). This lack of holistic, contextual management has led to criticisms that the British system places 'its emphasis on preserving individual buildings as monuments, while, as a nation, we treat our historic towns, cities and villages badly' (Powell 1992).

Though 'character' and 'appearance' were inevitably criticised for introducing amenity 'by the back door' into a purists' realm of protection (Mynors 1984), there is a growing concern to address context. While 'place' is not a new concept (Relph 1976; Johnson 1991; Urry 1995), it has gained ground after years of the modernist planning proclivity for eliminating area-based character in favour of providing universal 'space' – a blank sheet for development needs. Indeed, Worthington *et al.* (1998: 177) conclude that 'placemaking is now at the heart of conservation'. Certainly the EHTF is promoting place management as a central component of good practice for local authorities (EHTF 1998). It is also having an impact on official conservation thinking: providing a 'sense of place' has appeared in government policy as a justification for conservation; however, its meaning receives scant elucidation (PPG15: paras 6.1–6.2). Urban designers have been championing the concept for years and it is arguable that conservation is outmoded. Embracing a concept of 'place' and promoting sustainable environments are perhaps the two main challenges facing conservation practice (Dean 1992). Particularly given the political ascendancy of sustaining the natural environment (Mageean 1999), it is questionable whether built environment conservation has been 'left behind' (EHTF 1992: 5).

The extent of acceptable change (preservationism . . . conservationism)

Owen (1976) comments that conservation is one end of the spectrum of appropriate techniques for dealing with development. Despite the philosophical and practical confusion between the various interpretations of preservation and conservation, they are defined by the same root: 'the management of change'. 'Preservation' and 'conservation' have almost become self-parodying defences erected by different groups – architects confronting planners or conservationists against developers – from which they can cast aspersions on the others' interpretations of 'acceptable' change.

Ashworth (1997) considers that the preservationist legacy has monopolised protection control in Britain for the past century. With an antiquarian bias, preservation halts the temporal decay of a relic, leaving it as an archival record. This initial ethos could not foresee how the conservation regimes were to evolve; 'the more successful the movement the more is created to preserve' (Ashworth 1991: 25). Relying on the ability of the owner to pay the maintenance costs, preservation became increasingly untenable since prohibiting change restricts a building's capacity to generate income: preservation was perceived as a liability by owners.

During the 1960s, the introduction of conservation areas increased the number of buildings subject to protection control. A professional desire to break from the preservationist mould accompanied the promotion of a more creative use and integration of these old buildings: the 'enhancement' of areas (Maguire 1998). Government policy emphasised conservation as a positive responsibility, tolerant of appropriate new additions and revitalising buildings (MHLG 1967b).

However, conservation areas have not been characterised as representing a progressive approach (O'Rourke 1987; Morton 1998). Irrespective of local planning authority management, the reluctance to be progressive is often blamed on a fear of change, a continuing reaction against desensitising modernist post-war urban redevelopment (Relph 1987). Some writers highlight the limits of the human capacity to deal with extensive environmental change (Toffler 1970; Marris 1993). Arguably, the architectural profession's candour for building a bold future is not always shared by the general public (Stamp 1996). It places the planning profession in a particularly difficult position in balancing the 'public interest' over acceptable change, while wishing to avoid accusations of repeating previous mistakes.

Despite such criticisms, two agendas have influenced the perceived degree of acceptable change over the past 20 years. The first has been the increasing emphasis on sustainable conservation. In most interpretations this provides a resource-based economic rationale for bringing old structures back into use. The second agenda may be partially due to the success of the first in changing attitudes. Developers have been more eager to pursue conversion than new build, particularly if the associated 'heritage' value of an old building adds to the commercial profit. The message regarding re-inventing buildings and areas rather than re-creating them is percolating the profession (Latham 1999). Such conversions and their contribution to urban regeneration schemes are increasingly being stressed by EH (1998, 1999). These statements about EH's role indicate the direction in which conservation practice is heading: rather than being a desirable end in itself, conservation would be further applied as a tool of economic regeneration, driven by an urban development agenda rather than an art-historical, cultural one.

The basis of conservation's support and legitimacy (minority interest . . . popular interest)

The early preservationist pioneers are easily characterised as an elitist minority of upper-middle-class intellectuals. Their evangelical concern for saving ancient monuments was overtly historicist and their connection to a lamented 'golden age' was wholly romantic (Kennet 1972). However, their concerns accompanied a radical social agenda which drew inspiration from the spiritual and aesthetic beauty and continuity provided by these features (Macmillan 1993). Considering that this emancipatory agenda motivated some conservationists, the contrast with the present situation is all the more startling as conservation now appears to be part of 'the establishment' and is generally accepted as a good thing by the majority of people. On the face of it, this consensus seems so widespread as to be beyond reproach; Delafons (1997b) notes the lack of ardent criticism levelled at the conservation system. Its popularity appears to give conservation political legitimacy.

The literature tends to present conservation's broadening appeal as a cycle of increasing public awareness as certain important buildings are threatened with demolition; the reaction to protect them raises the value and profile of a particular style or period of architecture. It is an educative process as certain 'taste-leaders' transform public preferences (Stamp 1996). The formation of various interest groups (now the statutory amenity societies) in response to these watersheds has provided convenient pegs on which to hang an analysis of the broadening appreciation and appeal of conservation.

However, such an approach focuses on the evolution and appreciation of architectural taste, of legitimating ever more recent pieces of architecture for conservation's attention. It neglects the wider cultural appreciation of the past outside these architectural manifestations. The rise in popularity of the 'heritage' – a range of interests and activities loosely associated with the past – has undoubtedly seen a broader and more popular appreciation of the relics of history. Such a perspective, irrespective of its depth or credibility, does oppose the elitist attitude which formed the preservation lobby (Samuel 1994). There remains a cultural or even class distinction surrounding 'the heritage'. Whereas Hewison (1987) cites local museums, conservation areas, heritage shops, and so on as being biased towards the middle-class ghettos of England, Samuel (1994) criticises him and other heritage-baiters of inverse snobbery in their pillorying of heritage as 'low-brow' mass culture.

The extent to which popular interest resides in this more heritage-oriented sphere rather than an architectural one may be quite anomalous for the 'consensus' supporting conservation. A distinction ought to be made between an interest in the past, an interest in the past manifest in the built environment and an interest in the past which can be accommodated or expressed through conservation controls. The consensus may be questionable if its popularity is due to a wider interpretation of interest in the past than those factors which conservation planning recognises. If this is the case, then it begs the question, who defines the consensus or public interest?

National policy in PPG15 cites 'processes of consultation and education to facilitate' broad public support as being a 'key element' for conservation planning (DoE/DNH 1994: para. 1.7). From the emphasis placed on public participation in the Civic Amenities Act, government policy has encouraged local authorities to involve the public in conservation area designations (MHLG 1968). However, the continuing vitriol against development pressures over-riding local objections questions conservation's response to popular concerns. Recent research suggests that although conservation is well supported, public understanding of conservation controls, justifications and presence is low or misinterpreted (Townshend and Pendlebury 1999). Though conservation officers believed in engaging local opinion, confusion arose over whether this process was intended to educate or to learn from the public (Pendlebury and Townsend 1999). Conservation may be popular but does its statutory incarnation necessarily represent a popular interpretation of values?

The interpretation of features' interest (architectural and historical . . . societal and cultural)

> The long development of architectural restoration has provided the theoretical and practical support for urban conservation since the last century.
>
> (Zanchetti and Jokilehto 1997: 38)

The term 'special architectural or historic interest' has long been established as a central definition in conservation planning (Delafons 1997a). There appears to have been little criticism of the phrase because it has successfully accommodated shifting interpretations: PPG15's definition of 'interest' is certainly far broader than previous policy under the same legislative criteria (DoE/DNH 1994: s.6). Yet the suitability of the term merits review precisely because of its policy longevity.

It is arguable that the ethos pervading the whole urban conservation system is based on an architectural understanding of value, to the relegation, if not exclusion, of other types of value perception. Not to highlight its shortfalls or any alternatives would be to accept it as the dominant ideology of conservation. There are two arguments to challenge its primacy. The first involves the different scope of architectural, as opposed to historic, interest and the second the extent to which the extrinsic value of features is recognised in or is even compatible with the statutory framework.

While the phrase is cited as one indivisible term, 'architectural interest' and 'historic interest' have been developed and interpreted in different ways, involving not only different standards but also potentially conflicting philosophies. Although the original 1946 'Instructions to Inspectors' were remarkably broad in recognising the social dimension of historic interest, subsequent listing practice has 'concentrated heavily on architectural interest . . . it has always been easier to defend buildings whose interest can be described principally in terms of their architectural interest' (Earl 1997: 115). PPG15 continues to emphasise architectural over historic interest. Features of architectural interest are more likely to be

listed irrespective of other similar examples, whereas features of historic interest require a more selective consideration against similar examples (DoE/DNH
1994: para. 6.13). Architectural considerations may justify a listing irrespective
of any other factor, yet historic interest, though it may raise the grade awarded,
in itself is usually insufficient to merit listing (ibid.: para. 6.15).

Historic interest, in comparison with the objective professional recognition
that determines architectural interest, is a less tangible concept. It is characterised
by relative judgements and the consideration of historical circumstances which,
by definition, are unique and therefore difficult to compare. There was clear
evidence that the original Instructions to Inspectors stated the importance of
reflecting social history. In contrast, some commentators now see conservation
as being undermined by the inclusion of features whose historic interest is better
recorded in paper archives rather than by their physical preservation (Morton
1997).

Undoubtedly there has been an expansion in the importance and consideration of historic interest. In reporting EH's intentions to list wartime domestic
prefabricated chalets, Powell (1992) notes Pevsner's dictum: that a cathedral is
architecture, a bicycle shed is a building. The interest relating to the social history
of a structure far outweighs its architectural value, and so with the thematic
listing of twentieth-century buildings, the interpretation of 'historic' has significantly changed, with legitimate status given to social values.

The second set of considerations affect the perception of value from an
extrinsic, rather than an intrinsic, perspective.

> Although there is a need for objective methods in the definition and assess-
> ment of the urban structure, there is equally a need for a new consciousness
> of heritage values. After all conservation of cultural heritage is fundamen-
> tally a cultural problem.
>
> (Zanchetti and Jokilehto 1997: 38)

Despite the broadening appreciation of features in the built environment, the
institutional framework remains tied to this academic, architectural orientation.
The recognition of a feature's value has traditionally followed a formal aesthetic
approach whereby the interest is intrinsic to the object – it possesses qualities
and characteristics presented as universally recognisable. However, the value of
a feature may also be extrinsic, residing in people's experiences of these environments (Punter 1994; Ashworth 1997). The established appreciation of value in
conservation, while acknowledging this socio-aesthetic perspective, has never
ventured to include this type of value; it is perceived as too subjective and diverse.
By turning attention to experiences of the object rather than the object itself,
the apparent exclusivity of the conservation expert to define 'interest' is dealt a
hefty blow.

The introduction of conservation areas illustrated this point by limiting their identification to architectural or historic interest alone. Though townscape analysis was lauded as the more holistic approach, it suffered from concentrating solely on the physical relationship between buildings and spaces. As listed buildings were intended as an *aide-mémoire* to planning, a scant exposition of value in describing architectural features sufficed.

Attempting to define the 'character' of an area involves wider contributions from visual and social factors, the use and function of areas and their cultural significance (Suddards and Morton 1991). Evidence suggests that character analysis is poorly addressed in local development plans (Punter and Carmona 1997). Character requires the consideration of issues which planning, bounded by physical land-use concerns, may be unable to address. However, conservation ought not to neglect these issues simply because it cannot directly control them, though it is only relatively recently that addressing character has been officially tackled by EH (1995a). Protecting the palimpsest is the weakest area of English conservation practice when compared to international approaches.

Perhaps this is symptomatic of a peculiarly English approach to culture. Though suggestions to widen the compass of protection to include a cultural dimension have been made from the top of the profession (Page 1990), it seems the profession's response has been relatively lukewarm. In contrast, the Burra Charter, the Australian adoption of the ICOMOS charter for protecting cultural heritage (Earl 1997: appendix 4), is perhaps the most progressive recognition of the cultural significance of, and need for, conservation. Similarly, UNESCO has displayed a tradition of maintaining and promoting the continuity and stability of cultural significance through place identity and association (Shankland 1975).

To achieve this, conservation must recognise such personal, social and cultural appreciation of meaning and symbols. It involves understanding how elements of behavioural psychology (Hubbard 1993) and environmental perception (Lowenthal 1985) can be used to justify protection on the grounds of psychological needs for indicators of stability and continuity in the environment (Lynch 1972). The more recent literature approaching the concept of 'place' observes that understanding the cultural symbolism and representation in features is essential for strategies of conservation (Boyer 1994; Hayden 1995).

The hierarchy of significance (special, national interest . . . familiar, local interest)

> [T]he identification of cultural values in relation to urban structures happens mainly through the use of symbolic systems of reference, such as history, aesthetics (art), or, quite simply, age . . . and is thus related to political power games associated with the process of forming images, memories and representations in a given society.
>
> (Zanchetti and Jokilehto 1997: 41)

Since features (and processes) in the urban environment are vehicles for trans-ferring social meanings, the question of whether conservation emphasises national or local interest reflects the power to replicate certain values and pref-erences over others. Ashworth (1991) has noted that the strength and priority given to the level of protection measures (national, regional, local, site specific) is the main difference between various countries' approaches. It reflects the value that society places on the contribution of the past towards a local and more reflexive, or a national and official, use of those resources. Inevitably the distinc-tion between national and local interest is partly a control issue. With different bodies responsible for national and local concerns there is a power relationship to determine who sets the agenda for conservation objectives – this aspect will be dealt with more specifically later in the chapter (p. 75).

This relationship, through the definition of 'special' interest, determines the boundaries of legitimate concern for conservation control. Arguably, 'special' represents a quality control mechanism, particularly necessary in the light of the burgeoning mass of stock already subject to conservation controls.

Although it is opportune to stress 'national significance' corresponding to the tourist potential of exploiting national heritage, to describe listed buildings as being of active national interest is something of a falsehood. Apart from the initial identification of national interest from a largely academic perspective, it is local authorities, not national organisations, that have the greater influence over features' care and management. However, the framework for assessing special interest highlights an unequal interpretation of 'special' when considered against the premise of national importance.

Policy emphasises that the listing of buildings is based on their 'national significance' (DoE/DNH 1994: para. 6.16) – this distinguishes the buildings which have special interest from those which do not, presumably those with only local interest. The apparent objectivity, centralised scrutiny and rigour of listing, in addition to the strength of listed building controls, have consolidated the strength of this interpretation: 'special' equals 'national'.

In contrast, local interest can be defined only in relation to either conserva-tion areas or locally listed buildings – mechanisms which are both reliant on local authorities' interpretations of value. The challenge of independently recog-nising such a diversity of local values without suitably developed tools or concepts to define area-based character, coupled with weak controls over devel-opment in conservation areas, has undermined enthusiasm to equate 'special' with local interest. So when local authorities come to define the 'special archi-tectural or historic interest in the character or appearance' of their areas, perversely they are forced to do so with a definition of 'special' largely derived from its use relating to listed buildings and not conservation areas. Local interest will persist as the poor relation so long as the vehicles for conserving local interest are so inarticulate in assessing or expressing local value. The approach of listing and national significance will continue to dominate what is considered 'special' in the urban environment (Shelbourn 1996).

In attempting to protect the local and familiar cherished scene, conservation runs up against real difficulties because of the whole reliance on special, and implicitly national, interest. As Wright (1985) has noted, the more institutional view of the past and history emphasises the protection of the state or national type of relic. To illustrate this, consider the influence of tourism on conservation. Urry (1990) proposes that any individual tourist expects to see historic scenes or features which conform to a pre-determined conception of the picturesque, contrasting with the everyday environment – in other words, a stereotype. It is this way of perceiving an environment or the 'tourist's gaze' which characterises the identification of special features.

The non-tourist does not perceive that same environment in this way. In contrast, their 'everyday historical consciousness', whose strength Wright advocates, identifies 'familiar' elements in the environment as equally valuable. P. F. Smith (1974) has stated that the protection of familiarity is such an emotive force that it shapes public hostility towards or approval of new planning developments. The ordinary and commonplace serve as symbols and carriers of meaning in this environment; equally, they comprise the character of the area and any assessment must address the whole palimpsest (Bold and Guillery 1998). There is no distinction between the special and the familiar, yet the tools available to protect familiar elements are ill-equipped to address their qualities.

The influence and variety of knowledge and experience (expert opinion . . . lay opinion)

While legislation and policy set down the guidelines and criteria for conservation, they are shaped by, and are subject to, the interpretation of the people implementing these processes. Through their opinions and judgements, particular interpretations of value are consolidated as the legitimate scope of conservation. Though there is evidently a conceptual difference between 'public interest' and 'public preference', the evidence of having explored either in relation to conservation is conspicuous by its absence (Hubbard 1994). Considering that 'public interest' is a nominal basis for conservation intervention, it is desirable that those people involved in conservation recognise and include any commonly shared values.

Fowler (1981), among others, has identified the spheres of interest and opinion in society relating to people's 'sense of past'. These range from a core academic interest of scholars, through a wider popular interest, to apathy and total neglect. Although this may be stating the obvious, it is important to recognise the validity of each perspective and to ensure that control is representative of many opinions rather than just those of a paternal minority. 'Conservation is pursued within a distinct philosophy to which many may subscribe, yet only a few are engaged in establishing and implementing the necessary rules' (D. Smith 1974: 133). Professionals may happily operate under a notional public interest which widens the disparity between their professional perceptions of value and those held by non-professionals. It questions not only the relationship between the conservationist and the public but also that between the conservationist and planning officers.

The professional perspective, as Ashworth (1997) notes, reflects a formal aesthetic approach whereby the value of the feature is inherent in the object. Given sufficient training and knowledge, experts see a building's value as self-evident (Earl 1997). Hubbard (1994) comments that the professional socialisation of groups, through a shared professional language, background and values, implicitly excludes others from contributing to the realisation of legitimate values. It is an exclusive and exclusionary practice. Macinnes (1993) stresses that the artifice accompanying the various academic and professional value distinctions actually hampers integration and co-operation between disciplines. Maguire (1998) even cites academic research as contributing to the severance of listed buildings from an everyday existence by treating them as archival 'documents' instead of stimuli of emotional responses. It is an important distinction that can arise just as much between conservationists and planners as it can with conservationists and the public.

Often, design professionals claim that the public do not understand or have no taste appreciation: 'such an appreciation gap is frequently used as a justification for excluding the public from the design process' (Hubbard 1994: 271). However, there is little qualitative evidence of the public's lack of understanding conservation value (Datel and Dingemans 1984).

In practice, mechanisms to involve the public have not had the desired effect. Advisory committees accompanying the introduction of conservation areas were intended to engage the local community in harnessing conservation for their needs and aspirations. Rather than see increased public participation as a positive step, some have felt that such 'government by plebiscite' (Heap 1975: 36) would open protection to the fickle nature of public opinion (Cherry 1975).

Simply providing mechanisms for participation will continue to be inadequate as long as the public's perceptions, values and language are seen as incompatible with the professionals' and thus the 'legitimate' scope of conservation. Initiatives have made conservation more open, for example the public consultations on post-war thematic listing (Cherry 1995). However, it is open to question whether such moves represent expansionist attempts to gain public acceptance of the professionals' values or whether they are opportunities to acknowledge some of the wider conservation values that may reside in non-professional interpretation.

Townshend and Pendlebury (1999) acknowledge this discrepancy between the public's holistic perception of environmental value and the professionals' 'elitist didactic' orientation. The exclusivity of such expert interpretations creates a widening gulf between the popular and professional aspirations for protection. Studies have illustrated the variance between these preferences (Morris 1981; Hubbard 1994) and it has been suggested that practice ought to become more responsive to grass-roots interpretations of, and association with, place. However, these studies also illustrate a low awareness among the public regarding conservation's aims and provisions (Larkham 2000).

Comparison may be sought from other areas such as environmental perception (Tuan 1974, 1977) or sociology (Merriman 1991; Marris 1993). Certainly as regards design control, Hubbard (1994) concludes that there are consistent and identifiable aspects of lay appreciation of the built environment which planners do not account for. Mere visual stimulus is considered of equal importance to appreciating relics for their specific architectural qualities (Hubbard 1993). Bourassa (cited in Hubbard 1994) has suggested that the perspective of a planning professional remains external and detached, with less appreciation of the interaction between local users and their environment.

In a similar vein, Jones (1993) comments that professional conservation practice still identifies value irrespective of the cultural analysis required to understand the variety of meanings perceived in the landscape by other social groups. If this exclusive practice continues, the process becomes an end in itself, cataloguing and selecting valued features to serve the purposes of planning and administration. In contrast, when landscape value is seen as comprising different meanings and symbols for various cultural and socio-economic groups in society, the role of the professional alters to facilitate the comprehension of these extrinsic interpretations – conservation becomes a tool of cultural analysis.

Aspects of heritage valuation (formal 'historical' knowledge . . . the past as a cultural collage)

It is quite conceivable that contemporary interest in the past is more active and widespread than at any time since the Victorian age (PSI 1995). Though 'heritage' is pilloried in some quarters yet praised in others, its impact cannot be understated, partly for its breadth of interpretation, but also for its consequent revision of conceptions of the past and 'pastness'. Perhaps because heritage has not been centred within architectural debate, conservation has not fully addressed the influence of heritage to the extent that other cultural conservation disciplines have, such as museum curatorship (Merriman 1991). This is not to say there are no significant issues for built environment conservation to address.

The use of architectural or historic interest to evaluate listed buildings owes much to an academic interpretation of the features that give rise to the interest.

The preservation of a relic's authenticity is paramount for a 'genuine' representation of the survivors of past ages. Conservation protects those genuine features which have survived the years and have retained a proportion of their original elements. This singles them out as being special and the feature is then conserved for its authentic representation. However, some, like Ashworth (1997), have criticised this academic concept of authenticity. Though it is widely acknowledged that survival of one relic has been at the expense of many others, this process of selection is wholly dependent on a feature's good fortune in the face of contemporaneous economic or political circumstances. Both Lynch (1972) and Ashworth (1997) note that the 'authentic' state identified in the listing process is serendipitous and illusory – it does not represent the original, authentic feature. Certainly, once a feature has been selected for protection, for example through listing, it is 'sacralised' and removed from the natural cycle of decay and obsolescence to which the rest of the environment is subjected. Thus the 'historic environment' portrayed by conservation policy is far from being an accurate representation; areas have changed differentially over the years. Such distortions by chance and later conscious selection lead Lowenthal to conclude that authenticity is 'a dogma of self-delusion' (quoted in Ashworth 1997: 97). They raise the question that if authenticity is as weak a basis for protection criteria as some argue, what could other interpretations of 'special' contribute?

An alternative would be to consider the value which is perceived in the feature. A person's association with the qualities of a feature's past is quite independent of the actual age of the relic. Rather, as Wright (1985) notes, it arises from everyday experience and associations with familiar themes and elements in the social environment. The authenticity of a feature is of less concern to everyday experience: the important value is what a feature represents. In this view, the past is more a resource to be used than something to be preserved for its authenticity.

Rather than 'historic environment', Lynch (1972) prefers the term 'temporal collage' to describe features of the past in the present, particularly as 'historic environment' suggests something static, pre-determined and separate from an everyday experience of the environment. This temporal collage is the juxtaposition of past and present in a complementary relationship, not merely architecturally but with the mental associations and layering of meanings created by that context (Jones 1993). Wright (1985) too stresses that the eclectic context surrounding a relic provides more emphatic interest than the relic itself. Such symbolism and representation are used in postmodern architecture as a creative resource, in contrast to modernist rejections of the past (Jencks 1991). Lowenthal (1985) advocates that this ought to be leading us to a more creative use of the past, rather than one so venerated that it becomes untouchable (Thomas 1994).

It is indisputable that the 'past' is far from static, and increasingly, features that are decades, rather than centuries, old are being protected. As the past catches up with the present, some argue that heritage is (and always was) an emancipatory tool which challenges the homogeneity of objective history. In being able to re-use, re-invent and revitalise areas and people's lives through the use of 'historic' buildings, resources or themes, a heritage-based approach moves away from authenticity of the object to the authenticity, or quality, of experience evoked in the user. As the value of the built heritage lies in its variety and juxtaposition of components (Bold and Guillery 1998), so the scope of heritage allows conservation diversity of interpretation beyond its traditional confines. By treating features as carriers of contemporary cultural meaning (Jones 1993), heritage is about the renewal and adaptation of value. Now that heritage is no longer the transmission of stable, 'self-evident' values, the recognition of heritage values means that conservation is as much a discourse of the present as of the past (Merriman 1991).

Economic pressures and their impact on conservation (intrinsic value . . . commodity value)

It is only relatively recently that the literature has explicitly addressed the prevailing economic and political climate affecting conservation. While political support and economic circumstances have inevitably influenced the success of conservation, the literature has traditionally seen these as separate from the concerns of professional conservation. Hence there is less literature exploring these realms' effect on conservation, but considering the wider picture is imperative.

Although conservation of the built environment may isolate certain aspects for their cultural interest, it is not as easy to isolate these features from their necessity to generate revenue. The artifice of conservation controls over natural obsolescence in the face of development pressure has been noted elsewhere (Larkham 1992, 1996); changing economic forces have introduced significant revisions to the traditional perception of conservation.

In the existing literature, the effects of economic considerations are generally treated in relation to direct costs of the purchase, repair and sale of buildings. More specifically, the availability of repair grants and their respective tax regimes warranted attention. The orthodox view saw conservation, a regulatory mechanism, as an inevitable obstacle to development, an additional cost which prevented profit maximisation. This necessarily implied that without an extra layer of control to protect such features, the market would not recognise or respect their conservation value.

Indeed, as evidence from empirical studies has shown (Larkham 1996), balancing, or even demonstrating, the tangible value of conservation against hard economic forecasts of profitability is difficult. Conservation value is relatively amorphous and resides in more diffuse community benefits. In actual development decision-making, conservation issues often require buttressing by additional, cogent economic arguments.

Attempts to define the economic benefits/value of conservation have largely remained either academic exercises or isolated case studies recommending further qualitative research (Scanlon *et al.* 1994; Allison *et al.* 1996). Garrod *et al.* (1996) note the practical extent of the public's commitment to conservation by its willingness to pay for it through indirect taxation. Lichfield (1988, 1997) has been more comprehensive in defining a method for such analysis, yet such approaches remain under-represented in national policy guidance, let alone local planning authority practice. One common problem has been the inadequacy of methods (such as the contingent valuation method (CVM)) to reveal the complexity and subtlety of economic value to a community whereby conservation encourages investment in a higher-quality environment.

The most significant change affecting the consideration of economic factors has been the move away from perceiving the cultural built heritage (CBH) as a resource to be conserved solely for economic prudence (e.g. SAVE 1979). It is equally adept at generating its own income solely on the basis of its conserved status. It is a tradable resource which town and city authorities are employing in the competition to attract investment and development (Urry 1995). The evidence for such conservation-based economic regeneration is overwhelming (Skea 1996; EH 1998). As Strange notes (1996, 1997), changing patterns of local economic development necessarily require urban regions to emphasise their distinctive qualities over competitors with similar attributes. Though Ashworth (1991, 1997) considers that such a heritage use value offers the potential to consolidate conservation and development pressures, the demands of tourism and heritage exploitation result in acute conflicts with more traditional interpretations of conservation (Barrett 1993). Indeed, the saleability of 'pastness' can result in the creation of historic imagery through appropriate marketing, imagery and pastiche reproduction. As this use value dominates, the value of historical *image* subsumes features' intrinsic qualities; the protection of the past is no longer a cause in itself but a means for fulfilling ulterior motives.

The influence of political agendas (purity of choice . . . a political tool)

Exposing economic winners and losers in the community draws conservation into a more politically sensitive area. This is unusual, as conservation has managed to retain a relatively apolitical air. Throughout the statutory development of conservation, from 1940s Parliamentary debates regarding listing to the Thatcher administration's support of heritage, there appears to have been a tacit political consensus for conservation with appreciable mutual benefits for both. Conservation enjoyed a degree of political tolerance which furthered its cause, while politics could trade off conservation's popularity. However, the ease of conservation's political acceptance has been a double-edged sword. Based on professional art-historical objectivity and afforded the luxury of taking the high moral ground under an apolitical guise, conservation has, according to Delafons (1997b), neatly avoided scrutiny of its inherently political, social and economic consequences.

Conservation, like planning, involves the management of finite resources and a political consideration of the development and conservation merits. However, while conservation may claim that a feature's value is intrinsic and objective, the threat of development can often distort this evaluation. It is increasingly difficult to sustain 'pure' conservation arguments without reference to the local and national political agendas which shape their outcome. Worskett (1975, 1982) notes that conservation is not an end in itself and must operate in tandem with broader socio-economic policies. To secure financial assistance for conservation (money being a good indicator of political support), the aims and objectives must be directed towards fulfilling the wider political objectives of the relevant institutions. The important issue is the extent to which conservation must 'progress' or stray from its traditional concerns to fulfil a political agenda, which may set up conflict between the two.

This process may be seen at two levels. The first is competition within organisational structures – the power relationship between central and local government. National conservation advice, in line with much planning policy, is becoming increasingly centralised, allowing for little autonomy and discretion by the implementing local authorities (Allmendinger and Thomas 1998). Funding regimes and competitive bidding for national moneys along strictly defined criteria reduce responsiveness to local priorities in favour of matching any local circumstances to criteria that will attract funding. State and economic restructuring has affected local governance to a significant degree, yet, as Strange (1996, 1997) observes, relatively little is known about the effects of enforced privatisation and partnership on the local political economy in historic towns.

The second aspect is the potential difference that may arise between local and national policy objectives. Under Labour's administration since 1997 there has been a distinct shift in conservation politics, away from the 'national heritage', tourism enterprise of the Conservatives and towards an ethos of urban regeneration and social integration (Larkham and Barrett 1998). As national resources are arguably directed away from conservation, EH has been quick to portray itself as a regeneration, rather than a conservation, organisation. Similarly, the devolution of economic planning to the Regional Development Agencies has persuaded EH to reorganise along similar lines. While EH may stress that it is merely reiterating the importance of one aspect of its continuing work, consciously manoeuvring to gain political headway in terms of ensuring vitality and a continuing rationale for funding may set up potential conflicts within conservation activity.

While there is a distinct emphasis on regeneration at a national policy level, it remains to be seen whether local authorities – their members and officers – perceive the position of conservation in the same way. As EH has been compelled to reposition itself to align with strong political directions, so at a local level conservation officers will be subject to the political directions of members who may or may not support conservation. It may place success in the hands of those officers who are more politically astute than those who necessarily concentrate on the traditional work of conservation.

As mentioned at the outset, there has generally been tacit political support for conservation. But there is no place for complacency, especially since the evolution of statutory protection can be seen as a series of cumulative policy responses to successive threats. The past 20 years have not experienced any major upset to test this again; it is not inconceivable that the shift towards regeneration may represent such a re-orientation under a new conservation paradigm.

Research issues

The literature has provided ample evidence of the many tensions in conservation. Examining these in greater detail has resulted in a framework of ten themes which highlight particular issues of contemporary concern. In examining the 'big picture', it would be inappropriate to concentrate on specific questions raised

Table 3.2 The thematic framework

---

1   The nature of conservation planning
The relationship between conservation and statutory planning
The spatial focus of conservation controls
The extent of acceptable change
The basis of conservation's support and legitimacy

2   The interpretation of value in the built environment
The interpretation of features' interest
The level of significance
The influence and variety of knowledge and experience
Aspects of heritage valuation

3   The influence of external factors
Economic pressures and their impact on conservation
The influence of political agendas

---

within the context of this review. Indeed, the themes noted are heuristic and many issues embrace several aspects of this categorisation: it is essential to maintain a holistic approach. To summarise, the themes which can be used to explore and to understand contemporary conservation planning are set out in table 3.2.

It would appear appropriate to continue this broad tripartite approach in defining the research issues. As the point of the study is explorative rather than necessarily seeking definitive answers, it is more appropriate to leave these issues as open ended as possible and not to set specific questions. But inevitably, as there will be further questions raised in exploring the national- and local-level operations of conservation policy and practice, a firm base of inquiry is helpful.

1   How does conservation relate to planning in principle and practice?
2   How is value in the built environment perceived and interpreted for conservation purposes?
3   How do economic and political pressures contribute to or undermine conservation?

These questions provide certainty and grounding to the study and ought to be borne in mind throughout the following chapters presenting the study findings. They will be specifically addressed in the concluding chapter, chapter 8.

PART II

Conservation values in practice

'Be sure that you go to the author to get at his meaning, not to find yours.'

(Ruskin 1865: 24)

4 Survey of national conservation organisations

Introduction

The development of conservation is clearly not one single entity and can be more accurately characterised as a series of potentially contrasting value positions. The evolution of statutory conservation planning has been mainly in response to successive development threats, whereby new policies and value justifications were placed alongside existing ones, forming an increasingly complex web of principles in operation across various levels of practice. However, difficult questions remain unanswered. Where are the tensions within these themes? Where is the conflict, where is the consensus? How has actual practice responded and evolved? Part II attempts to answer these questions by looking at how these issues arise and are accommodated in reality.

It is worth briefly reviewing the factors influencing how the study was conducted. The existing research literature on conservation planning noted a gap between separate discussions of abstract conservation generalities and detailed investigations of specific, isolated locations (Larkham 1993, 1996). Neither approach seemed to meet the other satisfactorily, or accounted for the different tensions and pressures that exist in, for example, national or local conservation practice.

In addressing such criticism, the study embraced two operational levels to look at their distinct spheres but also their inter-related considerations of policy and practice. First, those organisations contributing to a culture of national conservation policy were surveyed. Second, selected local planning authorities, with conservation responsibilities over their particular environment, were explored in greater depth. This approach was intended to access both the normative, principled orientation of standards at a higher strategic level, and the application of these ideas as interpreted by a local decision-making authority. The approach was necessarily inductive, attempting to draw out themes and issues from practice rather than trying to observe and test the application of existing theories. This approach was designed to be holistic and raise general issues for discussion; it is recognised that these findings will not represent the whole of conservation practice.

A focus on individuals' perceptions

Identifying the values and justifications underlying conservation involved the exploration of policy and practice to far greater depths than just the analysis of documentary sources alone could ever provide. While mission statements, annual reports and development plans illustrate formal conservation responsibilities,

Euston Arch, London: the 1960s appetite for renewal prevailed over political apathy towards the protection of this Victorian monument it is the people involved in the conservation planning system who create, interpret and reinforce these norms. Certainly, much of the heritage literature (Lowenthal 1985; Wright 1985; Samuel 1994) concentrates on individuals' personal reactions to the past. These opinions coalesce and can be represented and reflected in the behaviour and attitude of institutions. Though prevailing structural forces may determine the general framework of conservation, it is fundamentally the agency perspective that is of more interest. Individual people's attitudes are highly influential because their personal values act as a filter and conduit for the information and knowledge legitimating conservation activity. However, this is not to disregard the significant effects of large-scale forces, such as economics, politics and both cultural and structural inertia, against which the individual can appear powerless.

A qualitative approach involving individual interviews offered the flexibility to explore each respondent's unique position and role, their values and opinions. While the potential for bias and inconsistency is acknowledged, the depth of material required would not be accessible any other way. For all the interviews, the thematic framework in chapter 3 provided an outline interview schedule, highlighting key themes with which to explore and categorise peoples' explicit and implicit views of conservation.

Table 4.1 National conservation bodies interviewed

Government and sponsored organisations
- Department of Culture, Media and Sport
- Department of the Environment, Transport and the Regions (as was)
- English Heritage

NGOs – voluntary sector
- Ancient Monuments Society
- Society for the Protection of Ancient Buildings
- Georgian Group
- Victorian Society
- Twentieth Century Society
- Civic Trust
- Royal Fine Art Commission (as was)

Other professionally oriented bodies
- Royal Town Planning Institute
- Institute of Historic Building Conservation (former Association of Conservation Officers)
- English Historic Towns Forum

The national level of conservation policy and practice

It is difficult to define what is the 'national policy culture' for conservation. Who comprises this esoteric realm and who sets the agenda is no more identifiable in relation to conservation than any other activity. Naïvety aside, policy discussions are as likely to be held in public houses as in the offices of the institutions responsible for the heritage. This presented a potential hurdle for selecting who was most relevant for interview. Within conservation there are a wide range of players whose influence and standing vary with the nature of the topic under discussion, be it new contextual urban design or the ecclesiastical exemption.

Evidently not all organisations with an interest in conservation could be accommodated. A sample of those bodies involved with national policy and the practice of conserving the built environment was selected (Table 4.1) on the basis of PPG15: appendix A, which lists 'key bodies and organisations'.

Larger organisations and government departments presented difficulties with navigating internal hierarchies and identifying relevant interviewees who could represent the corporate whole but also be sufficiently self-reflective about the policy issues under discussion. In these larger organisations, a diagonal slice of personnel across the hierarchy was selected to represent the range of views across the corporate body.

For smaller organisations, a single respondent was chosen from each to represent its respective views: generally people in a senior, if not the senior, position. It was notable throughout this national sphere that individuals often played several conservation roles, sometimes simultaneously across the public, voluntary and private sectors; therefore it was not always entirely clear whose loyalties and agendas they were expressing. Identifying one clear institutional line proved difficult and perhaps unrealistic for later analysis, both at this level and in the local authority case studies. For that reason, the views expressed by respondents throughout Part II are not necessarily the corporate view of the institution to which they belong. People mostly represented their personal view but their institutional background and current role inevitably strongly influenced their opinions.

Omissions

Since this study was undertaken, several bodies have become more prominent in national conservation. In particular, the Heritage Lottery Fund (HLF) has obtained direct control of conservation grant aid from EH and, following the creation of its Townscape Heritage Initiative, has gained more influence. In hindsight, perhaps there were also one or two other organisations that would have been interesting to approach, such as SAVE Britain's Heritage and English Partnerships, given the emerging emphasis on heritage-led regeneration.

However, the omission of these bodies does not undermine the strength or validity of the research findings.

Indeed, there have been major changes to government departments: the Department of the Environment, Transport and the Regions (DETR) became the Department of Transport, Local Government and the Regions (DTLR) and then the Office of the Deputy Prime Minister (ODPM). Conservation planning responsibilities *per se* have not been affected by this specific change, but it is likely that they will be subject to internal reprioritisation following changed agendas within the Office.

Identifying the issues

While there was some consensus of opinion among respondents in relation to single issues, there was no over-arching view running through any one type of organisation, for example among all the national amenity societies (NAS). Respondents' wide-ranging views could not easily be categorised along organisational lines, nor was there necessarily a unifying perspective among similar professionals within organisations. Rather than holding firm single views on a subject, individuals frequently expressed a certain duality of opinion, according to the particular aspect of conservation under discussion and the subtle influence of their background, experience and profession. The frequency with which this inherent diversity of views, even contradiction, can be seen throughout the interviews highlights a latent tension in the perceived values and aims of conservation. That these tensions can be seen as occurring *within* individuals as well as within and between institutions emphasises the amorphous nature of the activity and the potential incongruities for the interpretation and application of these policies. Though this spread is partly to be expected in qualitative work, which involves personal interpretations of value, there were strong themes that can be picked out from these national interviews.

Conservation planning: an inherent specialism

There appeared to be a general consensus among respondents that, nationally, conservation was enjoying a relatively healthy period, reflected in PPG15's comprehensive and flexible policy framework. Overall, the systems appeared to be working well, requiring only slight, if any, modifications. However, concerns were expressed over local authorities' inconsistent application of national conservation policies and internal prioritisation due to a local lack of resources, funding or, more importantly, a supportive political climate.

Despite this consensus, responses did reflect a spectrum of views. At one end, the non-statutory bodies were more likely to consider conservation as being integral to planning – managing change within the existing environment was seen as absolutely fundamental to land-use regulation. Conversely, some bodies viewed planning as a less suitable vehicle, conservation being superior to and beyond planning, rather than central to it. The NAS emphasised the particular specialism of conservation, while a greater cross-current of ideas characterised views at EH. Notably, perceptions of the conservation–planning relationship varied with the aspect under discussion, manifest through its principles, processes and professional relations.

In principle, respondents emphasised conservation's centrality to planning

In principle, many respondents wished to see conservation at the heart of planning. The comprehensive redevelopment characterising 1960s planning and the memory that statutory planning could actively endorse such 'destruction' were considered persuasive reasons for conservation's continuing presence. More fundamentally, conservation was seen as an essential planning purpose as it involved the promotion of the quality of the existing environment. Indeed, it was viewed as a discipline of environmental management and a corollary of sustainability. Similarly, regeneration was seen as the 'flip side of conservation', the revitalisation of areas and re-use of buildings being the sustainable recycling of historic features. A strong message from EH was that in terms of:

> the contribution [that] conservation of the man-made heritage can make to an overall sustainable approach to development and the contribution conservation can make to regeneration, I think we are still some way from conservation, in that sense, having its proper status. It should not be something which is dealt with by conservation officers in the planning department. The conservation philosophy should be something which underpins all of what local authorities and central government are doing.

Apart from raising the question of what is the 'conservation philosophy', it was an interesting perception that conservation's 'proper status' had not yet been achieved in wider environmental governance and practice. A respondent at EH commented that EH had to 'play the role of a regeneration agency' – an emphasis which tended to resound more strongly higher up the political hierarchy, not only in EH, but across government too. In fact, to make conservation work, it needed to correspond with broader political currents, promoting conservation in other areas of government activity where otherwise it might not have been influential.

Though the NAS look after a specific area of concern, and may be seen as quite distinct from this broader political agenda, the desire to see conservation recognised in a central role was still prevalent:

> [C]onservation loses by being regarded as elitist, as an add-on, as an extra when it's absolutely intrinsic to planning. After all, you can't indulge in town and country planning now without falling over a listed building or a conservation area ... it is literally impossible to separate conservation from mainstream planning.

Professional bodies also emphasised the desirability of manoeuvring conservation into a more prominent position in planning:

> [C]onservation is a major land-use policy decision – it should be seen like that, it should be treated as that and I think there could be wide opportunities [to] encourage using the local plan [more] constructively as far as conservation is concerned.

Conservation was viewed as analysing and managing the townscape – an essential planning activity. Some saw a much broader scope, considering that both planning and conservation were central components of urban management strategies which included wider economic and environmental considerations.

In practice, the separateness of conservation processes was emphasised

In contrast to the principled centrality of conservation, most respondents considered that implementing conservation was a function distinct from and (almost morally) superior to planning.

Conservation was seen to benefit enormously from the planning process, not only for the legal framework of permissions and consents but also for the added legitimacy it conveyed (though this is largely dependent on a particular conception of the planning system). Despite creating frustration for respondents, planning's 'vast balancing act' ensured that all sectional interests were accommodated within a comprehensive decision-making framework. As planning provided channels for public consultation and debate, conservation itself could remain a distinct, technical and almost apolitical discipline.

Especially after the reduction in scope of conservation area controls following the *Shimizu* case, all respondents agreed that these controls were grossly inadequate, though their opinions differed as to an appropriate solution. Though the NAS generally wished for new legislation, EH officially endorsed the revision of the General Permitted Development Order (GPDO) within conservation areas in line with various planning organisations' recommendations. The perceived legitimacy and transparency of the planning process could benefit the beleaguered and criticised management of conservation areas, which to EH meant that:

it would be a lot clearer as to why they were being designated and what the local authority were trying to achieve, what they were trying to protect against change, and I think [it] could again tie back much more effectively to the broader planning system.

The concept of area-based protection had been seen as unfortunately underplayed in mainstream planning practice; the planning organisations were particularly critical, arguing that activities such as townscape analysis, urban design and town centre management were integral to an area-based, holistic approach to conservation of the built environment.

However, suggestions for listed building consent to be incorporated into planning permissions (Mynors 1998) incurred a very different response from EH:

I mean, given that there is a special PPG and a special part of the Planning Acts and a special place in a lot of people's hearts too for conservation, then I think that justifies having a special scheme to deal with it and that there is something special about it . . . it's not the same as . . . all the other planning bits and pieces.

There was a slightly derogatory view of 'mere' planning in contrast with a 'special, express consent' by which applicants would 'know that it is a serious business': '[T]here is an argument for saying that to extend a Grade I country house is different in kind to any old planning permission and there ought to be an express permission.' It would suggest that respondents perceived a substantive shortfall between what planning could address and what conservation required. Respondents from DCMS considered that in proposing a single planning permission,

the heritage sensitivities . . . would not be apparent to the planning officer, who wouldn't think much of it. It would just go through the planning committee without any serious assessment of the conservation issues . . . it would be harder to identify the conservation element in the planning proposals than it is now.

Such attitudes may imply that conservation is not as central to planning practice as its principles would aspire to make it. Though a minority of respondents believed that the over-burdened legislation needed a radical shake-up, the majority still preferred separate consents.

Professional expertise and relations

Respondents from those national bodies approaching conservation more from the planning perspective stated that conservation was all about good quality design. Following PPG1's (DETR 1997) inclusion of design guidance, after years of neglect in government advice, planners were more confident in proactive design control strategies. Aesthetic judgement was an area in which planners should 'fight their corner', rather than let other professions encroach. One professional body noted that managing townscape was 'one of planners' key jobs in urban areas', aligning planning and conservation through design competency. However, many respondents from the NAS and EH believed that conservation represented more than just an approach to design or aesthetics. Conservation involved intricate technical knowledge which required specialist interpretation; the fact that planning personnel did not understand conservation merely reinforced the separatism. One respondent at EH commented that listing 'involves a series of decisions and a mind-set which is quite unlike that which you require for ordinary planning, it seems to me. Some planners can do it and some planners can't.' Moreover, some respondents considered that archaeology and sustainability were actually encroaching on their professional territory and distracting attention from the conservation specialism. While many were happy to use environmental quality as a principle for conservation, few embraced the different technical approaches involved.

Regarding local authority conservation practice, respondents believed that a dedicated post of 'conservation officer' demonstrated best practice. In lieu of having a specific officer, some authorities claim that all their planners are sensitive to conservation issues, but these 'national' respondents believed that not having a dedicated officer is generally detrimental for conservation. Despite the desire to see conservation as central to planning, many respondents felt frustrated by planning officers' apparent general insensitivity to conservation. The quality of local authorities' conservation officers raised some concern: most were very good but one NAS respondent noted that some authorities appeared satisfied with a virtual 'school leaver with an A-level in geography'. Planners were often seen as pigeon-holing conservation, invoking conservation advice as and when they saw fit, or just when the alarm bells of requiring a listed building consent were set off:

> [I]f you have a specialist section they can produce specialised knowledge based on their understanding, but they may get disregarded because they are seen as the man in the sandals with the funny hat or . . . the girl with the beads. They do the conservation – put them in a box and turn them out when you want them.

Several respondents at EH noted this, that the standing of the conservation officer in the planning service was inevitably shaped by many factors, but there was a perception for the conservation officer to be branded as separate and distinct, as the 'effete ponce from the planning department who likes old things'. The influence of particular personalities could reinforce the separation of conservation, in terms of knowledge and procedures, from planning. 'I actually fear [the] "ghetto-isation" of conservation. Having some degree of experience in professional life, you will find working in this field that from time to time you will be frozen out of a critical piece of decision-making.'

Geographical and spatial priorities

Respondents criticised planning's inability to address conservation concerns spatially and temporally. Planning, being concerned with broader land uses and activities, was perceived as insensitive to the intrinsic value of a building's fabric. Planning did not address this 'micro level', allowing conservation to fall through holes both in the development plan and in development control. Additionally, some respondents saw planning operating on a totally different timescale, being too short-termist and oriented to helping the property market rather than to the intrinsic qualities of the existing environment. There was something in the aims of conservation which brought a more responsible attitude in determining 'acceptable' long-term change.

Given the focus of these national organisations, it is perhaps unsurprising that responses predominantly concerned the listing process. However, the extent to which listing was portrayed as a stronger and more defensible regime than conservation areas raises concerns over the dominant professional interpretation of conservation.

Listing perceived as a strong and competent system

One EH respondent summarised the general view that listing 'is specific to the actual building and in theory has nothing to do with its surroundings and setting . . . it is still a relatively objective process'.

The rigour of listing's specific standards, particularly with the variety of checks and statutory bodies involved, was a reason for the perceived strength of listing's status – and more so for NAS respondents, for whom the protection of the fabric of listed structures was of paramount importance: '[W]e're more interested in products of buildings as products of a [specific] period and so . . . preservation of the fabric is pretty important.' Their emphasis was on ensuring the quality of repair for these buildings' re-use, concentrating on the small details that planning could not address. The weighting was towards the micro-scale rather than to broader townscape concerns.

Area-based conservation suffered from a variety of interpretations

In contrast, there was serious concern over conservation areas. While national respondents were less involved in the operation of a conservation area, they saw its value as being 'essentially much more subjective'. However, where respondents were more involved in the planning process, most felt that conservation areas were treated 'almost as a second-class concept'.

The strength of the controls available in conservation areas was of concern across the board, the small and incremental incursion of uPVC windows, stone cladding and satellite dishes being cited as key offenders. 'Death by one thousand cuts' is how one respondent described the assault on the character of areas. Most respondents perceived a need for stronger controls over minor, yet cumulatively significant, alterations. However, there was an official reluctance to broaden the scope of what conservation could control for fear of undermining its support within planning.

For some respondents, mostly those professionals in contact with the statutory development control framework, conservation areas were viewed as a potential leader in managing environmental concerns, rather than isolated fragments, incorporating urban design and holistic management strategies. In this respect, conservation was perceived as identifying place characteristics and ensuring that towns retained and cultivated their individual uniqueness rather than turning into 'everywheresville'. Some respondents felt that local authorities failed to realise local qualities and dimensions to conservation and merely paraphrased PPG15 in their policy frameworks. Conservation area character appraisals could address these difficulties, being more defensible justifications for action, yet few had been produced.

The scope of legitimate coverage for either listed buildings or conservation areas was perceived differently too. There was support and encouragement for listing's continued expansion in re-appraising value in buildings. Yet many considered that any widening of the concept of area-based value was taking it too far beyond what was originally intended, since 'as a general rule, most areas which should be conservation areas are now conservation areas'.

A further distinction can be made between the different professionals' support for different aspects of conservation. One respondent noted the encroachment of archaeology and sustainability, eroding the traditional province of building conservation. Another emphasised the professional distinctions involved:

> [H]istorically the sustainability and green issues have tended to be, if you like, the remit of rural and countryside people and historic buildings and conservation area issues tend to have been the remit of building professionals, architectural historians and more urban-based people, architects, designers and the like. I don't think the two fit together terribly well and I don't think they quite understand each other's language.

The extent to which sustainability was embraced as a further rationale for conservation may illustrate this distinction. Some welcomed its revision of value in more quantifiable resource terms but many felt it to be an empty rhetoric of 'in vogue' words.

Shaking off preservationism

Without exception, all respondents emphatically believed in conservation as a process of accommodating 'organic change' in the built environment. One respondent summarised this well, saying that conservation 'is the art of intelligent change'. A similar emphasis was prevalent at EH to rebut the image of conservation stifling development: '[W]e are interested in encouraging development and re-use which respect the historic or architectural interest in the buildings concerned, the areas concerned, which also make a positive new contribution as well.'

However, while unanimity suggests consensus, there were subtle distinctions apparent in the interpretation of change itself. Differences between respondents were shaped by their own organisation and their position within it. There was also a contrast between the way that professionals defined acceptable change and how they considered the public interpreted it.

Accepting or promoting change?

It is notable that several respondents cited how the acceptable degree of change was pre-determined by the particular regime of protection control. Ancient monuments were generally preserved, with change being resisted, for their intrinsic, didactic interest, whereas conservation of listed buildings and areas necessitated a more flexible approach to promote features' continuing use. However, one or two NAS respondents considered that one of conservation's qualities was seeing change within a much longer timescale:

> [W]hat we [have] found many many times is that when we've actually appeared to take an unreasonable line in opposing something on the grounds that something better may turn up in the future, in many cases something better does turn up in the future and very rarely are things much worse. So clearly a delaying tactic can actually be to everyone's benefit. And particularly in the light of a building which may be 100 years old, 500 years old or whatever, a 20-year delay may actually be of no consequence at all.

While some respondents considered that planning is too short-termist, their acceptance that change is inevitable and must be addressed is hardly profound in itself. What is more interesting is the degree to which conservation is perceived as reacting to change, regulating it or actively promoting it.

The NAS stressed their willingness to be seen as embracing change, distancing themselves from popular characterisations of them as being restrictive bodies.

Indeed, they gave the impression of vying among themselves to emphasise their ascendancy to be the more progressive. However, their predominant interest in structures' historic fabric can be seen as contradicting this. Many of their concerns, and those of other respondents, cited the gradual erosion tolerated within the vagaries of listed building consent – 'a very blunt instrument' which sanctioned an alarming amount of damage. Slower changes through the cumulative effects of minor alterations were a greater problem than larger-scale changes or demolitions in the built environment.

A distinction arose between more senior respondents in EH and other conservation professionals within and outside that organisation. The former emphasised conservation as contributing to regeneration initiatives, being a leader in investing in and revitalising features and areas which commercial markets had passed over. Some professionals appeared more cynical about their leaders' appreciation of how far change and renewal may transgress the boundaries of conservation. Many respondents had entered the conservation profession driven by a passion for the architectural integrity of historic fabric, and therefore the sacrifice of it to enable development or preferable political approaches was abhorrent.

A couple of respondents noted the development of the profession following the Civic Amenities Act and the appointment of specific conservation officers. Previously, those involved in conservation had been architects who might have followed the SPAB philosophy, allowing and appreciating overtly modern insertions into the historic fabric. However, training, education and a developing culture of professional conduct separated conservation as a specific entity in itself. A discrete conservative attitude emerged, drawing back from allowing obvious insertions and contrasts and preferring a more conciliatory approach. One respondent noted that Duncan Sandys might not even recognise his vision of conservation in today's concept, whereby even features of minimal interest are sometimes zealously protected.

One respondent considered that conservation had actually been 'a victim of its own success'. In some areas, the preservationist legacy had been so great that the only way to obtain a planning permission for new development was to fit in with the context, except that '"fit in" is interpreted as meaning "fake up" some old something or other, which you're not likely to do very successfully anyway'.

The insertion of new design in the historic context created further splits in the 'consensus' supporting change. Anomalously, respondents argued that they had nothing against modern design but considered that there was little evidence of good modern design sympathetically complementing the surrounding historic context. Whereas some conservation professionals felt that the quality of architecture could be appreciated irrespective of its age, others considered that they were not necessarily well placed to pronounce on the quality of new architecture as it represented a different language and sphere of competence.

Public support

Irrespective of their organisation, respondents were of the unanimous opinion that conservation enjoyed widespread public and political support. A firm belief in this consensus provided a strong defence against criticisms of conservation as being too elitist or exclusive. However, the perception of public support appeared to rest on particular concepts of 'the public' and the nature of interest shown by various sections of society.

Perhaps because NAS are supported by members' subscriptions, their respondents were most forthright in expressing popular support for conservation. One respondent commented that conservation was 'strongly entrenched, particularly by public opinion'. Another noted that the societies were 'pushing a public position'.

> There is obviously a great deal of core goodwill and affection for old buildings, associations or whatever. So people, when they see a development taking place which involves the destruction of old buildings, which is practically every one these days, feel a sense of loss which translates through to protests. And that's been a phenomenon in this country for at least 60 years or more.

The country's antique-worshipping culture and the prolific membership of the National Trust were cited as examples reflecting the strength of the public's interest in the past. The institutions of conservation, to some extent, were seen as resting on this popular mandate, particularly as it added weight and legitimacy to what might be perceived otherwise as an exclusive activity. One NAS respondent commented that:

> a lot of the decision-making, a lot of the opinion forming is done by a small minority of people who have the time, who have the education, who have the passion. The great majority of people will endorse and ally themselves much more easily with the cause than [just] the devotees or, if you like, the fanatics, but no, I don't think it is elitist.

This strength of opinion was considered instrumental in promoting conservation, particularly since many statutory conservation bodies had at one time been lobbying groups:

> [U]ntil the people themselves value these things . . . until they value a particular type of building in large enough numbers, then all the bureaucracy that anyone could imagine paying for is not going to help . . . it's just not going to happen at all until there is a movement of valuing old things at large amongst at least the educated, influential classes.

A particular kind of public

However, while there was a genuine belief in the public's support, it would appear that this depended on a particular conception of the public. As revealed by the last comment, the 'educated, influential classes' – that is, the more culturally active middle class – were perceived as the established backbone of support. Those with the passion and time to devote to conservation will always be more involved, one NAS respondent noted, than those 'living in miserable areas who are exhausted by work; that's an inevitable reflection of the social make-up of the area'. All the NAS respondents felt that 'the chief source of the enthusiasm of the preservation argument comes from the residential side'. Indeed, some of these respondents noted that the NAS exist to support owners of historic properties, encouraging and guiding them to do the right thing by their building. Such ownership and property considerations inevitably reflect the interests of particular socio-economic classes.

A striking feature of the professionals' responses was their view of the public's perception of conservation. Professionals emphasised their acceptance of change, yet they considered that the public interpreted conservation as a very negative control. This was evident in the public's misinterpreting of 'conservation' to mean 'preservation' and also the extent to which the public actively supported restrictions:

> [F]or a lot of the public who don't really go through a planning process, they see listed buildings and conservation areas as the only two ways of stopping a development, and if the situation they're dealing with doesn't fit in with those criteria, they get very cross.

Among other respondents, particularly those from the professional organisations, there was a concern that residents' support for protecting buildings and amenity, under the guise of conservation, was in fact 'all about defending their status and their territory and I suppose the bottom line is defending the value of their property'. They characterised a popular opinion of conservation as being a good idea, but it was equally 'an ambivalent view until the issue happens next door [and] suddenly conservation is the thing that will stop something that they don't want happening'. Similarly, a government department respondent noted that people are generally 'pretty neutral' about conservation; they like the idea of living in a listed building or a conservation area until they find it restricts their own use of the property. Put more succinctly, 'I think that people believe conservation is there to stop other people from doing things.' Public support was seen by some as only catalysed by a threat to private interests. Otherwise, the public acceptance and support for conservation was perceived as tacit and understated.

The judgement of a beneficent expert making decisions on the public's behalf may not accord with the public's view of conservation. One respondent acknowledged that they were still perceived by the public as 'being in the slightly cuckoo band . . . a bit in the lentils and cloth sandals brigade'. Conversely, another respondent noted that conservation unashamedly relied on the pioneers, the eccentrics, the lone voices who would champion a cause that the general public would otherwise ignore or even actively decry.

Commentary on the scope and focus of conservation controls in relation to broader land-use control issues

The relationship with planning

While conservation and planning were perceived as compatible, the responses illustrate many more incongruities in principle and practice.

The idea that conservation is central and fundamental to planning was widely held but may only be wishful thinking. Conservation's contribution to wider planning agendas – sustainably re-using resources or promoting economic regeneration – was emphasised but may be largely rhetoric, espoused in order to survive political reprioritisation rather than being a genuine philosophical revision shared across the profession.

More fundamentally, while conservation is seen as being at the heart of planning in principle, it is questionable whether the processes of conservation control and their attendant professional distinctions actually inhibit this central role for conservation. The actual mechanisms are separate, and the perception of their value is in their separate status from 'mere' planning. Is this compatible with closer integration? It may challenge traditional assumptions, as one respondent noted, that previously conservation had been regarded as 'just good planning'. Conservation was described as 'the art of intelligent change', but is not planning already the art of intelligent change? If it isn't, does planning need conservation to make good its deficiencies? Could it imply that planning and planners do not necessarily appreciate the extent and subtlety of environmental change as successfully as conservation and conservationists? Is conservation something beyond the scope of planning? These are questions which can be addressed in the local authority case studies that follow in chapters 5 and 6.

Planning has become more concerned with a market-facilitative, user-oriented approach. Conservation, at least in its statutory incarnation, is still fundamentally a regulatory activity. The desire to place conservation at the heart of planning equally reveals respondents' conceptions of the planning system as being based on more traditional notions of 'public interest', rather than client service. Resolving the two is essential, particularly when there is pressure to move conservation area controls into the planning mainstream. If government department representatives believed that an integrated planning permission would preclude a serious assessment of conservation issues, then what are conservation's prospects in local planning practice?

Where is the focus?

Admittedly, listed buildings and conservation areas have different focuses, yet their utility is perceived in specifically different ways. For historic (rather than logical) reasons, current practices place most weight, in terms of standards and regulatory powers, on the value of specific buildings identified through listing. However, if these systems were to be re-created from first principles, many considered that recognising context and understanding the 'milieu into which change is to be slotted' should be paramount. This is significant for the definition of value within each regime, listing or conservation area, and its contribution to conservation value as a whole.

The strength of listing, as a process and an end, was stressed through both its actual controls and the legitimacy conferred by a systematic scrutiny of value. In contrast, area-based conservation was seen as much weaker in terms of regulatory control and vague definitions of 'character'. Paradoxically, the desire to prevent the erosion of character in conservation areas by advocating tighter controls over minor alterations and development addresses only a very narrow consideration of area-based character. This view may be inherited from a mindset which treats environmental aspects in a similar manner to a listed building – that is, as a fabric-specific process.

Notably, there is an inherent bias, illustrated by the national organisations' greater involvement in listing and therefore lending greater profile and legitimacy to a fabric- and structure-specific interpretation of value. As long as conservation areas are viewed as more of a general planning consideration for local authorities, there will not be the same national institutions in place to develop and consolidate area-based valuations of character with their inherently more diffuse and amorphous concepts. If such a division is prevalent in conservation attitudes, it is questionable how far other disciplines, such as urban design and townscape analysis, can help consolidate this shortfall.

What is acceptable change?

While respondents emphasised conservation as the acceptance of environmental change, a question remains as to whether this is an attempt to distance the profession from its preservationist legacy or whether conservation practice accepts and actively promotes renewal.

The message of 'accommodating change' has been interpreted and adopted differentially across sections of the profession. Those involved in determining listing building consents perhaps show a stronger resolve to retain control over, and a certain reluctance to see too many incursions into, their scope and competency. The desire to see tighter use of listed building consents and stronger conservation area controls to prevent the cumulative erosion of features reinforces a more regulatory view of conservation.

However, respondents of higher political status tended to emphasise conservation as having a regeneration role. Considering the spate of recent publications and press statements, particularly from EH, this is not surprising. The interesting question is whether this message represents a genuine reconsideration of the conservation agenda or is, for political purposes, tessellating with the impetus for urban regeneration under the current government's agenda.

Indeed, there are potential discrepancies between professionals regarding their own competencies to comment on new design. The more recent literature has painted a conciliatory picture of modern architecture and conservation coalescing in one communal concern (Stones 1998; Worthington *et al.* 1998). However, professionals still distinguish the new from the old, the contemporary from the conserved.

The type of public support

Determining acceptable change is also seen as dividing professional and public opinion. Though some professionals lamented the public's lack of understanding conservation, an alternative explanation may be that the public simply value different aspects of the built environment. The differences in strength of public support are dramatic, ranging from genuine widespread support to a superficial acceptance.

There is a general perception that public support still provides a legitimate mandate for conservation. While the 'beneficent minority' responsible for statutory conservation consider that they uphold the same value orientations as the public, this executive model is satisfactory. However, questions are raised when respondents consider the public's interpretation of value straying from their own; it may undermine conservation's legitimacy to act in the public interest.

The literature presents the development of conservation as a progression of taste-leaders' crusades championing public appreciation of a new period of architecture, but perhaps there is greater uncertainty in reality. Traditionally, the educated middle classes furnished the support for conservation, though respondents also considered that support was more widespread, as evinced by other social and cultural trends. Respondents' conception of the public and their support influenced the type of public involvement with which respondents felt comfortable. Public debate generally centred around a fairly orthodox architectural appreciation of value, which limited contributions to those already educated in these spheres. Therefore, public participation may be criticised for involving

BISHOP BURTON COLLEGE

only a certain section of people who share, or at least can access, the professional language of conservation.

The reliance on a particular section of the public – middle-class residential interest – also raises difficulties. While this section may be seen to comprise the bulk of public support for conservation, it is incredibly difficult to unpack a 'public interest' since the interest may be no more than a collection of individuals' desires to protect private residential quality and amenity. More significantly, this bias may exclude many other sections of the public with a legitimate, yet unaccounted for, interest in conservation.

Special interest

All respondents considered the legislative criteria of 'special architectural or historic interest' to be a satisfactory definition of conservation value. Crucially, they perceived a distinction between the concepts themselves and their application, and also between the relative strengths of *architectural* and *historic* interest as two separate concerns.

The statutory criteria

The statutory criteria were universally seen as a strong 'intellectual construct' defining the direction and boundaries of conservation's legitimate concerns. Their continued use over 50 years of listing practice had consolidated a broad and germane definition, flexibly evolving to include new aspects. One respondent commented that this flexibility was the reason why listing had never needed reform. Others noted the criteria as being 'extraordinarily comprehensive' and commented on how they had 'managed to absorb an enormous diversity, richness and variety, different categories of buildings, different forms and functions and now the historic landscape and environment, and [they've] done so without any tremendous strain on definitions'. The concepts were so well established as to be almost placed beyond criticism: most respondents appeared surprised to be asked about their contemporary suitability. A lone respondent did confide that their ubiquity and frequency in working use did obviate the need to consider their deeper nature.

While the concepts were seen as sound, their breadth of application and the significant discretion involved in their professional and personal interpretation divided opinions. In response to criticisms that conservation (and architecture and design for that matter) were essentially subjective issues, some respondents argued that there was an objective basis for appreciating value, characterised by the strength of 'special architectural or historic interest'. However, when respondents were pressed, the concept of objectivity held by many instead turned out to resemble a shared idea held within a professional group. The definition of interest was 'a relatively objective process, according, admittedly, to a fairly specific level of objectivity . . . a sort of rolling consensus of all those people who think about these things'. The objectivity of special architectural or historic interest was considered a distinct strength, particularly in contrast to the perceived subjectivity inherent in defining cultural or social value. The latter were seen as so amorphous and ambiguous that trying to include them within any policy definition of value could undermine the legitimate valuation of architectural interest.

Despite many respondents' belief in the objective quality of the criteria, others admitted that the listing rubric had been dramatically stretched. For example, one respondent's experiences of listing buildings in the late 1970s evinced younger professionals' broadening of the scope of conservation interest beyond the more establishment interpretations of older colleagues. Subsequently, architectural interest was broadened to cover vernacular architecture in addition to the 'polite architecture' which had previously dominated listing mores. Similarly, the social and economic historical interest of buildings was accounted for, whereas previously the national, political and military significance of history had dominated: 'consequently the bald phrase "historic interest" did a virtually 180-degree turn'.

Relative values

While the criteria are cited in a single indistinguishable phrase, discrepancies arise between *architectural* and *historic* interest. Most respondents spoke in architectural terms, used architectural examples and referred to features' fabric and detailing to express value. This expression of aesthetic interest was most pervasive: 'I have to say that the first [thing] that triggers you to defend something is its beauty.' However, this respondent then exemplified value in terms of the associated activities over the passage of time which really 'tugged the heartstrings'.

In considering the age of features, contradictory views arose regarding architectural appreciation. While one respondent lamented the preponderance of the antiquarian prejudice – protecting old buildings simply for their age, irrespective of their quality – others surmised that age and survival in themselves were a positive aspect and 'in a sense non-controversial . . . people accept the fact that pre-eighteenth-century buildings ought to be preserved'. An appreciation of architecture was seen by some as a universal perspective through which any period of architecture, ancient or modern, could be enjoyed.

The association of events and uses accrued with age were seen as a corollary supporting the main interest in the architectural fabric. Historical interest was specifically described by some as 'the much poorer relation'. As one NAS respondent observed, this may be due to the fact that because there are more groups in conservation concerned with architecture, the perception of value is necessarily focused on this physical evidence. Though the passage of time inevitably affects features, the value of temporal relationships was considered 'more difficult to assess'; certainly it was less well defined in policy statements. One or two respondents considered that the fact that a particular person or event was associated with a building/structure was of minor consequence since this association left no physical trace on the building. For them, conservation, as a physical control, ought not to be over-influenced by this; conservation ought merely to address architectural history.

A prevalent attitude among many respondents was that non-architectural value was merely an expression of sentimental nostalgia. While such emotions' potency was undeniable, they were not legitimate conservation interests; they lacked recognisable principles and logical arguments.

A cultural dimension

Historical interest starts to move away from the purely tangible and physical evidence in features. The association of uses, events and symbolism adds a variety of layered meanings to the feature over time. Some respondents highlighted the 'cultural weight and value' of conservation. Turning away from the orthodoxy of 'regarding a building as having a certain intrinsic value both as a fabric and for what it demonstrates about the history or the aesthetics of its time', some respondents noted that cultural value is a 'continually changing thing', which English practice is relatively weak in addressing. For example, one EH respondent cited the morphology of urban areas as:

> a very big cultural artefact, the management of which is a great deal more than worrying about design or the amount of archaeological fabric that has survived ... for us to simply deal with it in terms of our architecture, of historic interest residing in a particular building is not at all how people feel about the patina of history.

Cultural value and character were interpreted in a variety of ways. For instance, in the move towards conservation area character appraisals, some saw the process as no more than a comprehensive townscape analysis, while others supported the introduction of a greater cultural dimension. However, proponents of the latter view were cautious in accommodating cultural values, as these could expose planning law's limitations in only being able to control activities specifically relating to land use:

> I think the character issue is, has been, somewhat shirked because it tends to raise these difficult issues and will continue to raise difficult case law

really. [It] will result in difficult cases where brave conservation officers wander off down a very, very thin twig in attempting to protect something which is undoubtedly of the character, on the one hand, but is perhaps not defensible in planning law at all.

One aspect of the cultural dimension of conservation was a generational review of value. Several respondents noted that the succession of new amenity societies was instigated by the young generation re-appraising their grandparents' heritage, recovering it from their parents' critical denigration. Such revision allowed the 'latent' values of certain buildings and periods to emerge.

Several respondents noted a further aspect of the cultural dimension of conservation emanating from the status of listed buildings. Listing itself creates a certain expectation of genre and an important symbolism. This may be illustrated by one respondent's distinction of listing as a process for identifying academic interest in, rather than the actual merit or popularity of, a building's design. The symbolic value of listing can be seen reflected in the political endorsement of decisions that represent certain cultural values. A couple of respondents anecdotally recited the previous, Conservative government's explicit removal of suggestions for the listing of post-war buildings on the grounds that listing certain modernist, collectivist buildings would be legitimating a politically unpalatable 1950s socialist ethos.

'National' interest

While the statutory phrase 'special architectural or historic interest' defined the orientation of value, respondents unanimously considered 'national interest' to be the yardstick for defining and defending features' special qualities. In contrast, 'local interest' was universally perceived as subjective and far less quantifiable. However, identifying a 'national interest' involved various contradictions.

National interest

Respondents from organisations predominantly concerned with listing considered that 'national interest' set the standard for identifying features' value: the taxonomy of maintaining this high quality was essential. By working with the 'set of recognised criteria' as laid out in PPG15, all professionals evaluated features against this national interest: 'it's just a pure measure – it's on the list'. Similarly, EH noted that 'having the courage of saying, "that is one of the finest buildings in Britain and should be preserved and this one is of less importance", this is something we do as a national body.'

However, the common purpose of upholding national interest must be seen against a variety of respondents' comments which cumulatively challenge this concept. One respondent noted that the national status of listed buildings was an unintended consequence of the abolition of non-statutory grade III band (buildings of local interest), which implied that the remaining grades (I, II* and II) were automatically of national interest. It created 'the slightly absurd position that in theory there are 350,000 buildings in the country all of which the nation, *the nation*, cares about. Now in fact that can't possibly be true.' Local lists were seen by most respondents as mere window dressing, good for the local authority's state of knowledge but little more.

Government funding regimes do not appear to demonstrate a national interest in listed buildings, either; as one EH representative said: 'We are not going to be able to keep more than a tiny fraction of them as state pensioners, we shouldn't do that.' The restriction of national grants to grade I and II* properties (through the HLF) has been partly influential in considering whether some grade II listed buildings could be re-assessed in order to qualify for vital, yet otherwise inaccessible, repair funding.

If listed buildings are truly of national interest, it is also anomalous that there is no national system of monitoring. Unlike in the case of ancient monuments, neither the government, EH, the NGOs, nor indeed the local authorities supervise whether all listed buildings are well maintained. In effect, 94 per cent of listed buildings (grade IIs) are of local interest and are the responsibility of local authorities. This is a concern among listing professionals that 'the fact that the lists are national is a kind of fiction. . . . I don't know that there will ever be an explicit recognition of the fact that these buildings are purely local.'

Citing particular examples may illustrate the potential confusion over what constitutes a national interest, and there may be a distinct hierarchy, with listing still embodying the 'traditional value system of polite architecture' which constitutes the 'official heritage of the country'. The message is still confused within EH:

> [O]f course we must recognise and protect the best. I'm not saying that a prefab in Birmingham is as worthy as Lincoln Cathedral, but I am saying that prefabs in Birmingham are as worthy of statutory protection. It's not just about legal protection – I mean there's an assumption that if you extend the heritage, you're either going to interfere with more things or you're going to dilute the degree of protection you can give to a building – which is absurd – that you can give the same protection to a prefab as you can to Lincoln Cathedral.

The gravity and authority of listing standards appear unshakeable. In contrast, the significance of features at a local level, exemplified through conservation area designation and other initiatives such as local lists, was perceived to be a far weaker concept.

Local interest

Perhaps given these national organisations' administrative concern with national interest, it is unsurprising that many respondents considered that a discussion of local interest was more appropriate, and indeed convenient, to leave to local authorities. While one respondent noted that a significant local value ought to constitute a national interest, this was somewhat against the general sentiment, which viewed the importance of local interests somewhat pejoratively: 'Now if you have buildings which are assessed by their interest as structures or works of art, then the fact that they have a local sentimental value is a difficult factor to have in a national system.' There appeared to be an overwhelming perception that local interest is primarily subjective, amorphous and unquantifiable. In contrast to the special, recognised criteria of listing, many perceived local value to be supported by 'quite inchoate reasons': [W]hat we hope, obviously, is that [local] decisions are logically based, not guided by pure unalloyed emotion, and that they do follow the criteria given by central government.' Other respondents, while noting the importance of local value, also perceived it as either thinly veiled self-interest in protecting private amenity, or sentimental nostalgia characterised by irrational, emotional responses to environmental change. Measuring and accessing 'local interest' – what is 'special' in a locality – was perceived to be too difficult a task and, regrettably for some, something which those with national responsibilities had 'shied away from'.

However, some respondents endorsed attempts to encourage local assessments of value. Although there were problems accessing and interpreting these values, respondents considered that these should not prevent local authorities from attempting to do so. Some noted a worthy local orientation of value equating to a more holistic view of the built environment: '[People] feel very strongly about conservation concerning the way in which the familiar and cherished scene . . . is underpinned by historical background.' At the local level, issues of conservation and history, both local and national, became 'so conflated in the common mind that they're almost unpickable'. The expression of local value fulfilled a cultural need to recognise the 'patina of history'. Another respondent noted that valuing only architectural or historical value was a false distinction: people were equally likely to consider familiar and everyday aspects of their environment to be 'special'. Perhaps there are distinctions between what lay members of the public value in their environment and how professionals choose to interpret value?

Public and professional paradigms

All respondents explicitly distanced their expert interpretation of value from their perceptions of how the public considered value. The surprising aspect was the relationship between these perceptions, exemplified through the extent of individuals' education and involvement in conservation.

Professionals' craft

A recurrent feature expressed throughout concerned professionals' firm belief in their objectivity and rigour in evaluating the 'special interest' in a feature. This skill, interpreting value relative to standards of national interest, distinguished the professional from the interested amateur. Respondents did not articulate their skill as a specific acquisition of knowledge – although many professionals were of an art-historical background; these abilities were undoubtedly a result of years of training and experience. In fact, because their everyday work comprised so many unique cases, many respondents considered that a set of general principles was of only limited assistance. Instead, defining value was portrayed as a refined skill, a craft, and ultimately having a professional 'eye'. Notably at EH for example, the 'collegiality of professionals' was considered a major asset, allowing instant access to specialised areas of knowledge and collective discussion of cases' merits.

Informing the public

This professional culture, developed over decades of official recognition, has the potential to distance conservation from the public's immediate understanding. As one civil servant noted, 'It would be a bold man or woman who could say that the public was very clear [over] why conservation investigations and controls apply.'

Given this consolidation of professional knowledge, most respondents were eager to ensure that the esoteric nature of their pursuits did not obscure why they were doing them. A senior EH officer noted the relationship between professionals and the public:

> I certainly would never say that public views should not be taken into account. I will say that where there are issues that require a certain degree of specialist understanding, then it is very, very incumbent on the people who are doing the consulting to make sure that they explain why they are trying to do things.

A listing professional cited the intricate descriptions of buildings on the lists illustrated the unnecessary obscurity that can cloud conservation:

> [They] are very inexplicit. . . . They usually don't go beyond that to its value . . . the ordinary person finds list descriptions very baffling and, importantly, needlessly baffling because they could say why the building had been listed . . . all of that is clear to the illuminati but it needn't be so to the layman.

Most respondents noted that part of their role was to ensure that the public understood and, ideally, supported their professional interpretations. Such dissemination arguably is determined by the accountability of public servants; the responsibility to inform the public is a consequence of taking decisions on their behalf.

However, one respondent criticised EH for lacking transparency in the way it explicitly states its reasoning when supporting listing advice. If the information is to be meaningful, it requires a receptive audience that understands the concepts, reasoning and language employed. As one EH respondent stated:

> [W]e're not just saying, 'we think these buildings are important and you should agree with us', we'd say, 'we think they're important for these reasons and see if you agree with us or not'; this is why they are important.

Promoting public understanding also operated proactively, with several EH respondents highlighting the necessity of persuading the public ahead of an initiative in order to gain popular acceptance of potentially unpopular issues. Without this work, insufficient public response may otherwise cause a new initiative to flounder:

> [W]hen we announced our post-war listing campaign, we had a campaign for hearts and minds. The first proposals failed because we didn't do the evangelical work . . . we had to do a lot more education and consultation, we did it and I think it paid off in terms of getting public acceptance which we would never have got . . . before.

The emphasis continually appears to be on *informing* the public; few respondents wished to give 'the public' any further say or power in conservation. The degree of participation permitted under statutory planning mechanisms was seen as 'about right'. As this responsibility fell on local authorities, representatives at this national level noted that: '[Local planning authorities] should take the whole [process] in a more advanced participatory and consultative way, take the public with them, ask for views and explain very carefully and exactly what the whole business is about.'

The public's response

There is certainly a desire to interest the public in conservation, but what is the perceived nature of the public's contribution? Respondents distinguished the knowledge bases and appreciation of value held by different sections of the public. This could be said to affect the desirability of involving these sections in conservation. While traditionally, interest in conservation has come predominantly from the middle classes, their support permissibly closely aligned itself with the professionals' art-historical orientation of conservation value. One respondent noted that in so far as this section of the public is always involved, the conservationists are forever preaching to the converted.

However, in terms of conservation responding to other, possibly more populist or heritage-oriented interests in the past, respondents were more pejorative. Public taste and appreciation, while admittedly fickle, was also considered somewhat anti-intellectual and too poorly informed to be seriously taken into account. For example: 'the preference for fake Victoriana I'm sure would take us even further down that route [of fake heritage]'. A preference for mock-Tudor Barrett homes, or for heritage-inspired boutiques in old dockyards, contributed to some respondents' viewing 'public taste' with disdain. Lay sentiments were often described as nostalgic or sentimental, possibly indicating a dismissive attitude towards their legitimate value, particularly in contrast to the professionals' 'objectivity'. However, one NAS respondent nevertheless felt the strength of the public's expressions:

> I'm always amazed by how strong the level of support is when a particular local building sometimes of not much architectural quality is threatened. Immediately [there is an] extraordinary reaction amongst a surprising range of people – without being patronising, not very articulate people who write in green Biro letters to the local planning authorities. [They] haven't quite got the buzzwords that everybody else has got but just express through that letter how strongly they do feel over a building which sometimes would be quite hard to defend because it's very mauled, altered or out of context, but for them it matters a great deal.

If such sentiments are so strongly felt, then on what basis are they considered inappropriate for conservation? Few respondents actually mentioned the wider resource pool that such local knowledge, sentiment and experience can contribute to conservation. After all, one respondent noted:

> I mean, ultimately it [the value of listing] only matters because people think it matters . . . you can argue, well what is the intrinsic worth of anything? It doesn't have any intrinsic worth, it only has value because we think it does.

Heritage and culture

While the influence of 'heritage' culture was generally acknowledged, respondents displayed mixed opinions regarding its contribution to conservation. Though sentiment was finely balanced, the prevailing view favoured broadening the scope of conservation's attention, but with some strong caveats expressed about undermining the basis of conservation, which ought to remain focused on buildings' historic fabric. However, themes relating to the temporal collage perceived in the environment appeared too abstract an idea to discuss. While this may reflect a pragmatic professional approach, it is interesting to report that an important strand of philosophical inquiry is somewhat disregarded.

Wider interest

Many respondents embraced this rising popular interest in the past as evidence of welcome support for conservation. Some highlighted the proliferation of groups and societies concerned with less traditional aspects of the past as indicative of a 'democratisation' of what constitutes a legitimate conservation interest. It mirrored a general broadening of conservation's focus from being narrowly defined by the 'great and the grand, whether we're thinking about buildings or art or whatever'. This may represent a move away from the national or official heritage which had previously monopolised the attention of previous generations involved in conservation. Key players in EH believed the inclusion of other considerations of the past was essential:

> We need to look across the whole history. The heritage isn't just about high heritage or Christian heritage or landed gentry heritage or whatever – it's about the whole of our past and the wider it goes and the deeper it goes the happier I am.
>
> One of the things about understanding the past is [that] you've got to understand all of it.

Striving to accommodate 'the whole history' inevitably presents problems with a selection process designed to ensure a representative sample of conserved buildings. Listing was lauded for its recognition of twentieth-century structures some of which arguably belonged to the 'minor history' of the country – for example, the listing of inter-war pre-fabricated domestic chalets. However, broadening its compass was perceived as beneficial only in reference to the objects of conservation rather than the processes or means of interpreting value.

A significant section of respondents considered that heritage was a debasing influence; conservation ought to concentrate exclusively on the historic fabric of features. One EH respondent observed that 'heritage is what you visit and conservation is what you live with'. For example, in relation to archaeology, another respondent noted how many colleagues had difficulty in accepting the premise that archaeology is the study of the past right up to the present day rather than the uncovering of the lost past. This illustrates a perceptual problem with the legitimate concerns of conservation and the merits perceived in heritage.

'Dumbing down'

The criticisms of heritage, which appeared well rehearsed, covered, first, the objects of heritage's attention, and second, people's interest in it. For instance, one NAS respondent commented: '[W]e all tend to dislike the term "heritage" – nobody likes it; it sounds too rustic, too retrograde, [has] associations with the heritage industry, et cetera.' A DCMS respondent noted:

> I've got no idea of what [heritage means]. It's become a bunch of abused words which people then use as a crazy name to justify their own particular interests or concerns, 'it's part of our heritage' or whatever. . . . But I think that's a different issue, the one that concerns, or I suspect that concerns, most people; it's almost like it reflects a primitive nostalgia for the past, things which should or should not be changed.

In characterising any appreciation outside the sphere of credible academic interest as 'primitive nostalgia', this respondent appears to be branding heritage as lacking an intellectual constituency. This is an emphatic dismissal, considering that many respondents also observed a pervasive interest in the past as a national trait. When considering heritage, many respondents considered that the side effects of commodifying the past are incredibly damaging – not only to the fabric of structures, in attempting to make them accommodate inappropriate uses, but also to attempts to represent the past accurately. Commodification, they believe, downgrades the diversity and richness of the features subsequent generations inherit. In attempting to reflect continuity in the environment, an obsession with heritage is liable to produce a homogeneous design solution. One NGO noted:

> An awful lot of local authorities think when they come to urban regeneration schemes, 'what do we do?' 'Let's try and make the best of the old docks' or 'we've got this disused Victorian station and let's build our heritage sort of regeneration around that', which is fair enough and fine. It's just [that] sometimes it can go too far and you end up with, you know, terrible tweeness and fakeness, and so on. Even then people like it, I mean that's the kind of paradox.

Other respondents echoed criticisms that the pastiche creates a new, characteristically uniform aesthetic that in no way reflects the actual past of an area. This acceptance (by the public and also by planners) of such imitation was seen as having a very negative effect on the accuracy of representations of the past and of real environments.

Commentary on the interpretation and articulation of value in features attracting conservation interest

Interest in buildings

There was a unanimous acceptance of the definition 'special architectural or historic interest' as the basis for conservation. Concentrating on a feature's architectural detailing, and the effects of time on it, creates a system propounding intrinsic value. Extrinsic value, on the other hand – cultural meaning, experience, sentiments and association – was generally perceived as less critical because it is secondary to, or dependent on, the fabric.

Re-appraising the more recent past highlighted a significant collision of values. Values were often presented as intrinsic; they were latent and waiting to be discovered. However, the inherent flexibility of interpreting special architectural or historic interest according to a 'rolling consensus' of professional opinion means this view is somewhat flawed. In reality, values are created afresh and are representative of contemporary culture just as much as they are immutable principles. The essence of professional interpretation is relative to the generation, location and context of the culture in which it occurs. Yet anomalously, there is concerted opposition to the official extension of legitimate conservation value to include cultural and social interpretation of value (lying outside the profession), which is currently dismissed as sentimentality or nostalgia, frequently without due consideration.

The interpretation of the current statutory criteria reflects a definitive preference for architectural over historic interest. The ability to recognise and evaluate features in architectural terms does offer a more universal template than historical evaluation, which is necessarily dependent on the unique historical circumstances affecting specific features. Whereas a building's architecture is obvious (structural occlusions aside), its history is not. Historical interest, to a far greater extent than architecture, is constrained by a process of legitimisation: certain types of history are more readily admissible and supported. For instance, it is only relatively recently that social history has been a legitimate factor within listing's value rubric. In the continual revision of acceptable or legitimate values, further questions arise. Is admitting socio-cultural perspectives resisted to the extent that it is because architectural interest is paramount? Is cultural context merely acknowledged or can it be actively embraced to revitalise an interpretation of conservation value?

What is national interest?

The consideration of the legitimate types of history is more likely to include the 'national' history. Listing operates by a recognised set of criteria, distinguishing grades of national interest, yet it is debatable whether the buildings that are listed are actually of interest to the nation as a whole.

In fact, the notion of an identifiable 'national' standard is actually relatively recent: only the thematic twentieth-century listing review has involved a consideration of individual features' merit in relation to a recognised national scale. The routes to achieve listed status – original survey, accelerated resurvey, spot-listing, or thematic – involve different types of information, produced for different reasons in order to get a feature listed. The transparency of the standards applied is in no way assisted by the exclusion of explicit statements of value on the list description itself.

The variety of routes to listed status, the lack of national monitoring of features, and the lack of financial and national support for the bulk of the grade II properties all question the commitment to the 'national interest'. Though change is unlikely in the foreseeable future, Ashworth's (1997) suggestion of a revised grading scheme of local, regional and national importance may address this.

However, a more fundamental problem was the maintenance of national kudos at the expense of local significance. The level of perceived importance, local or national, is the distinguishing mark of different countries' systems. In the UK, most of the curatorial responsibilities (for listed buildings and conservation areas) are heavily weighted towards the local level. However, the importance that has been given to recognising local value has been significantly underplayed at the national level. Admittedly, local value is, by definition, specific to a locality, but the negative perception of these values may contribute to hampering a strategic national development of the concepts required to explore and elucidate local value. Paradoxically, while conservation areas are facing increasing pressure to define and defend 'local value' via character assessments, list descriptions are remarkably free from stating 'national value'.

There appears to be a false assumption that local value is adequately represented through the conservation tools available to local authorities. The concept of a conservation area was never intended to mop up features of local interest that fell short of national recognition. The exclusion of local sentiment under the auspices of nostalgia may illustrate Merriman's (1991) proposition that national and official history is intellectualised above local and immediate emotive historical sentiment. The view of a minority of respondents supports this conviction, that the perception of local value is more holistic and requires greater cultural understanding. Perhaps historical context can appear a stronger force at local level in defining local interest, while architectural interest is the driving force at the national level.

A professional culture . . .

Throughout the analysis, the strength of the professional/expert consideration of value has been a prominent issue. A fairly small community of experts linked by a common cultural background, education and training is able to mould the interpretation of legitimate conservation value. For them, the value of conserving certain buildings was considered to be self-evident and appreciable for all those with a mind and eye to notice. While such experts are laudable for their immense work and knowledge, the professionals' collegiality or culture does appear to be a relatively exclusive one. It is proposed that the development of conservation as a statutory administrative system has created and consolidated a professional culture of conservation that, despite relying on public support, may be quite distinct from popular interpretations of value.

This is not a problem in itself as few would argue that there ought be a direct conceptual link between public interest and what the public is interested in. However, professionals have a responsibility to inform the public of the work carried out on their behalf. But if the public (in their many facets) hold valid perspectives of value beyond the comprehension or competence of the professional culture or indeed this administrative system, to what extent can the system genuinely be said to work wholly in the public interest? The degree of public involvement can range from the provision of information, to education to appreciate conservation, to the contribution of the public's own interpretations of value. By and large, the responses of the national organisations involved in conservation show them to be content to draw the line before the latter.

In the raising of public awareness, a further question is posed: who is the main beneficiary in this process? Is it the public who enjoy increased awareness through a democratic debate about conservation? Or is it the profession/ organisations who require public acceptance of, and therefore support for, new conservation initiatives? In which direction is the significant flow of information – up or down? How far are the public really able to contribute to conservation? Education, in these terms, may be seen as little more than legitimisation of the accepted view – a one-way transfer of information.

Respondents generally characterised any further involvement of the public as being a function of the planning system. Those lay views which did not accord with the received way of interpreting value were rejected from the discussion. Public nostalgia or sentiment is undoubtedly a reflection of people's attachment to, and the significance of, particular features in the built environment. There appears to be far less opportunity for other sections of the public, outside the minority with an architectural understanding, to contribute their evaluation.

The direction in which legitimate interest flows can be illustrated thus. Interest flowing from the professional to the public legitimates professional values. Information flowing from the public to the profession, expressing sentiments and interest in aspects of the environment not considered 'worthy' under orthodox means, creates the potential for greater dispersion than support.

. . . but a populist heritage

One such example of this flow of legitimate knowledge surrounds the role of heritage in conservation, particularly regarding the accuracy of representation – in other words, how authentic a feature is.

Most respondents supported the broadening of interest, recognising more diverse architectural pieces for listing. However, this revision remains within the traditional architectural scope of value. As heritage interest strayed outside the confines of architectural assessment, even though related to the built environment, there was a tendency to dismiss these issues as being fickle, emotional and irrational responses often driven by unbridled sentimentality or primitive nostalgia. While claims are made for conservation to represent the whole of the past, there cannot be an accurate representation of the past.

It is arguable that conservation is oriented towards being more 'true to form' in architectural and design terms than it is 'true to time' through the vagaries of historical interpretation. As both Jones (1993) and Macmillan (1993) have argued, heritage can be a creative re-appraisal of conservation value, as the emphasis shifts from intrinsic value to experiential value based in groups' and individuals' experiences of their environment. The evidence from these interviews suggests that creating a framework for allowing wider interpretation should be encouraged generally, but many professionals feel that this would be taking conservation too far beyond its principal focus, which remains grounded in the architectural tradition. However, if heritage is perceived as an undermining element, conservation may be excluding a significant and refreshing perspective.

The economic imperative

Respondents' attitudes towards economic issues did not coalesce into a common view, except the view that ensuring any building's continued economic vitality requires a 'flexible approach' to decision-making. Consistently throughout the interviews there was less discussion of this issue than of others, which could reflect respondents' belief that really these issues mostly affect local authorities. It was clear that the causes and effects of economics on conservation had created a diverse reaction.

Promoting growth

Conservation was frequently portrayed as a major contributor to the promotion of urban regeneration. Buildings and their associated heritage were portrayed as assets requiring careful management to ensure their continued use. In this respect, conservation was facilitating rather than regulating the market. For instance, '[The former] Chief Executive at English Heritage is utterly convinced that conservation *is* regeneration and if we don't understand that we will perish.'

Pursuing this enabling role of conservation, one key EH respondent noted that the state could not afford to keep vast numbers of listed buildings as 'pensioners'; rather, viable market solutions had to be found. One of conservation's advantages was viewed as its capacity to take a longer-term perspective and maintain buildings until property markets became sufficiently buoyant to take them over. From this perspective, the impact of economics on conservation could not be overstated. One respondent considered that 90 per cent of what happened to historic buildings was determined by economic factors, and that any intervention explicitly in the name of conservation came into play only in a minority of cases. Less positively, NAS respondents viewed the influence of economic pressures as inevitably resulting in threats to, and the loss of, historic fabric.

Some interesting points were raised relating to economics' causal relationship with conservation – that is to say, how market obsolescence can create features that need protection. For example, conservation is increasingly concerned with the social history manifest in the built environment. The restructuring of the UK's manufacturing base has created a wealth of ageing industrial buildings struggling to justify their existence. Precisely when economic considerations demand these features' redevelopment, conservation is arguing for their retention and conversion. One respondent at EH lamented the difficulty of overcoming the perceptual and practical problems this has created:

> [T]he assumption is automatically made, not only that they [old buildings] are temporarily redundant, but that they must be redundant for all time. And the other assumption is that because they're not suitable for today's particular uses, they won't ever be suitable for any other uses again.

A couple of respondents from planning-oriented organisations presented a different angle on local authorities' use of conservation controls. With increasingly intense economic competition between towns and cities, distinguishing places' unique characteristics and qualities was essential for many local authorities. Historic towns faced formidable opposition from larger metropolitan and unitary authorities in terms of attracting inward investment and securing grants and regeneration funding. One strength of the former was being able to market their historic environmental qualities to attract jobs and residents, shoppers and tourists.

Weighing the benefits

Positively, some respondents commented that developers have appropriated the conservation message in converting redundant buildings seemingly based on a growing realisation of the saleability of 'pastness', combined with profitable, central urban locations: '[F]rankly, they started to realise the commercial value of the buildings and architectural heritage – they are selling things [for] a higher price because they are individual.'

Some respondents viewed developers' interest with cynicism. The conversion of such redundant buildings (often along a particular 'heritage' theme) was viewed as an easier route for obtaining planning permission if local authorities were keen to revitalise these deteriorating structures.

Away from the commercial side, many considered residential interest in conservation to be a double-edged sword. Increased prosperity and a cultural propensity for home-ownership made the kudos of owning a listed building a reality for a greater cross-section of the public. Home-owners improved and maintained properties that previously might have been neglected and left to rot. However, the increased incidence of such residential improvements brought all manner of uninformed and unsympathetic alterations to the fabric of historic properties. Indeed, the NAS considered that the majority of their casework involved over-enthusiastic home-owners' 'improvements' to listed buildings.

In controlling these commercial and residential aspects, many respondents considered that local authorities were too conciliatory to the economic pressures, and often threats, propounded in applications for planning permission. Local planning committees were seen to be too easily persuaded to sacrifice the intrinsic interest of a feature in order to secure a potential development; for developers, maintaining the all-important economic viability of a scheme was a powerful tool against a potentially vulnerable planning authority. Though many respondents recognised the inevitable 'trade-off' between retention and development, they considered that local planning authorities often deviated away from the recommended guidelines in national policy.

The politics of conservation

It is notable that, as with economic issues, respondents were less forthcoming in discussing the political aspects of conservation. It appeared that politics and policy were largely an influence on these respondents rather than being of definite and central importance. One respondent at EH noted that policy:

> gets talked about by those who wish to talk about it . . . it occasionally gets talked about [in terms of] whose technical responsibility it is at the upper levels, but that, broadly speaking, happens when they are kicked . . . it's just because they're all too short of time.

Moreover,

> [I]t tends to be very haphazardly done . . . so although we might, I hope, present a perfectly united front when a large issue comes up to the outside world, we don't spend our time endlessly churning over policy. . . . I think policy is rather under-loaded in terms of time.

Respondents chose to interpret political influence in different ways: first, party politics and its effects; second, the effect of political issues on regulatory relationships. Though national political issues were seen as paramount, local politics was considered much the stronger influence on conservation as it affected the actual physical results delivered in the name of conservation.

Politics

At a national level, time and time again conservation was portrayed as enjoying cross-party support:

> I think conservation is one of those things [that is] accepted by all political parties; it's intrinsic to all government advice now. I think it is regarded as just a given and no political party could hope to gain power or respect if it announced tomorrow that it was abolishing listing . . . it's just not a vote-winner.

This conviction of conservation's stability, in a fashion, has permitted conservation to continue its operations with minimal political interference. One EH respondent noted that even when 'Thatcherite Britain [was] in full flood', EH still managed to get the 'presumption in favour of preservation' accepted in PPG15, much to the consternation of developers and the construction industry.

However, it has already been commented upon that political preferences are shaping conservation's orientation, at least in EH's representations. At the time of investigation, the UTF was creating tangible uncertainty for the future role of conservation in urban development. Thus while some maintain that political influence may appear minimal, this is not to say that there aren't political values in conservation: indeed, it may create some of its own.

Political values

The extent to which conservation advice remains apolitical is open to question, particularly when one respondent sarcastically commented: '[I]t must be the Secretary of State's decision on the impartial advice from a disinterested advising group and of course *that is what happens every time.*' Evidently there are political biases and preferences that affect the apparent impartiality of decision-making. Indeed, some respondents noted how protecting a feature from development by spot-listing could involve considerable political expediency to justify its protection, and thus potentially distort the significance placed on the intrinsic interest of the feature. Other recognisable biases involved the division of conservation responsibilities between two political masters in the then DETR (now ODPM) and DCMS: 'It's an amazing split and it's totally dysfunctional; it doesn't work properly and it's actually extremely difficult to be working to two masters with different agendas.'

Conservation's relationship with planning also influences the way in which conservation can access politics. Many respondents considered that in cases of protection or development, politically sensitive outcomes, whether intended or not, were a matter for planning, not conservation. This perspective allowed conservation to retain an apolitical stance. For instance, one respondent highlighted the conservation programme in Bologna through which the local Communist administration introduced a socio-political agenda for conservation. In UK practice, few, if any, conservation initiatives were even discussed in (right- or left-wing) socio-political terms. Where gentrification occurs, some respondents saw it as legitimately assisting properties back into re-use, having encouraged the new owners to uphold conservation aims. Although conservation could create social problems, these were beyond conservation's competence and could be left for planners and politicians to adjudicate.

Central–local relations

Most EH respondents saw their work with local authorities as a partnership, encouraging and overseeing local conservation practice, supporting the, often lone, local conservation officer. EH's added weight and legitimacy emphasised the national responsibility of conservation, a responsibility which local politics might brush aside. However, the diversity and autonomy of local authorities, while inevitable in a democratic country, presented great difficulties in securing conservation's place high among local priorities. Particularly for NAS respondents, local authorities could as easily present a hindrance: 'You know, local planning authorities can do what they bloody like as far as I can see in listed building consent cases.'

The power relationship between the tiers of government is a sensitive one. Listing can be imposed: '[I]t doesn't cause a problem if the local planning authority doesn't want it – one just sits there and says "tough!" Conservation areas are a nightmare because the local planning authority really is the one who designates.' The local political agenda generally poses a problem for national organisations in ensuring that conservation receives consistently high-quality treatment. One respondent, with a background in local authority politics, noted that while conservationists are immersed in the subject, they must be politically astute too:

> [I]f conservation is going to survive, it's got to survive in the murky polit-
> ical world . . . conservation is one of many elements in the planning process
> – it's not a unique one and it has to fight its corner with other subjects – it
> doesn't have a divine right to be listened to.

It was noted above that many respondents considered PPG15 to be a high-
water mark in national conservation policy. In spite of this, several respondents
lamented local authorities' lack of imagination in implementing its guidance.
Most local plans merely paraphrased national conservation policy, with little
attention being paid to identifying local characteristics and priorities. This may
be indicative of the balance of power between local and central government,
which has shifted in favour of the latter over recent years. However, it does not
necessarily mean that all local authorities are inattentive to their conservation
responsibilities. A couple of respondents noted some local authorities' desire for
further layers of conservation control: some authorities want the political imperative and autonomy – in terms both of actual control and of recognition for the
quality of their local features.

Respondents also perceived the influence of power relations within local
authorities, between officers, as affecting the local success of conservation. The
implementation of good conservation schemes was widely recognised as dependent on the quality, relative status of and respect shown to the conservation officer
within the planning service. The generation of support and political goodwill for
conservation in an authority was often the result of the individual conservation
officer's enthusiasm, persuasiveness and tenacity.

To what extent do economic and political pressures affect conservation?

Generally speaking, economic development was considered either a force which
conservation can harness or an obstacle to successfully maintaining buildings'
architectural integrity. While all respondents emphasised that keeping buildings
in use was their main concern, actively encouraging re-use and an emphasis on
economic viability affected where the fulcrum was placed in the delicate trade-
off between retention and renewal. EH's self-proclaimed role as a regeneration
agency represented a significant change in the organisation's outlook, and will
require a further set of criteria by which to measure the effects and performance
of its activities in this arena.

Economic effects are particularly difficult to measure, given the intricacies of
calculating the economic value and benefits which conservation may either
accrue or contribute. Some studies have attempted this (Allison *et al.* 1996), with
limited efficacy given the contested nature of quantifying cultural and social
value as opposed to economic ones. Ashworth's (1997) argument that conserved

117

structures ought to be more productively recast as marketable heritage resources attempts to address this economic turn, yet it would appear that there is not a great deal of support for any such reconceptualisation of values. Lichfield (1997) has perhaps come closest to producing a framework for calculating conservation's economic contribution, but the point is that the more that economics is brought into the fray, the weaker the non-economic benefits of conservation appear in contrast, as they appear to be less quantifiable and therefore less defensible. This revision may have quite profound effects, given the criticisms levelled at local authorities by respondents for too easily sacrificing conservation to development pressures.

But it seems that economic and political pressures do go hand in hand. Conservation was perceived to have fairly robust political backing at a national level, yet at the local level it was decidedly more vulnerable to other political pressures. This may reflect a problem that conservation bodies face in making their message relevant to local authorities. Local politicians may want their locality to look attractive but they may not support conservation because it appears to be a luxury in the face of more urgent priorities. The portrayal of conservation as an art-historical concern through national policies and select local conservation professionals may actually reinforce this distinction. On this reasoning, conservation needs to demonstrate that it can engage with and contribute to wider socio-economic priorities if it is to overcome local political apathy and even cynicism. Purists might oppose such a move, but it may be essential to re-appraise what conservation is and does, in order to achieve the sort of local political consensus which is seen as supporting the whole system nationally.

Concluding observations on the national survey

A relatively small survey of the principles, policy and practice among selected national conservation organisations can never hope to present a definitive and universally accurate picture of these issues. But in representing a sample of key players, it is illustrative of the shared values and also contradictions which are seemingly inherent in this sphere.

Although it was difficult to establish completely coherent positions for organisations, it was surprising to find such a high degree of correspondence between these bodies' views. Perhaps this was consolidated by their united front in campaigning for conservation. The question is, however, how far do these similarities necessarily indicate an identifiable set of national values in conservation? Answering this involves addressing two observations: first, there was an intellectual vagueness characterising respondents' expressions which masked underlying tensions in their opinions; and second, there may have been an over-arching professional perspective or culture which might account for their answers.

First, the apparent consensus on issues holds firm only for general, unassailable statements, such as believing that conservation is the management of change. When individuals' responses were unpacked, the cumulative impression these statements gave was one of confusion and vagueness rather than illuminating clarity and consistency. The intellectual basis for conservation remained elusive and ephemeral, even apparently for those professionals engaged in its operation on a day-to-day basis. Though tensions were mostly implicit, the contrasts were sufficiently disparate to expose a variety of competing interpretations to challenge superficial consensus. Moreover, the tensions were evident not simply between respondents but also within individuals' own attitudes.

Such inconsistency may be unavoidable, having been created by the structural tensions inherent in conservation. Time and again, respondents, particularly those involved with casework applications, noted that their practical work could not be performed according to hard-and-fast rules. This is not to say conservation ought to rely on a universally consistent intellectual basis for its actions, nor should its absence *per se* be criticised. It may appear wholly unrealistic to clamour for greater consistency in conservation when professionals place such faith in the discretion and flexibility available to them.

The second consideration is acknowledging the influence of professionals' background and training. The issue is first raised here as it has not appeared in the conservation literature to date. There was a significant degree of employment mobility within the national conservation sphere, with individuals moving into and out of posts across the private, public and voluntary sectors. Thus any one organisation could be staffed by a significant number of people who have held positions in other conservation organisations. To some extent, this may account for the difficulty in distinguishing corporate viewpoints from individuals', if opinions have been formed by education and by experience influenced by several roles in different sectors. This may indicate that these conclusions can only represent the values of a shared professional culture among key players at this level.

So in response to the specific question 'is there a set of national conservation values?', the answer appears rather tautological. While there is common agreement at a superficial level as to the general direction and parameters of conservation, the diversity of interpretations and values supporting this consensus is sufficient to undermine it. However, it is also arguable that there is a shared and somewhat exclusive professional culture born of similar education and training, which influences this deeper level of value diversity.

From the extensive material amassed from this survey, presented below are the significant points worth highlighting and taking forward to examine in further detail in the context of the local planning authority case studies that follow in chapters 5 and 6.

The nature of conservation planning

There was a widespread desire to present conservation as a central component of all levels of governance and land-use planning. However, conservation practice was seen as a distinct specialisation that benefited enormously from separate legislation, consents, professionals and responsibilities. Any measures to integrate conservation further within planning were dismissed as potentially obscuring vital conservation issues.

It appears that the legitimacy gained from closer integration with planning was of less importance when compared to the benefits of having operational distinction. It is significant how far conservation's mechanisms, relations and professionalism may actually inhibit how it develops, as the *status quo* is continually used to justify conservation's special status.

The distinction in specific mechanisms and consent regimes between listed buildings and conservation areas further emphasised this split of competencies between planning and conservation. When conservation was more closely entwined with planning practice it was perceived as weaker in terms of control mechanisms and as a theoretical concept. Urban design and townscape management were alternative ways of accomplishing similar objectives, but conservation's strength was perceived in its specificity towards historic fabric. Planning, by and large, was far too blunt an instrument, in terms both of the controls available and of planning officers' ability to appreciate conservation issues. A distinction in professional design competencies provided a further contrast.

Conservation was seen to enjoy considerable public support, an interest almost bordering on a national pastime, which not only gave the profession a platform but also accounted for the perceived political consensus supporting conservation over the past 30 years. Such public interest lent moral power to the elbow of the conservation profession.

Inconsistencies arose when the public was viewed as distinct sections rather than a homogeneous whole; public support then varied from tacit acceptance through to apathy and lack of interest. While it was incumbent on the profession to explain and educate the public, this raises the question of how far the conservation profession responds to public interest or opinion or, alternatively, sets its own values.

The interpretation of value in the built environment

The statutory criteria of 'special architectural or historic interest' were universally considered an appropriate and flexible basis for interpreting value in conservation. The importance of the 'architectural' appeared to eclipse the 'historic', despite some broadening of the latter to acknowledge social and economic history in the built environment.

Respondents focused on the intrinsic value of historic fabric. More significantly, listing was implicitly held as the torch-bearer in identifying new interpretations of conservation value. The concept of understanding the character of areas was under-developed largely because it was the responsibility of local authorities. An area's character, more so than the character of a building, was difficult to define since it involved a greater cultural dimension which conservation had not traditionally encompassed.

The national interest of features provided a benchmark in the taxonomy of conservation. While the processes of affirming 'national' interest were considered rigorous and relatively objective, it is questionable whether the absence of national monitoring, comprehensive grant schemes and controls means that the nation is actively interested in conserving all these buildings.

Local interest was considered much more subjective, and in general, respondents were satisfied to leave this concept for local authorities to develop. However, relatively few authorities analysed local interest or applied the concept meaningfully, and national bodies had little power to demand better performance.

The definition of 'interest', although defended as a relatively objective standard, is created by a fairly small community of experts. Their relatively exclusive interpretation can operate as a value filter and, given their strength of conviction in their professional judgement, it would appear that this collegiality, more than anything else, provides the intellectual basis for conservation. When professional disciplines become closed to wider societal evaluations of value, conservation risks becoming a self-serving administrative function (Jones 1993).

As mentioned above, the consideration of the broader cultural dimension of conservation has created problems. While respondents recognise its importance, there was a reluctance to broaden the parameters of conservation beyond the art-historical paradigm. For instance, the effects of heritage have promoted a revision of conservation value, but only in relation to pieces of architecture. Heritage has not widened the legitimate routes open to cultural interpretations of conservation value.

The influence of external pressures

It is significant that throughout the interviews, respondents were less ready to discuss these external pressures. Economics and politics were generally considered more appropriately addressed by local planning authorities in determining conservation's effects rather than being the major considerations at a more abstracted national policy level.

Conservation was continually battling against the inherent economic obsolescence of buildings. Although the exploitation of the heritage was increasingly recognised as marketable and profitable, respondents were sharply divided about whether to ride the crest of this wave or take shelter from its inevitable fallout.

Ultimately, most agreed that conservation still suffered from having a weak bargaining position in contrast with hard economic arguments, especially within local authority decision-making.

In political terms, there were strong perceptions that the government had, through its hesitance to take positive steps in favour of conservation, signalled a change in the political patronage for conservation. Consequently, the key players in conservation have felt the need to re-orient their conservation practice, or at least the rhetoric, to tessellate with a political agenda that puts urban regeneration at the top of the list of planning priorities.

From principle to practice

The survey of issues from this national level is interesting, but to understand how conservation operates and implements certain values and justifications, examining the practice of local authorities is imperative. There are some salient questions raised in this chapter that are worth bearing in mind for the case studies in chapters 5 and 6.

- How does conservation activity interact with statutory planning in local practice – is there a similar value placed on its 'separateness'?
- Is there grass-roots support for conservation in a locality?
- Does the intrinsic architectural value of historic fabric enjoy the same prominence or does the presence of local area-based protection engender a more holistic approach?
- Is there a distinctly local, in contrast with the national, perspective regarding conservation value?
- Is there still a core set of professional values defining conservation?
- To what extent do economics and politics dictate conservation's influence?

5 Conservation in a post-industrial mill town

Introduction to the local planning authority case studies

The previous chapter examined the range of values and attitudes within what might be loosely termed a 'national policy culture'. Evidently this is merely half the story: what happens in practice on the ground can be far removed from more strategic, perhaps even esoteric, discussions of value. There is evidently a different set of considerations in force when decisions are taken locally, the gritty realism of determining planning applications.

Previous conservation studies have been criticised for concentrating on the minutiae of particular locations and then being constrained in their capacity to extrapolate findings to a wider context. On the one hand, the comprehensive coverage produced by canvassing all local authorities has to be balanced against the quality and depth of examination which is possible by concentrating on a few selected case studies on the other. Every local authority will be influenced by a unique set of circumstances in its handling of conservation issues. Conversely, there are likely to be generic issues in dealing with the cultural built heritage which will be common to urban authorities not only throughout England, but also in other developed countries.

Focusing on just one town or local authority would have been too restrictive, and so instead two different towns were selected in order to compare and contrast their approaches to conservation. The idea was to contrast a town exuding a traditional historic image with a town comprising similar conservation responsibilities and resources yet whose image was far removed from the archetypal 'picture postcard' heritage.

Existing literature provided detailed information about the nature and management of some local authorities' conservation management. In particular, the studies by Pearce *et al.* (1990) and the English Historic Towns Forum (1996, 1997) proved invaluable. The last study, comprising an assessment of all the local authority conservation practices of EHTF members, surveyed nearly all the 'traditional historic towns' in England. The criteria set out in table 5.1 were used to short-list suitable authorities.

Since the Four Towns Study (Buchanan and Partners 1968; Burrows 1968; Esher 1968; Insall and Associates 1968) there has been a tendency to focus research on the historic 'gems' (Larkham and Jones 1993). Unfortunately, doing so is not particularly representative of problems facing most local authorities, so less high-profile 'conservation' towns were selected.

For a second authority with a contrastable image and character, the former metropolitan county councils across the north of England provided the most

Covent Garden, London: a high-profile success for the conservation movement in saving the fabric if not the spirit of this renowned square

© Francesco Venturi; Kea Publishing Services Ltd/CORBIS

Table 5.1 Criteria used to identify suitable local authority case studies

Criteria used to identify suitable local authority case studies

- Number of list entries (not necessarily listed buildings numbers) in the authority's area
- Relative breakdown of the grading of listed buildings
- The general character of the protected building stock – architecture/period
- Number of and type of conservation area designations
- Presence of local initiatives such as local lists, local 'buildings at risk' register
- Presence of public participation forums such as conservation area advisory committees
- Funding arrangements – CAP schemes, internal grant aiding

suitable candidates. These areas, shaped by nineteenth-century industrial development, boast significant numbers of listed buildings, and contrast well with the pretty shire image of a more traditional market town. A suitable contrast, in terms of town size and conservation responsibilities, was found between a northern industrial town and a market town in the Midlands, and the two cases are examined in this chapter and in chapter 6 respectively.

The investigation of each town's conservation planning was identical in so far as was practical. The first objective was to provide a contextual background to the authority's conservation operations through examining local policy, strategic documentation and unpublished authority documentation. As the culture largely

Table 5.2 Respondents interviewed in both local authorities

Respondents interviewed in the course of exploring the contextual background of the local authorities

- Planning Chair
- Planning Committee Members
- Executive level officers
- Chief Planning Officer (or equivalent)
- Planning Service Section Managers (and equivalents at relevant county level)
- All DC planning officers dealing with applications covering the main urban area
- Conservation Officer (or equivalent)
- All other conservation section personnel
- Recently retired or relocated officers who played a significant role in conservation
- Representatives of local bodies interested in conservation – for example, the Civic Society or prominent residents' groups

resides in people's minds, interviewing local key players and stakeholders was essential. Being able to cross-reference their opinions and personal interpretations of events, institutional arrangements and priorities provided a much better picture of this fairly intangible culture. For as representative a sample as possible, respondents at various levels of seniority throughout the authority were interviewed (table 5.2).

The second objective was to see how the values apparent in conservation policy were actually applied in particular developments involving significant conservation issues in considering a grant of planning permission. Several commentators (e.g. Barrett 1993) have noted the importance of exposing conflicts and arguments in the crucible of actual development control (DC) cases. Using real examples of decision-making and implementation provided a rich source of material with which to test and challenge the conservation values of a range of players beyond the institutional scope of the local authority, as well as to illustrate the implementation of certain policy positions.

The research literature on urban morphology stresses the importance of recognising the variety of agents active in the development of the urban form (Whitehand and Whitehand 1984; Whitfield 1996). The study adapted this classification to cover different types of development and developers (table 5.3). Four individual planning applications and their subsequent land developments in each local authority were selected.

The available material in the planning files outlined the negotiations between the various parties, who generally comprised the applicant, the agent, the relevant planning officer(s), the conservation officer(s) and any other third parties. These parties were then interviewed and the issues raised by the respective developments used as a basis on which to question the attitudes and opinions of a wide

Table 5.3 Criteria used to select the development case studies

Sampling strategy criteria used to identify four different development cases in each authority

- The development must be in the urban area of the main town
- The development must be complete, or at least have received planning permission
- The development occurred within the past three years for ease of respondents' recollection
- Two cases concern residential use/issues and two concern commercial use/issues
- In these residential/commercial groupings, one case should be a listed building case, the other an unlisted building in a conservation area
- Furthermore, the four cases ought to involve one application each from a developer of commercial property, a local private business, a developer of residential property and a private householder

range of players. To minimise the potential for systemic and personal bias in these interviews, the thematic framework provided a robust tool for an outlining the interviews, categorising the amassed evidence and analysing emerging issues.

Since the research was actually conducted, there have inevitably been changes in the administration and staff in both local authorities. Without doubt, the national agenda has also moved on and it is possible that certain local pressures have become more dominant in the intervening period. The development cases themselves have much longer histories, with some applications dating back to initial discussions in the early 1990s. Evidently, the parties interviewed and organisations concerned are likely to hold different views now as compared with those expressed during this research. This is only natural: the values present in any system are determined by the continually shifting factors influencing the society and culture in which that system is located, and this study can only ever attempt to convey a snapshot of these values. However, the themes emerging from this work embody significant features which continue to be equally relevant today.

An illustrative background

This industrial town in the north of England is a little-known architectural treasure: the local authority has responsibility for well over 1,000 listed buildings. While many of these listed buildings represent the mills and industrial heritage of the town, there are outstanding highlights of the town's grand Victorian and Edwardian architecture.

During the Industrial Revolution the town grew exponentially on the basis of its international textiles industry, which still exists today in a much slimmer form. While the town also has a strong base in the chemical and engineering industries, an over-reliance on ageing manufacturing industries has taken its toll economically, seeing a heavy rate of closures and redundancies throughout the 1980s. The town has a population of around 120,000.

A brief summary of past achievements

The council was created in 1974 in the national re-organisation of local government. Over the years, the internal structure of the authority has changed repeatedly. While conservation has always been an integral part of the planning service, it previously used to sit alongside development control (DC).

The forerunner to the current departmental arrangement was loosely divided into two teams, one dealing with specific DC advice and the architectural detailing of listed building consents, and the other taking a more project-oriented approach to urban renewal. The latter was broader-ranging, working outside the conventional boundaries of planning, often in tandem with other departments such as housing.

The council's officers in general were eager to retain as many conservation responsibilities as possible at a local rather than county level. Several conservation initiatives through the 1970s and early 1980s illustrate the benefits of that decision.

In terms of listing, the original lists of historic buildings for the area, dating from the 1950s, were of little practical use to local officers. By the early 1980s, with national concern over the listing surveys' sloth, the former Department of the Environment (DoE) sought to speed up the national listing process by co-opting local authorities to produce provisional listings. The EH listing inspector began the process with zeal, using the opportunity to champion the wealth of eighteenth- and nineteenth-century vernacular buildings and the impressive Victorian civic architecture in the town. Following his initiative, the authority was invited to conduct one of these pilot listing projects for the rest of the authority's area, which fed into phase 1 of the accelerated national resurvey. A local specialist, an architect, was commissioned to prepare provisional lists, which despite reduction by the DoE have today left the authority with a considerable number of listed buildings. The initiative not only produced lists representing greater vernacular interest, but also illustrated how listing itself can alter perceptions of a place. At the time, the council welcomed both the appreciation and the kudos, though some members saw listed building consents, particularly in the case study town centre, as an unwarranted obstacle to the town's economic development.

A further accolade was the introduction of a local 'buildings at risk' survey to support the authority's own historic building grants scheme, which actually put it ahead of most other local authorities' practice in the mid-1980s. With EH's backing, every listed building was photographed and recorded, and the methodology employed formed a basis for EH's subsequent national 'buildings at risk' surveys. The concern for features of predominantly vernacular interest was a significant innovation, valuing the locally undervalued and providing a platform for local conservation officers to consider their conservation practice the equal of those prestigious towns which boasted a more established conservation profile.

A reversal of fortunes?

In contrast to the pioneering spirit characterising the first 15 years, conservation's status arguably diminished during the 1990s. With the abolition of the metropolitan county councils in 1986, further responsibilities were transferred to the local council, and conservation had to vie with new challenges and priorities on the political agenda.

Economically, the 1980s were not easy years for the north of England. Like many others, the town suffered a long decline in its traditional industrial and manufacturing base and tried to encourage growth based on a more diversified economy, through service industries and retailing. The drive to stimulate inward investment, creating new jobs and prosperity, while always important, appeared to transcend all other priorities. As in many other authorities, the planning service was increasingly being pressured to apply developer-friendly policies and approaches. Though this initiative fell mostly to the economic development section within the planning service, some local politicians considered the regulatory and restrictive ethos of the planning service to be an obstacle. This attitude resulted in the creation of a separate economic development unit, leaving the planning service with a reduced strategic and proactive role regarding local development. While the restructure was portrayed as providing clarity and definition to the planning service, some planning officers saw it as a diminution of planning's local political status.

Subsequent budget reviews similarly reflected the council's political priorities. The council frequently suffered central government capping, which meant that virtually all council services received an annual cut. While the planning service consolidated its staff under these reductions, a series of unfortunate cases where conservation was blamed for causing delays for well-connected developers further undermined conservation's political support. Conservation was not considered an essential function and it received a series of deeper annual budget cuts until the resulting loss of staff through natural wastage and demoralisation left the conservation section severely depleted.

It is difficult to summarise such an extensive history in so short a space but over a 25-year period the value of conservation's contributions, to planning and politically, has evidently altered. Politically it has been eclipsed by other more pressing agendas. While conservation is still praised by all as a worthy activity, as a separate section, distinct from statutory planning responsibilities in the DC and policy sections, it may face a far greater threat of marginalisation. While recollections of past practice may be positively remembered through rose-tinted spectacles, there is no denying that the authority undertook several pioneering initiatives, supported by national conservation institutions. Latterly, the scope and support of such practices appears more confined. While planning has been stripped to the essentials and possibly outflanked by the economic development unit's proactivity, so conservation has been characterised and pigeon-holed as a minor regulatory responsibility. Such a perception does not bode well for reclaiming active political support.

Current structure, operation and priorities

HEI section

The Heritage, Environment and Implementation (HEI) section is divided into Conservation and Design (C&D) and Implementation (see figure 5.1). The

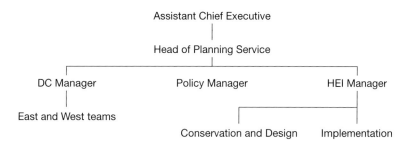

Figure 5.1 Structure in 1999 of the council planning service of the first town studied (a post-industrial town in the north of England)

Implementation team assembles bids for all external grant applications, drawing funding into the authority for regeneration projects, and also manages existing grant schemes in close liaison with external stakeholders. The C&D team are the Council's design advisers, dealing with referrals from all other council services, but mostly from DC, on specific aesthetic matters.

C&D comprises two officers under the Team Leader. This is in stark contrast to just two years ago, when the section had five full-time officers. The loss of staff has been debilitating not only for the loss of institutional memory and expertise in the field but also because the budget cuts and perceived lack of commitment to conservation higher up in the authority had created significant push factors for staff.

The priority facing HEI, as outlined by principal officers, is to become oriented to pursuing more proactive and project-based conservation. In order to survive as a valid planning activity, conservation needs to prioritise cases and not treat each feature as an irreplaceable marvel. The section ought, it is felt, to concentrate on the authority's wealth of grade I and II* responsibilities, some of which were in desperate need of attention, rather than more ordinary, mediocre listed buildings. The latter should be left to an accomplished DC officer, who, given appropriate pre-emptive design guidance, could deal with them appropriately.

The view from within C&D

Opinions within C&D differ from the corporate vision. Unfortunately for C&D, principled conservation arguments can often seem to become lost as they wend their way through the planning service and committees, leading to a lack of appreciation of, or consistent approach towards, conservation. Aside from the Unitary Development Plan (UDP), there is no guidance, no corporate statement and little design training outside the C&D section. The lack of support for conservation principles leaves it more vulnerable to the development pressures to which development control officers are continually exposed. Several recent cases have highlighted this, and the opportunities for C&D to influence DC decision-making have been perceptibly reduced.

Rather than seeing it as just an element of design, the conservation adviser views conservation as reflecting people's awareness of space–time relations: features in the built environment help orient experiences of the present. Criticisms were levelled at national conservation policy for not accounting for specific qualities of locality and place. Certainly this neglect of context has been a major criticism of modern architecture – in which professional arrogance pays scant attention to surroundings, spatially or temporally.

From a wider perspective, C&D officers believe conservation can be most successful when accompanied by public interest and co-operation, either in submitting sensitive applications, or through active conservation lobbying. However, conservation may be seen locally as a luxury rather than a priority by a majority of the public; this is partly reflected in local political attitudes. If the public do not appear to take an active interest in conservation, it is all the more important to act on their behalf. Unfortunately, the public may not appear interested in conservation because lack of familiarity with the professionals' design language precludes members of the public from taking part in the debate.

DC section

While the planning service has been subject to budgetary cuts, the DC section has retained a large staff to ensure swift processing of planning applications. The section deals with all the planning applications made to the authority, including all listed building consents.

Senior planning officers consider that the planning service has a good reputation based on its DC officers' flexible and sensitive approach to achieving a mutually satisfactory arrangement with applicants. Planning was viewed as a balancing act of policies and principles with the need to have a purposeful and pragmatic service to deliver results. In contrast, some planning officers considered that a planning authority upholding an ethos of 'public interest' ought be less conciliatory to applicants' desires. Evidently there are tensions throughout regarding the practical and normative function of planning.

Operational relations with HEI

Previously, in the early 1980s, the conservation section had advised on all planning applications involving conservation issues – that is, all listed building consents and most applications where the character or appearance of a conservation area was affected. However, the intervening years have witnessed a gradual decline in conservation's priority in, and influence over, DC. Rather than being a significant element of the departmental position on conservation, C&D now acts as a special adviser to the DC section, where its views may be more than countered by opposing perspectives. Although consultation guidelines were formally developed in the early 1990s, subsequent staff and resource reductions in HEI have made these arrangements impractical to follow and somewhat irrelevant.

C&D is automatically consulted over works to grade I and II* buildings, but for the rest – development in conservation areas and minor listed building consent work – consultation is discretionary. DC officers have been encouraged to take greater responsibility for the majority of 'ordinary' conservation issues. Despite welcoming C&D's specialist advice to supplement their own self-admittedly meagre conservation knowledge, all DC officers qualified the appropriateness of this advice. Sometimes conservation guidance was taken with a pinch of salt, as C&D's approach might involve imposing many further conditions on a planning permission. In day-to-day work, consulting C&D could be onerous and created unnecessary duplication and delay. For that reason, conservation could become a victim of its own rigour as DC had to prioritise issues, perhaps along different lines from C&D advice.

DC perspectives on conservation

Many DC officers, especially those with several decades' experience, considered that they could unilaterally deal with most planning applications involving conservation issues. Undoubtedly the interpretation of 'conservation' differed between C&D and DC. Whereas C&D's main concern was the integrity of the whole building, DC attitudes mainly focused on what was immediately visible. If a contested detail was not obvious to the public gaze, DC officers were more flexible regarding its treatment. While acknowledging C&D's specialist architectural knowledge, DC officers believed that the conservation discipline essentially concerned buildings' features and then, more generally, urban design. Apart from the real gems of evidently impressive grade I and II*s, there was little to distinguish dealing with 'run-of-the-mill' conservation work from any other design issue that crossed a planning officer's desk.

The senior management agreed, trusting every DC officer to deal competently with the majority of building casework involving conservation issues. The introduction of design guidance on common aspects of conservation, such as replacement windows or suitable mortars, was intended to assist DC officers with their devolved responsibility. However, with fewer HEI staff to write it, this supplementary guidance was already two years overdue and DC officers were not necessarily in a position unilaterally to make an informed decision over certain applications.

Although a lacuna in detailed policies had been created, most DC officers did not miss this extra layer, considering that the UDP and PPG15 already provided sufficiently intricate conservation guidance. Several officers preferred not having any design guides, considering that inappropriately applied conservation (i.e. without the intellectual rigour of the conservation expert) had led to a dumbing down of design standards, a lack of creativity and no representation in the town of a late twentieth-century aesthetic. In requiring traditional materials or construction, or new designs alluding to accepted and familiar forms, applicants were not encouraged to be creative even on sites of minimal conservation interest. Certainly many planning officers were frustrated by their members' preferences for safe architecture and copies of traditional buildings.

Wider influences and accountability

Policy and politics

During the 1990s, planning policy was located in different documents in the authority – the draft UDP and the former old development plan. The UDP had taken over seven years to complete and had undergone many significant revisions as two swings in the local council elections, from Labour to Conservative and back again, altered the political imperatives placed on planning. For instance, under the Conservatives the encouragement of enterprise and development initiatives perceptibly contributed to undermining the position of conservation.

Chapter 4 of the UDP contains policies relating to the built environment based on a broad approach to urban design, emphasising the quality of design contributing to improving the existing environment. Particular sections are dedicated to listed buildings and conservation areas respectively, with particular policies which in effect paraphrase PPG15 and outline the authority's statutory responsibilities. There are references throughout the chapter to conservation-oriented themes which coincide with wider policies, particularly town centre management. To accompany the consideration of new design, a series of character statements for each conservation area is contained in the appendices. However, as this comprises a one-sentence description of the area's physical appearance, it is questionable how far such meagre descriptions could contribute to or enhance the quality of planning officers' decision-making.

Among council members, opinions varied over the value of conservation. Conservation measures were supported because they improved the look of the town centre and thus enhanced the town's image to potential investors. Yet others contended that there were too many listed buildings in the town, which created undue restrictions for new development, especially given the tight profit margins determining developments' economic viability. Moreover, design considerations *per se* were viewed as a luxury which the authority could not always afford to pursue in planning. The drive for economic regeneration, attracting investment, jobs and services in competition with other towns, was imperative.

These contrasts may account for planning officers' concerns over the lack of a coherent conservation commitment across the authority as a whole. While such a lack may be an inevitable repercussion of planning in such a marginal economic area, it does little to assuage members' perceptions of conservation as anything other than a peripheral activity. It appeared that at higher levels in the authority, conservation (and planning) were considered a responsibility rather than an opportunity. It is questionable whether conservation issues entered the decision-making for the council's longer-term strategy, in either the administrative or the political sense. The upper limit of conservation's influence appeared to end with the head of the planning service; only the sheer number of listed buildings forced conservation on to the political map.

This priority of attracting and accommodating development in the town has similarly characterised the Planning Committee's treatment of conservation. Officers noted that conservation was usually approached on a case-by-case basis in committee, and with no clear guiding strategy, conservation concerns were usually subsumed by development pressures.

Following the 1998 local elections, a new Planning Committee chair resolved to place conservation and heritage matters on a higher footing. After years of apathy towards conservation and design, this statement marked a significant change in attitude. The new chair considered that the authority's conservation practice, partly shaped by national conservation policy's focus on the integrity of buildings' fabric, had become too blinkered. Conservation should give greater importance to the identity and characteristics of places, and positive and inte- grated measures taken towards enhancing local distinctiveness. This approach aligned conservation with regeneration activity: raising the quality of the local environment and attracting the type of service and cultural industries that could stimulate this regeneration. The large number of listed buildings was seen as an under-valued asset which could contribute to this repackaging of the area in tourist and cultural terms.

At the time, it remained to be seen whether the initiative could succeed but officers had noticed some softening of attitudes and greater debate in committee over conservation issues. A Scrutiny Commission, comprising selected officers and members, was to review conservation's role within the planning service and its contribution to the authority's wider political priorities. Although the prospect might be encouraging for conservation, any lasting success depended on changing existing political attitudes. This challenge came, not least, from within the then locally controlling Labour group, where divisions had marked out conservation as liberal middle-class luxury; if these attitudes persisted, conser- vation would continually be placed below measures for improving the quality of life for those most in need in society.

Perceptions of the public interest

There appeared to be a consensus across the planning service that the public in general were not particularly interested in planning except to prevent someone else's development. While there existed good working relationships between the authority and recognised groups interested in conservation, there were questions raised over how representative these groups were of the 'public'.

Broadly speaking, planning officers recognised that many members of the public did not appreciate the quality of the buildings in the town; features were familiar and taken for granted. Indeed, C&D officers felt very strongly that this increased their responsibility, because they had the training and knowledge to appreciate architecture, to protect the town and its listed buildings on the public's behalf.

Development cases

The second tier of investigating the local planning authority's conservation culture involved in-depth studies of four separate development control cases. This not only provided a unique insight into real circumstances in which the

Table 5.4 An outline of development cases' attributes

The Lodge
- A medium-scale residential development of a grade II listed building with further enabling development on-site
- Site owned by a local builder and thereafter taken over by another local (to the region) developer – both mainly involved with residential development

The Yard
- An unsuccessful application to demolish an unlisted building in a conservation area and erect a replacement retail unit
- Site owned and developed by national commercial property developers: commercial tenants involved

The Square
- Conversion of a grade II* listed building in a conservation area into a retail outlet
- Owner applicant of freehold – local small business owner

The Mount
- Conversion of a grade II listed building in a conservation area into a single dwelling home
- Private residential owner-occupier

rhetoric surrounding policy could be tested but also identified a range of parties with differing experiences and values relating to conservation in the locality. A range of developments and applicants, involving different aspects of conservation control, were selected. Table 5.4 outlines their correlation with the selection criteria in table 5.3. The case names have been changed, so as to respect respondents' anonymity.

The Lodge

A summary of the development

Left to rot

The Lodge is a large, two-storey grade II listed building lying just south-east of the town centre. Originally it was constructed in its own grounds on the edge of town, but council housing now surrounds the site on three sides. Although the focus of the study is the final planning application, it is worth exploring the history of the site, which created so many problems for the authority.

After the council's social services stopped using it as a residential home in the early 1980s, the building remained vacant until it was sold to a local developer in 1987. Under his ownership, several planning permissions were granted for conversion schemes ranging from institutional uses to intensive residential development. While in planning terms these uses were non-controversial, the schemes frequently encroached on the setting of the listed building. As the planning authority was pursuing a hard line to obtain a high-quality restoration scheme, C&D advice on repair and renewal had been largely upheld. Certainly this first developer considered that the conservation measures imposed on him – comprising several tree preservation orders and the listed building consent – significantly reduced the financial viability of his proposed schemes. The approved permissions were never implemented, fuelling scepticism that the developer was waiting for the listed building to fall down, thereby gaining a clear site and a clearer profit margin.

Site problems

The building had been persistently vandalised, suffered numerous small fires and was starting to attract the antisocial behaviour of local youths. The roof had been stripped, allowing the elements to accelerate its deterioration; the first floor had already fallen through. Most parties, except C&D officers, considered the building way past renovation. The authority approached a second developer, with experience of building housing in the area. He noted how the building 'was derelict literally, we hadn't much to work on' – and held the council at least partly responsible for the lack of maintenance under council ownership. There was nothing left in the shell to imply any value; it would have been better either to de-list it or to demolish it. Planning officers presumed that there must have been some 'national interest' in it at some time but most believed it had lost any credibility as a listed building.

Apathy and lack of interest characterised most local residents' attitudes towards the building. Indeed, local council members doubted whether anyone would have even noticed the building but for the antisocial activities occurring on-site. The authority was not receiving messages of support to repair the building – it was neither a local landmark nor an object of local sentiment. The developer noted that despite its condition when listed, 'it really didn't say to you, "I'm a listed building, people should come and look at me"'.

C&D officers commented that 'the majority of people are not very visual – they can't imagine it being lovingly restored, they just see it as a problem'. They noted that the building, like that area generally, had been 'left to rot', and although the listed building could be the focus for broader area-based regeneration, there was insufficient vision (though probably resources as well) to achieve this. If it was possible to restore the building properly, 'the effect of such a building in a milieu of dross is quite uplifting. If you do one thing right, then at least people have got something interesting there.'

The first developer's scheme

Plans were submitted in August 1993 to convert the main listed building into flats, to replace some out-buildings with new houses and to erect a new dwelling block at the front of the property. At the time, planning officers considered this front block wholly detrimental to the setting of the listed building, yet the developer argued that 'setting' was inherently subjective, '[as] demonstrated by the conflicting opinions of the two successive principals of the historic buildings team'. He contended that 'when [this building] was conceived, [the area] must have been so different as to be almost unrecognisable today. The setting has changed completely, the site now being an island among council housing and somewhat "downmarket"'.

In contrast, planning officers thought the listed building was well shielded and could be treated independently from its wider surroundings. This difference of opinion divided the parties and the authority characterised relations with him, after seven years of fudged compromises, as embodying 'total conflict and failure to find any solutions'.

Complaints to the council about antisocial activities on the site – vandalism and drug abuse – became more frequent. While the authority commended its planning officers on their ability to balance conservation needs against addressing these social problems, the latter appeared not to include any concern for the building itself. As a local councillor became involved, the prominence of residents' concerns increasingly politicised the problem. The developer was described as leaving the site 'littered with broken promises'. The councillor's personal loss of faith, combined with the public complaints, was the catalyst for the authority to serve an Urgent Works Notice in November 1994, overcoming the authority's concerns over incurring potential financial liabilities. Though the Notice was respected, it marked a turning point in attitudes regarding the site: the political will to see that the site did not deteriorate further and the developer's realisation of a lost cause.

The second developer's scheme

The surrounding council housing had previously deterred private purchases of this large house and consequently limited the site's commercial development value. The authority looked for potential rescuers, one of whom was a local builder and developer in the region. Negotiations led to a private arrangement whereby the site ownership was transferred; grant money already secured for developing the site and the final profits of the sale were to be taken by the first and second developers respectively.

Such political sensitivity invoked the rare personal intervention of senior members of the planning service, who had the local political support to resolve the case expediently. Approving the new scheme appeared far less problematic, partly because of the incentives offered by the authority to ensure development. Certainly the developer appreciated this:

> [B]ecause of political pressure and through the good sense of the planners, we had to progress with the work very quickly. Some of the attitudes and provisions which would normally be used with a listed building were put to one side and we were allowed to do certain things both for speed and economics – it had to work.

The developers were in a privileged position, having been approached by and dealing exclusively with senior managers. They had been granted more freedom and allowed to pursue the scheme on the basis of its economic viability rather than its conservation merit; the authority's position had necessarily become 'more realistic'. Flexibility over permissible materials, scale and massing, and the removal of trees subject to preservation orders were significant shifts in the authority's consent, but all parties recognised the political and economic imperative of the situation. The developer noted that '[P]erhaps they went further than they would have done but there was political pressure to bear from one of the local councillors and from the local people.' Though no construction was permitted in front of the listed building, the consent did not stipulate permissible alterations to the listed building itself. The committee left approval of these to be decided by planning officers. The approved scheme demolished, rebuilt and converted the listed building into four flats, and demolished the out-buildings and replaced them with four new houses using the redundant ashlar stone. A further six houses in artificial stone were permitted to the rear, although the use of this material went against council policy. The developer stressed that a restorative scheme was not financially possible; the enabling development of 10 new houses was essential. His challenge was to do something new with the site rather than restore the listed building, which had already died: '[T]he main problem was making a silk purse out of a sow's ear.'

However, C&D was not consulted and was 'distressed to find that little remained. All but two walls, all internal features . . . and all of the roof structure had been completely removed'. The authority was satisfied with the demolitions on grounds of structural dilapidation and considered that the development had not gone beyond its authorisation. Under PPG15 a significant demolition to a listed building ought to be referred to EH. It was not. Planning officers described this as 'a bureaucratic mistake' but of minor consequence because no one appeared to care for the decrepit building; it was an irrelevant, though unfortunate, deviation from the correct procedure. C&D officers cared, stating that the authority had 'approved the demolition of the bulk of this building whilst congratulating ourselves on our success at saving it'. Their contention was that it was no longer a listed building: 'its whole history has gone'. Since the interior, the plan, the structural features and the outbuildings which all contributed to its interest had been demolished, it would be better to de-list it; there was nothing left to distinguish its 'national interest'. Thus the authority's views were split between hailing it as a success or regarding it as a failure, though the prevalent opinion championed the cause as a good example of a development addressing social blight through re-use of a listed building.

In contrast to the previous seven years of false dawns, the development had been completed in 18 months. Local residents and local councillors were satisfied, characterising the benefits in the wider sense of having cleared the social problems, provided new, affordable houses in the area and made the site look nice again. Concern for the listed building was significantly less important. The authority noted that although it was not the best architectural example of conserving a listed building, the wider benefits far outweighed the sacrifices, particularly as it had involved no cost to the council. The proactive attitude in which the authority approached the second scheme was presented as a salutary lesson to the C&D section: '[T]he results of their approach over seven years had been absolutely nothing and therefore [it is questionable] that the line that they took was actually ever going to achieve anything in a million years.'

Attitudes to conservation illustrated in this case

Planning is a balancing act

Despite the intense social and political problems with this case, in planning terms it was relatively non-controversial. There was no material change of use, so it was solely the listed building considerations that caused concern. DC officers did not consider that conservation involved any different philosophical or practical approach from any other issue they were required to account for; it was an aspect which just required some expert advice. However, this advice became increasingly seen as just 'purist input', and while DC officers welcomed the insight and undoubted expertise, they treated its practicality with some scepticism. Senior planners supported their officers, considering that the case illustrated the delicate balancing act that DC performed in accommodating a variety of competing interests. As the town's political and economic circumstances required planning to facilitate new development, DC's priority was to deliver a viable scheme. There was a tendency to see conservation, and the C&D section, as concentrating on buildings' physical problems. This was the distinction made between planning and conservation; the perspective of architectural history, while valid in itself, lacked an appreciation of planners' responsibility to the local community. It was perceived that this social element did not enter conservation practice at all.

However, presenting planning's priority as a community service may be incredibly altruistic. The view from a C&D officer revealed a different perspective: 'There is a basic tension between conservation legislation and planning legislation because one is about real human values in terms of how one wants to live on this earth, and the other is about making a quick buck.'

As regards the development site, there appear to be two opposing considerations. From a conservation perspective, the setting of the listed building meant the whole site, spatially and historically. Most other respondents viewed the wider context, within the council estate, as constituting 'the setting', which created contrasting priorities for the treatment of the building.

The building's state of repair significantly affected the degree of acceptable change. The developer considered that the spirit of the building had already died and that it was preferable to start afresh and create something new. This complemented the planning service's increasingly 'pragmatic' approach, though the C&D section was aghast at the results. It appears that as features or indeed areas become more decrepit, there is a stronger instinct to clear and redevelop them, thus eclipsing their potential re-use and regeneration. This instinct is all the more acute in such marginal areas where there *appears* to be no role for conservation to play. Certainly the contrasting views within the authority reveal intensely subjective interpretations.

The state of repair also affected locals' perceptions of the building. It did not represent a particular landmark or attract much sympathy, and some respondents asserted that locals were not even aware of the building, let alone its listed status. Nearly all the comments were received from immediate neighbours concerned by antisocial activities on the site which threatened their security and peace of mind.

Condition or conditioning?

While the building possessed sufficient 'special architectural or historic interest' to merit its original listing, its dereliction seemed to obscure any attempt, outside the C&D section, to consider its existing value.

C&D officers believed that returning the building to an impressive state would affect the surrounding area, physically in stopping the slide towards neglect but also psychologically in lifting locals' perceptions of their environmental quality. This 'quality of life' argument exists beyond the statutory and policy definitions of conservation and is difficult to quantify, but provides a powerful justification for intervention.

The building's state of repair eclipsed most people's appreciation of its value. Although PPG15 states that 'condition' is not a relevant consideration in assessing value, the abuse of the building reflected and reinforced its lack of gravitas; the physical deterioration in itself undermined its 'spirit', 'dignity' and 'credibility' as a listed building. It is interesting that respondents used such phrases as these, connoting sympathy, affection and emotional responses to the feature. Very few planning officers believed the building still possessed any national interest, especially given its lowly local regard. Instead they only presumed a 'national interest', reciting the phrase without seeming to believe in it.

Thinking that a listed building can lose its special interest through neglect is contrary to the conservation ethos. The prevalence of this view outside conservation circles raises two issues. First, some assert that the use of a building, as well as its architecture, is an important factor in appreciating a feature's worth. In this instance the building just provided a site for vandalism and solvent abuse. Second, it may suggest that there is a stereotypical perception of a listed building. Listed status conjures up a particular image, even among planning professionals, of qualities which people may actively wish to see or visit. When a building does not appear to fulfil the stereotype, it loses support, which consequently makes its alteration or destruction easier to sanction.

This attitude indicates a significant emphasis by most respondents outside the conservation profession on the superficial, visual impact of a feature. This is not to dismiss this basis as shallow and insignificant – far from it: it needs to be recognised and explored if conservation is to appeal more broadly. Many planning officers noted that in general an application may be acceptable 'if it looks

OK', despite more principled conservation reservations. That the front elevation remained unobstructed while all development occurred at the rear illustrates the potency of superficial visibility contentions. This view was particularly difficult to reconcile with that of a C&D officer who thought that any value had been destroyed: 'It's got this vernacular wrap on the front but it's not, it is not, a historic building. . . . Its whole history has gone.' Accompanying this dismissal was a rare preference to see it de-listed – remarkable coming from a self-proclaimed ardent conservationist.

Those members of the public expressing a view appeared happy with the development. A C&D officer considered that raising popular support for this building suffered from the public's inability to visualise a good-quality renovation scheme. The public suffered a lack of opportunity, either immediately in this case or more generally through the education system, to engage with any design issues. Consequently, highlighting the public interest in sensitive design solutions was all the more important. In wider terms, this view also reflected the degree to which executive officers could act on behalf of the public. For instance, where the public were considered to be better educated, sophisticated and able to engage in local decision-making, such as in the Cotswolds, there was less of a need to represent them. This has implications for accommodating public opinion, especially if conservation is justified in terms of its appealing to an innate sense of visual appreciation and yet the public's ability to express or convey this is dismissed.

Considering the surrounding area, one planning officer considered that the incursion of the council estates bordering the site removed any last trace of the building's original historical context, thus undermining its value and contribution. However, it is arguable that the relationship and contrast between the nature of the old and the modern environments actually provide an interesting temporal juxtaposition. It is counterproductive if surrounding non-contemporaneous development can reduce older features' value so drastically.

Political results mean popular results

During the early 1990s the economic climate had changed dramatically, and, given the additional problem of a stagnant housing market, the site's location limited development profit margins. In short, it would have been difficult to recoup any significant expenditure on the listed building. It was noted several times that had this site been in the affluent west of the town instead of the east, there would have been little problem in finding a private buyer who could restore the property as a family dwelling.

Rather than being a potential investment, the building was an economic liability. The less specific people's conservation knowledge was, the more they defined the value of the listed building by its actual use and the less by its architectural or historical appeal. Given this premise, the balancing of conservation interest and economic return becomes increasingly difficult since there is no common way of measuring them. From the developers' perspective, the architectural or listed value of the building was so slight as to rule out retaining it – there was a much weaker conservation argument to oppose these economic considerations. Conservation is only as important as the market economics of the situation permit.

One major factor in overcoming this restriction is the political will supporting a particular solution. Throughout this case, actions and decisions were influenced by the amount of political interest necessary to achieve an expedient solution. Local councillors were spurred to act by the antisocial activities occurring on the site rather than by any concern for the listed building. Indeed, there was a view that an accident of architectural perception (in listing) had left the authority with responsibility for too many listed buildings with little merit. It placed undue constraints on the planning service and on local development.

Internally, the political influence was manifest in several unique occurrences, such as the fact that the case was handled exclusively by the most senior planners. The hard line that the authority originally pursued was considerably modified once local politics began to dominate proceedings. Pressure to resolve the situation forced a number of compromises which had been intolerable in previous applications. The political agenda was perceived as quite different from the conservation agenda, though some considered it similarly distinct from the planning agenda. While catalysing results, the political input perceptibly undermined the authority's stance *vis-à-vis* the developers. However, without this political pressure it is conceivable that the site might have remained derelict to this day. To most concerned, except the conservationists, the final result was a success and the problems of the site cleared, so where does this leave the conservation argument in this case, particularly if it needs to rely on political support for its efficacy?

The Yard

A summary of the development

Improving the town's retail capacity

The greater part of the town centre is a conservation area and is subject to a CAP agreement. Located in one of the main shopping streets, the Yard is a modest late-Victorian building owned by a property investment group and has two commercial tenants: a shoe shop at street level and a family-run restaurant on the first floor. The authority received a planning application in July 1994 to redevelop the site.

The owners wanted to expand the unit to attract larger tenants, such as a major high street retailer, and the restricted floor space of the existing building was unsuitable for modern retailing requirements. The building was unlisted and the owners' architects considered that its poor state of repair and absence of architectural interest meant that a direct replacement would be suitable. The original floors and internal walls had since been replaced and a proliferation of piecemeal extensions to the rear did nothing to enhance the overall character of the building.

The application proposed demolishing the building and replacing it with an entirely new three-storey unit – a modern interpretation of the existing design with a larger footprint than that of the existing building extending over a rear yard and a side alley.

The first application: a 'postmodern' design

The applicants presented their scheme as a long-term investment in the town's retailing competitiveness within the regional hierarchy. The authority had initially considered the application to be acceptable, in policy and design terms. However, on closer inspection C&D noted that there was no structural survey submitted with the application. The necessity of demolition, on the grounds sanctioned by PPG15 that the building was no longer structurally sound and usable, had not been proven. The demolition could not be recommended on conservation grounds.

Although the building was not listed, C&D considered that it was a unique feature in the street: '[A]lthough it has been altered and refurbished, [it] still makes a significant contribution to the conservation area in terms of street façade (particularly the upper storey [fronting the] street), roofscape and urban grain.' The existing building was a component in a series of historic stone frontages; an adjacent building was listed and therefore C&D argued that altering this building would affect the other's setting. The age, materials, detail and scale of the surrounding buildings were all important in maintaining the overall harmony. Several other buildings in the street had received shop-front renovation grants and C&D believed this building could be similarly improved: '[T]he original form of the building is still intact and has the potential to be repaired and restored to its original character.' Furthermore, C&D considered that some internal features were worth retaining, such as the 'ornate coved and coffered ceiling'. For C&D, the proposed design employed materials and detailing which conflicted with those of adjacent properties. With its top-heavy, 'elephantine' façade and over-large fenestration, the design was 'postmodern' and unsuited to the area: it was considered 'a mere vernacular wrap'.

Aside from the design of the new unit, a further issue concerned extending its footprint over the side alleyway and a yard at the rear of the property. These 'yards' throughout the town centre are vestiges of the prolific woollen and textile industries of the nineteenth century. They formed the small trading areas of local merchants and they characterise the street pattern. This physical and historic connection with the town's commercial past has meant that some yards have been restored and new uses found for the small premises therein.

In contrast, the applicants considered that because the Yard was enclosed by windowless elevations, contained an electricity sub-station and provided no thoroughfare, it was a redundant service space which would be more profitably incorporated into the new development. However, C&D considered building over the alleyway and Yard contrary to PPG15, which emphasised the importance of retaining the historic layout of property boundaries and thoroughfares. Although the Yard had not been identified (as several others had) on the UDP map as an historic feature, conservation officers considered that it ought to be treated as 'an important and peculiar characteristic street pattern'.

DC accordingly revised their recommendation and the Planning Committee refused planning permission, but the applicants appealed. Both applicant and agent felt aggrieved by the authority's double standards, referring to another yard behind that street which had been converted into small retail units. The authority had permitted an 'abysmal' pseudo-traditional loggia at its entrance which was far more out of keeping with the area.

The second application: a more traditional design

Twin-tracking their appeal, the applicants then submitted a second, significantly amended application to demolish and rebuild the premises. The architects hoped that a more traditional approach would address the criticisms of the previous design, so that the:

> form and massing, height and scale of the proposals closely correlate with the existing building. While not a copy, the design of the new façade takes strong cues from the fenestration, double gable arrangement and proportions of the existing frontage. Allied to the use of traditional materials and detailing which complement the area's Victorian heritage, the overall effect is to provide a sensitive architectural solution to the townscape.

The revised footprint still built over the alleyway and Yard as the developers did not share C&D's belief that this space could physically or economically accommodate small independent retail units. Several identical units in an adjacent yard renovation scheme still lay empty and tenant-less. The agents were disappointed with the 'lack of response and co-operation', despite the design revisions, and thought the authority was taking a dogmatically preservationist stance over the whole site.

Again DC was willing to permit the application, recommending approval because 'a fundamental issue . . . is the merit of the replacement scheme'. But C&D considered the proposals did 'nothing to mitigate the problems originally highlighted'. The new design did reflect the essence of the existing façade, but merely reproducing these features could never capture the subtlety and patina of age which characterised the original. The replacement materials, such as aluminium window frames, were unsuitable, and the art-stone detailing would not weather as an ensemble. Moreover, with no appreciable difference in the proposals for the alleyway and the Yard, reservations concerning the loss of the characteristic street pattern remained.

The public want to use buildings, not just look at them

While the authority was preoccupied with design details, public reaction to the proposed redevelopment focused on the building's uses. The local Civic Society strongly supported the potential new retail functions and welcomed the long-term investment in the town centre. The society considered that replicating the previous design would provide 'an attractive "streetscape" in the familiar local vernacular' (in stark contrast to the authority's conservation objections).

Comments from individual members of the public concerned the threatened loss of the restaurant on the first floor; apparently its relocation within the town was not an option. A petition of over 900 signatures highlighted the depth of public feeling and generated several articles in the local paper. Letters to the authority expressed some recognition for the building's aesthetics, but generally people were concerned about the threat to the restaurant. Despite falling outside the sphere of legitimate 'planning issues', these comments were still influential.

The situation appeared desperate for the restaurant's proprietors, who wrote several letters to the planning service. Their tenor changed from outlining the loss to the town of their restaurant, to using conservation issues later on to bolster their protests. In their desperation they also wrote to EH (which, in hoping that the organisation would intervene, misconstrued its role).

The weight of national advice

The authority had consulted EH over the second application, and EH's eleventh-hour comments proved most persuasive in Planning Committee. The advice highlighted the building's continuing viable use, since the case for demolition was not proven on structural condition alone. The replacement would not enhance the conservation area because the burgage plot size ought to be retained, other-wise it 'would introduce alien detail and character'. Relying on this advice, the committee followed the conservation argument and rejected the application.

Although the applicants considered they still had a good chance of success on appeal, considering the slim profit margin and the withdrawal of their prospective tenant, they dropped the scheme to pursue other larger and more profitable developments elsewhere.

Attitudes to conservation illustrated in this case

What does a conservation area really mean in planning terms?

Irrespective of the building's location in the central conservation area, there were different viewpoints within the authority over its retention, a schism that was also clear to the applicants.

While DC initially believed that the building held little interest and that its replacement would contribute to the town's investment potential, many DC officers were content to keep conservation issues as a wholly separate sphere. Such an attitude concerned the EH officer, who believed that planning officers alone might not have the necessary training to deal with conservation effectively. The fact that the Yard was omitted from the UDP greatly undermined C&D's starting position and highlighted the importance of earlier policy decisions.

The relationship between the building and the surrounding area was heavily contested. Most parties considered that the building was no more significant than any other in the street, its mediocre condition and repair engendering this dismissive attitude. Such disinterest spurred C&D to emphasise its redeeming characteristics, analysing the demolition of the building along the lines set out for assessing listed buildings. This arguably reflects the impotence of area-based value as an effective planning tool.

> I liked the building; it had a fantastic interior, particularly the ceiling, but of course that was not an issue because it was an unlisted building – it was a driving force behind me, the vision of it, that gave me the bite, the real passion for the building.

Indeed, some planning officers questioned the whole street's intrinsic interest: 'I don't think that building is particularly attractive . . . I am not too sure that street should be a conservation area at all.' Such a view is indicative of the low esteem in which the conservation area concept is held in general. Certainly the applicant considered that conservation areas, unlike listed buildings, had only minimal value and were so loosely defined because insufficient thought, or courage to embrace change, led to blanket preservation. He considered that to the public and many authorities, conservation areas had become like green belts, simply prohibiting change. The agent echoed these reservations:

Towns where I think [conservation] goes wrong is where there is a very strict policy of maintaining say grey slate roofs, red bricks, three storeys high, red window frames or whatever and you end up with a town that has no soul.

The building's contribution to the street was largely considered in aesthetic terms. However, there were various interpretations of how any replacement could 'enhance' the conservation area. For the applicants, 'enhance' meant boosting the centre's attractiveness to investors. The EH adviser and several authority officers noted these difficulties: '[What] we have not really come to terms with on many sites where the buildings are of a minor quality is what replacement architecture or what good modern "in character" regeneration would be.' C&D officers shared this concern that there was a paucity of debate about regional and local character in modern architectural practice. The fact that coercive regulation was required to prevent an 'enhancement' illustrated that the conservation philosophy was not endemic to many people's thinking.

Local interest: a difficult concept to protect and enhance

Respondents questioned not only the quality of the conservation area, but also the quality of the building itself. The applicant thought it was 'a pile of rubbish' and, agreeing with his agents, considered that its mauling at the hands of previous occupants had displaced any inherent interest in its fabric or need to research its history. The extent to which the accretion of cumulative changes over time positively augments a feature or detracts from its 'genuine' qualities is questionable. While the argument was first broached by the SPAB, it is manifestly still relevant.

Many parties noted this street's lack of discernible qualities, as it comprised very mediocre buildings, and questioned its inclusion in the central conservation area. The immediate surroundings, the alleyway and Yard, reflected the historical significance of previous uses. However, their neglected state obscured these somewhat intangible qualities, emphasising instead the relative lack of any architectural features therein. The conservation adviser observed:

[Y]ou find that many buildings of local historic interest don't get listed at all ... listing authorities don't take any recognition of buildings of local historic importance, of old schools that might be just quite ordinary or something like that, or if they're by a local architect. Of course they're of architectural importance but they tend to be of historic importance as well.

Without recognising features' less obvious qualities it is much easier to portray them, as the applicant did, as 'wasted space'. There was no conservation area character appraisal, and while planning officers considered that their personal familiarity with the area sufficed to define its character, this was difficult to defend in planning terms without formal support. In contrast, the EH adviser approached cases by first considering a place's urban historical development; relating 'character' solely to building forms was considered a terribly restrictive practice, though most other parties were guilty of this.

The proposed replacement building also created difficulties, with neither the contrasting nor the traditional design proving acceptable. While the agent wanted to create an impressive modern frontage to complement the image of its new retail tenant, the design did not match expectations. The second design ultimately pleased nobody in the planning service:

> What I don't like is what that second scheme, in retrospect, was . . . just a pastiche of everything stuffed in and at the end of the day that's what you get out . . . a building that's got no integrity, it's got no logic behind it and it's monstrous.

This planning officer lamented that where conservation was poorly applied, it inadvertently created urban environments that failed to reflect any contemporary contribution. Despite its concessions to tradition, a C&D officer considered that the design was 'like a stage set – it wasn't architecture at all'.

Since the only protection regime involved was the conservation area, this ought to imply that the significance of the site was mostly local, except that there was little credence or even recognition of this interest. In fact, the absence of a character assessment for the area ought to concern EH, given its adviser's belief that conservation provides a framework with which to debate these features' value in a community. The tenor of public responses illustrated that the use, rather than aesthetic considerations, attracted or dispelled popular support for buildings. Conservation issues were often used to buttress retention of the current use, not for their interest *per se*. Ironically, it fell to a national body, EH, to add gravity to the local importance of this site, influencing planning officers and Planning Committee members in their support of the local conservation arguments.

The applicant held strongly opposed views, considering that local interest was a shaky concept to define, especially when left to local authorities. Unlike listing, where standards were universally respected, it resulted in false imagery. Conservation was appropriate only in worthwhile contexts, such as a cathedral city, but there was little British architecture worth saving outside such enclaves. He believed that misplaced conservation was creating an unrealistic and idealised image of the town.

Prime economic consideration is obtaining planning permission

Developing a prime retail site in a main shopping street will inevitably involve conflicts between profit maximisation and any form of regulation. However, the interesting aspect is the extent to which economic considerations altered the emphases on the existing building's qualities and, more generally, the purpose of planning measures.

The application portrayed the building as a dilapidated structure requiring replacement; the building's natural obsolescence was emphasised and convinced DC officers of the need to redevelop. With the UDP's emphasis on encouraging new development in the centre, the economic arguments proved acceptable and expedient. Yet the applicant felt frustrated by a sense that planners in local authorities generally were too insular to realise the economic pressures driving development. He viewed planning as inhibiting economic growth by antagonising those putting forward development opportunities and thought that planners should realise that planning should assist the market in developing and improving the environment.

The agents noted how the necessity of securing a planning permission relegated the aesthetic considerations: 'The revised scheme was deliberately biased to try and reproduce a lot of the features that were there already simply to obtain permission – but that is a cop-out.' Pursuing the safe option created further reactions from within DC:

> You've only got to look at what's happened on the [adjacent] development to see what crap that can turn out to be . . . I can understand to some extent architects' feeling that they're giving us the easiest form. [The] line of least resistance is let's go with what we expect the planning authority and the relevant planners to go for, which is traditional design, built in stone etc. etc. Whereas I think they have to take a bit more responsibility – they can't blame it all on planners and the planning authority – they are professionals.

In terms of political arguments there was a split between the case for upholding the building's interest and that for acknowledging local people's interest in that building. The case for promoting prosperity supported either the retention of the popular restaurant or the prospect of a new, larger retailer in the town centre, yet the weight of local opinion (and subsequent votes) supporting the restaurant's retention and was most persuasive in committee. Observers noted that the authority would have preferred the case to go to appeal, allowing an inspector to take the responsibility of making a potentially unpopular decision. However, it was EH's involvement and added kudos that lent power to the committee's elbow in supporting the building's retention. Without this extra support it is doubtful whether the conservation line would have been given political backing.

The Square

A summary of the development

Beauty may only be skin deep

The Square is a corner property, part of a grade II* listed terrace which fronts an impressive Victorian square, the focus of a flagship regeneration project comprising grade I and II* listed buildings. It is in the town's central conservation area, covered by a CAP and the local 'Victorian New Town' grant scheme to encourage sympathetic re-use of many vacant properties.

This mid-nineteenth-century four-storey terrace, constructed in ashlar stone, presents a classically proportioned façade to the Square. Despite a long frontage, the building is a mere 8 m deep, which proved problematic for accommodating alternative uses. On the rear elevation, the presence of hoist arms and lift hatches reflects its original use as woollen merchants' offices and for textile storage. While not particularly 'pretty', these are industrial features and reflect the building's functional history.

Though other properties in the terrace have recently been restored, a fire in 1990 and escalating repair costs left this property vacant and dilapidated. The roof had been shored up to prevent rain entering the building, but the fire gutted the inside, leaving only the central wall and chimney stack through all four floors. Though the main stone staircase to the first floor was scorched, it was structurally sound; a separate wooden staircase remained only to the first floor. The only other surviving feature on the ground floor was the original ornate plasterwork in the main entrance hall. While the upper floors had remained unoccupied, the ground floor's last use was as a snack bar. Renovating the building was imperative for the authority as it was deteriorating into an eyesore in an otherwise impressive area.

New retailing – new look

A local businessman bought the property without planning permission in 1997, attracted by a colleague's successful conversion of an adjacent terrace property into a café bar. An application was submitted in November 1997 to transform the building into a department-style designer menswear shop. This was the first planning application received since the fire and the authority was keen to encourage it, making grants available, not only from historic building funds but from other sources such as local Single Regeneration Budget (SRB) funding.

However, the applicant's retail vision was not necessarily compatible with the physical and legal constraints of grade II* listing. Given the extensive fire damage, the agent's design proposed refurbishing the whole interior to provide open-plan floors. A steel frame was to be inserted, carrying mezzanine concrete floors and the frame bolted to the exterior walls; a striking new steel staircase was to replace the two fire-damaged ones. Opening up the floor space proved the most contentious issue.

While wishing to restore the impressive façade, the application proposed lowering the ground-floor windowsills to maximise the shop's display area. Also, vertical 'banner-type' signage the height of the building would highlight its four trading floors. Since the building was so narrow, a separate goods lift and an alternative means of escape were to be placed on the external rear wall down into the service yard.

Behind the façade

Such significant alterations to a grade II* listed building were not acceptable to C&D. Some problems were resolved, such as the unsympathetic alterations which did not respect the façade's symmetry in the Square. The main problem throughout concerned the internal alterations, which constituted a significant demolition. C&D stated that 'it is obvious that the designers/architects are not appreciating the significance of listed status in that they are proposing to gut the internal [structure]'. The regional Victorian Society's response echoed these sentiments: 'In reality this scheme amounts to little more than the façading of the building.' The Council for British Archaeology was similarly concerned and quoted PPG15 (para. C58): '[T]he plan of a building is one of its most important characteristics. Interior plans and individual features of interest should be respected and left unaltered as far as possible.' EH reinforced many of these concerns: '[W]hile [the buildings'] special interest resides principally in their main elevations, there are elements of the interior and the rear elevations which merit preservation.'

However, EH's further recommendations differed from the local authority's conservation advice. In an initial letter, EH stated that while the building's plan form could still be discerned:

> [these elements'] individual form does not appear to relate to specialised functions [of the building as woollen merchants' offices] and thus some opening up of the floor-plan could be achieved without significant loss of special interest to enable the proposed change.

The two staircases and the 'rich decorative' plasterwork features in the entrance hall were considered worth retaining by EH, the former for their 'aesthetic and historic [functional] value'. With such a weight of objection, this first scheme was recommended for refusal, though the application was withdrawn for further amendment.

Structure and purpose

While new designs were being prepared, EH revised its original advice and following a site visit in January 1998, accepted 'a compromise which retains something of the special interest of the interior while accommodating the proposed retail use'. EH wanted to retain the entrance-hall features and main staircase, but stated:

> [T]he plan-form of the spaces generally is not critical to the special interest of the building. The chimney-breasts do not retain fireplaces of note, and do not retain prominent or decorative stacks. Accordingly English Heritage would not object to the level of opening up proposed.

This revised position contrasted with both EH's and the authority's previous recommendations to retain the timber floors over any concrete replacements. Negotiations also continued over the location of an additional staircase (fire escape) and lift shaft. Though C&D insisted that these should be internal, whereas EH would have preferred them to be internal, the applicant was adamant that these features must be located on the external rear wall to provide the requisite retail floor space.

Disagreement ensued between the parties over the cost and viability of the project. C&D remained convinced that 'the building is perfectly adaptable to retail use with intelligent and relatively minor alterations such as openings in walls'. It was particularly concerned by EH's apparent 'volte-face' in believing that 'some opening up of the building could be achieved'. C&D contested EH's acquiescence over additions to the rear elevation (i.e. the lift and fire escape) since there remained a significant degree of historical interest in the remaining functional features. C&D considered it incredible that EH had 'not heeded government advice' in PPG15 – that the plan form is one of a building's 'most important characteristics' – and had advocated its destruction.

The retention of the central chimney stack continued to split opinion. While EH saw little of interest in the interior, C&D contended that the chimney stack ought to remain as it retained the 'spirit of the building' (i.e. its traditional load-bearing construction). Without it, the revised plans for retaining a traditional floor construction appeared structurally unsound. The applicant's vision for unencumbered retail floors remained through a change of agents.

Despite C&D's concerns, the authority followed EH's advice and the committee approved the application. Conditions were added to retain the existing timber floors but the removal of the central chimney stack was accepted. The fire escape and lift were eventually settled to be external elements leading directly into the rear service yard. The only internal features to remain were the plaster-work in the entrance hall and the main stone staircase to the first floor.

At the time of study, the permission has remained unimplemented. The property is still in a dilapidated state and may continue to be so for the foreseeable future.

Attitudes to conservation illustrated in this case

Planning and conservation working for different ends

The case highlights a continual tussle between different priorities in conservation and planning. In planning terms, retail use in this building was non-contentious and satisfied other UDP policies encouraging town centre development. Whereas DC prioritised negotiating a planning permission for the applicant's business success, conservation was characterised as embodying some deeper principle, a quite separate issue and actually beyond the interest of those in DC. C&D considered that permitting such extensive alterations eclipsed planning's wider responsibilities to the building and to future generations.

For many respondents outside the authority, the planning service's advice appeared to vary according to officers' own personal interpretations of conservation. EH officers noted how this balancing act created further tensions, in the absence of a coherent authority-wide commitment to conservation: 'I'll deal with the planning officer because my objective is to influence the outcome.' EH cited the potential danger in having conservation as a mere consultee; being 'outside the mainstream planning decision weakens their ability to turn heads'. The applicant also perceived the invidious position of C&D within the planning service.

All respondents recognised and defended the building's prime contribution to the Square. Securing the building in this impressive arrangement dominated most discussions, except for those involving C&D, who were equally concerned about the building itself. This created different priorities and standards for respondents as the visibility of features diminished. The elevation fronting the Square never appeared in danger of alteration as opinion was overwhelmingly in favour of repairing every detail. However, most respondents considered internal and rear features far less important as they did not contribute to the Square. This meant that it was easier to sanction more drastic alterations to these features – even the agents were surprised at the level of opening up permitted – thus contrasting with C&D's belief in the integrity of the whole building.

The damage to the interior also undermined perceptions of the building's grade II* status. The applicant considered it a prime opportunity for renewal, as did some DC officers. Perhaps because the final proposals did not interfere with the front elevation, there was minimal public concern expressed over the changes. Perhaps the fact that it was a vacant, non-residential building affected support, but no comments were received from the public; a planning officer noted:

There doesn't seem to be a lot of public interest at all . . . there never does. Unless it's something like an extension and they think it's going to change the appearance of a building – that's probably the only time we have any comments from the public.

High visibility – high value

The visibility of features appeared to be a significant factor in treating this building. This revealed several distinctions between the public and planners, between different planning officers and even between conservation specialists. While listed buildings are defined as whole structures, with all features receiving equal protection, EH noted:

It's not II* for its interior. It's II* for its contribution to the formal square . . . the interior of the building was of grade II quality and the exterior of the building was of grade II* quality and that was obvious going into the building.

In general, there appeared to be a hierarchy of values emerging: first aesthetic, then structural, and third historical importance, each reflected in the quality of the physical remains. All respondents considered that the 'prettiest' features – the façade, the main entrance plasterwork and the staircase – deserved to be retained because they supported the building's grade II* status. Furthermore, C&D believed that the construction of the building displayed a significant degree of historic interest in itself. In providing the building's structural spine, the chimney stack and plan form reflected the original compartmentalised design, though admittedly taking this into account was extending the interpretation of 'historic' beyond PPG15:

I interpret historic interest [as] the construction interest as well, it's not just that Queen Elizabeth slept here or whatever, it has certain constructional interest as well from a technological point of view. It is pushing the bound-aries wider but I think that's actually quite valid because I think you do compromise buildings when you start introducing new constructions into a historic building.

The third aspect, the historical, was acknowledged as being of great interest in illustrating the town's development. However, features reflecting the building's original function – the hoist and so on – were considered of too lowly an archi-tectural quality to be worth protecting. It is interesting to note that EH considered these features at the rear (reflecting historic use rather than aesthetic interest) as being more appropriately dealt with as 'townscape' considerations. This is perplexing given that these features are intrinsic to the building and, being out of sight, at the rear of the property, contribute little to the townscape aesthetic. It questions conservation's manifest reliance on arguments for the architectural integrity of the building, especially when operating in a planning system which is oriented to dealing with context rather than content of buildings.

Interpreting the significance of value in a grade II* building relies on its national interest. However, EH noted that these values could not be pre-determined by set principles; they depended on each case's circumstances. The EH officer was able to identify the 'national' interest, over any local planning officer, as his judgement was based on experience of comparing listed buildings over entire regions. Given his remark that conservation value is heavily dependent on personal interpretation, his comments would suggest that the national standards buttressing listed buildings are open to far greater variation than is officially portrayed.

Economic prestige, economic prevention

Perhaps the strongest element driving this case was the applicant's commercial vision for the building, the applicant having been attracted by the kudos and prestige of the impressive façade. This image and association of quality were valuable for a business premises. While the façade served this purpose, the interior needed to be modern and functional. This vision narrowed the possibilities from the outset, precluding an assessment of possibility of retaining the interior. When the applicant spoke of value, it was predominantly in terms of land-use values, rents and profit margins. His investment in the property demanded that the application be successful.

The building's poor state of repair and the lack of previous applications worked in the applicant's favour. Its vacancy and destruction displaced many planning officers' perceptions of its being a worthy grade II* building, and so radical alterations to it appeared less offensive. The authority was keen to retain and negotiate this scheme for fear of losing this opportunity and seeing the building deteriorate further: '[T]he main priority was trying to get an acceptable scheme; I was eager for it not to be just abandoned and that was the problem.' These economic pressures divided the authority. Officers noted that members did not appear too concerned about the building itself so long as it was re-used. The economic development unit contributed forcefully to the discussions and offers of SRB grant assistance proved highly persuasive. C&D considered that the availability of alternative funding can undermine conservation initiatives:

> The whole thing was being pushed through by government grants encouraging businesses and thereby giving them too much money that allowed them to demolish the building. So you've got a government grant regime that was actually buttressing, it was supporting a non-viable scheme.

Certainly the potential contribution from SRB funds far exceeded a conservation grant. The agents noted its importance in the 'triangle' of their assessment – first considering PPG15, then the clients' brief, and third the likelihood of obtaining grants for any works. The extent of removals permitted surprised the agents: 'this thing has just been bulldozed through'.

These tensions also influenced EH's consideration of the issues. In liaising with the planning officer, not the conservation specialists, EH was perhaps more exposed to the pressures to redevelop. All parties noted that EH was far more flexible than the authority in its outlook; the agent noted, 'I think they [EH] bent over backwards because they wanted to see this building renovated, put to use.'

The Mount

A summary of the development

The Mount is a semi-detached grade II listed building situated in a suburban conservation area comprising predominantly large Victorian villas. The house, of stone construction, follows more classical proportions than the ubiquitous surrounding Victorian Gothic.

The current residents purchased it three years ago, wishing to return the property to use as a family home, as it had been divided into three flats. The work required some internal works and the removal of two external additions: a metal staircase from the side elevation and an ageing wooden conservatory to the rear.

Although the proposed work was potentially subject to both conservation area control and listed building consent, it fell within the permitted development rights of the householder and therefore did not require planning permission. The committee delegated the case to officer determination, which involved only a consideration of the conservation aspects. The HEI section considered the scheme acceptable, provided that the internal works did not comprise any larger-scale demolition than initially proposed. The consent was approved and the owners were able to carry out their alterations without further recourse.

Attitudes to conservation illustrated in this case

Conservation deals with the minutiae or the minor aspects of planning

As this application did not require planning permission, C&D dealt with the listed building consent exclusively. The scale and nature of these domestic works are perhaps more representative of applications received by the authority. In the previous chapter we saw that most national respondents spoke of conservation as falling through planning's holes. Conservation was required as a parallel system because planning operated on an unsuitable scale, spatially and temporally. This particular case questions the perception that conservation is 'separate' and 'special'. If DC officers can move such applications across their desks, it may well reinforce the perception that conservation is mainly concerned with minor, trivial aspects which planning disregards.

While the property was in a conservation area, only listed building consent was at issue. The owner considered it somewhat anomalous that the authority exercised the same level of control over works inside his property as those external works which affected the surrounding environment. He considered that controls were most sensibly applied to protecting the most visible elements.

His wish to return the house to its 'former glory' did not appear to raise any SPAB-oriented objections to removing the natural accretions and adaptations of the building over time. Evidently the low quality and disrepair of these features dispelled such considerations but it is arguable that striving for a particular aesthetic, while pretty, undermines the authenticity of the building. More generally, the owner considered that old buildings should be saved 'because the new ones that they throw up tend to be very much nondescript concrete and glass [with] no character to them at all'. The main problem for planning would appear to be the development pressure to replace the unique with the uninspired.

A particular expectation of a listed building

While estate agents may portray the acquisition of a listed building as desirable, the owners 'decided to live with the fact that it was listed'. They did not consider themselves particularly interested in architecture or history, though they were attracted to the house's period features, irrespective of its listing. While they were evidently aware of its status, they were not conscious of the reason why their property had been selected:

> Ours is relatively plain compared to a number of the [houses] and I sometimes wonder why they decided to list this one. . . . There are more substantial properties than ours, more ornate properties. . . . I mean there are one or two that look like castles, whereas ours is fairly straightforward, [with] clean lines. I suppose in that sense it may represent a certain style and be listed on that basis.

This may imply that certain types of building can be more readily identified as listable owing to their size or ornamentation. The quality of the stone and the classical portico were noted as potential features which may have attracted the listing inspector's eye.

The 'national interest' in their house was not necessarily obvious. They maintained the property not for any abstract duty, but out of respect for the building itself – changes ought to be in keeping with its character. Irrespective of the conditions of the listed building consent they would have replaced the sash windows and the cast iron drainpipes with the correct materials. They evidently knew of their building's listed status but initially they did not know they were living in a conservation area. The quality of the surrounding area was influential when they were deciding to purchase the house although the conservation area's designation was irrelevant and to some extent continues to be so. When they described the character of the surrounding area and indeed of the town centre, they defined it by reference to the class, use and function of buildings rather than to their architectural or aesthetic qualities. However, it was notable that the owners did consider that, irrespective of these qualities, conserving such features does 'provide an identity to the town and continuity'.

Concluding observations from the case study

The four development case studies and the issues raised by the authority's general approach to conservation provide a snapshot of attitudes and activities in the locality. While there are many similarities regarding individuals' opinions between the national and local level, it cannot be said that there is one prevalent characteristic national or local view on issues. However, there are a number of identifiable contrasts which challenge some of the assumptions made by national respondents.

The nature of conservation planning

How compatible are conservation and planning?

While PPG15 stresses the compatibility of conservation with planning, local authority practices illustrate equally important distinctions between conservation and planning in terms of process and professional attitudes.

Despite making criticisms of the associated delays and ephemeral nature of conservation advice, planning officers evidently recognised the importance of conservation principles. Indeed, the conservation adviser's personal zeal was often described as 'the conscience of the authority'. Pursuing a principled conservation line may be shared by conservation officers in other authorities, but it received a mixed response in this particular authority. In one sense, conservation practice was admired for its relative freedom to pursue design principles which were otherwise constrained in DC work, yet in another sense conservation was more sceptically seen as 'ivory tower' planning – a special consideration in only a handful of cases. The procedural separateness of conservation was not perceived by planning officers to indicate any greater specialness; if anything, conservation was more easily marginalised by this distinction.

Many respondents pigeon-holed conservation as only concerning old buildings and contrasted that with planning, which dealt with the needs of the whole community. All authority respondents characterised planning as a vast balancing act accounting for all manner of interests. Planning was portrayed as having less of a definite substantive goal or aim, instead being characterised by pragmatism, flexibility and the use of common sense. The main concern appeared to be assisting the smooth transition of planning applications from paper to physical development.

The interaction between officers over planning applications, while amicable, depended heavily on the personal discretion of DC officers to consult C&D. Evidently this is influenced by individual planning officers' awareness of conservation issues and their comfort and competence in dealing with it unilaterally. It highlights a curious tension among individual DC officers over when they consider they are dealing with a 'conservation' issue and whether it is sufficiently special to require advice. It is equally arguable that planning practice can reinforce planners' perceptions that conservation exists to deal with the more trivial detailing of buildings which, in the larger planning picture, ultimately might be irrelevant. Paradoxically, the planning service's strategic goal was to concentrate conservation on larger project-based work and grade I and II* buildings, leaving the minor control of less significant detail for DC officers.

It is questionable who is right in this relationship. Evidently a major concern of planning should be improving the quality of the environment, which in turn affects people's lives. But equally this is what conservation staff in the authority are aspiring to but with fewer resources to support their work.

Can conservation principles be applied beyond listed buildings?

A pertinent question is to what extent the planning service's structure defines conservation's main concern to focus on listed buildings or whether there is scope for developing wider aspirations to environmental quality. In policy terms, area-based value is not well explored: the UDP contains but a few sentences appraising the authority's many conservation areas. While time and resource constraints mean that C&D remains preoccupied with dealing with building-specific referrals from DC, the Implementation Team is left to conceive areas' value on more of an *ad hoc* basis to justify areas' character in proposals for externally funded regeneration projects.

The effects of this structure have inadvertently focused attention on dealing with the essentials – that is, statutory responsibilities – with the consequence that area-based policy is continually left underdeveloped. This is certainly not unique to this authority. The Lodge case showed how the relevant context of a building can be drawn tightly around the site or more diffusely as a component of the wider urban fabric. The former approach can lead to the defining of areas' value merely as a collection of buildings – as individual 'atoms' comprising the overall character 'molecule'. The Yard case illustrated how weak concepts for appraising areas' character were in comparison with those for listing in trying to defend the character of the area. This surely contrives and compromises the whole rationale for the conservation area, yet this is not explicitly addressed in policy.

DC officers considered that their professional training equipped them well to embrace, and take responsibility for, townscape or urban design. They felt confident to deal with conservation issues professionally on this scale. However, most were less confident with conservation issues on an individual building scale; in these circumstances they were wholly subordinate to the knowledge/status of the architectural professional. This raises a widespread problem throughout local authorities that there is a significant and questionable gap in urban design and conservation competencies between planning and conservation personnel.

Defining 'acceptable' change

Reflecting tensions in national policy, there are incidences of planning and conservation personnel pursuing opposing presumptions of retention. However, the important distinction is whether conservation, in practice, is unfairly equated with opposition to change and whether this is due to the personalities involved. Although the service wished to encourage a more proactive approach to conservation, on the ground this can be difficult when, as C&D emphasised, the historic fabric itself is a valuable document. Inevitably there were conflicts with national policy, which emphasised conservation's contribution to regeneration. The tensions over the renewal of fabric illustrated a common problem in defining which features could conceivably be altered and which were untouchable. As discussed below, the state of the building or area profoundly affected perceptions of its worth and thus the degree of change tolerated or desired.

This distinction arose most acutely in relation to conservation areas. Defining 'enhancement' caused arguments in the Yard case, yet officers were assisted by few strategic guidelines. Consequently, the difficulty in defining and supporting enhancement often created an easier fall-back position which relied on preservation instead. The case illustrated that the replication of an existing feature, or the qualities most readily identified with it, became an easy way to secure planning permission and could unfortunately lead to a reduction in the contribution of any late twentieth-century aesthetic to the town's urban fabric.

The public interest and the public's interest

The extent to which the local public were involved in, or appeared to care about, conservation was slight. This is not unusual in itself as public participation in planning is generally only modest. Evidently it is difficult to surmise public enthusiasm for conservation accurately, but officers' attitudes to the public's involvement can reflect the value of its contribution.

If the public got involved in planning only to object to proposals, low participation might indicate that the authority was performing satisfactorily. However, officers were more likely to think that the public do not care about planning or conservation. Aside from the local formal consultative groups, public concern was viewed more as a manifestation of protecting personal property interests.

Any expression of public interest in conservation occurred over proposals affecting the most visible aspects of existing features, the exterior of buildings, the street façade, and so on. However, public responses were not necessarily presented in language and concepts that constituted a valid planning issue. The local public were referred to as 'not very visual people' and their interpretation of phrases such as character, identity and attachment, while recognisable, could be potentially inadmissible as support for formal conservation arguments. The contrast with more affluent areas could be striking, particularly with areas where the public were more used to engaging in the planning process. There is an already widely recognised difficulty in encouraging members of the public to contribute their interest and an even greater one of representing that interest in planning terms when it is forthcoming.

The interpretation of value in the built environment

Seeing a particular type of interest

Environmental or area-based value was portrayed as far more malleable and subjective in comparison with defining the value of a building. This is not to say that a focus on buildings provided a coherent and incontrovertible interpretation of value. The conservation adviser considered a building as an integral whole, an historic document, with each component identifiably contributing to its overall interest. In contrast, those from non-conservation backgrounds appeared to disregard integrity, instead measuring the significance of 'interest' by the visibility of the features in question. The superficiality of 'visibility', contrasting with the deeper integrity of the building, reflects a knowledge-based contradiction in values.

The extent to which knowledge affects people's evaluation is really illustrated when someone's sensory perception of a feature is contradicted by their accepted knowledge of it. For example, of listed buildings in a poor state of repair, many people noted that these did not look like listed buildings because they lacked certain qualities. It suggests that there are certain preconceptions, even stereotypes, pertaining to a listed building. Generally the stereotypical qualities comprised: traditional images of polite architecture, though not necessarily a particular style or period; an allusion to prestige; a certain longevity; and some degree of contemporary attachment, care or use. There may be a further expectation of visual stimulation by its scale or by decoration, which produces something worth going to see; this equates with the stereotypes of tourists' expectations (Urry 1990). As mentioned earlier, the state of repair and the use/function affect perceptions enormously. Now a reason may be discernible because a poor state of repair or vacancy can undermine the preconceptions of a listed building stereotype.

The interpretation of special architectural or historic interest in these cases may reveal a hierarchy between these terms. In all the developments studied, the aesthetic interest was predominant, in either the visibility of features or their architectural quality. Historic interest, the most abstract and potentially intangible quality, appeared in all cases to be the subordinate interest. Though PPG15 states that historic interest must be supported by some accompanying architectural interest, this is only in relation to listing grading and not in the practice of consent approval. The conservation adviser had noted this anomaly too: whereas local, vernacular architecture was embraced in listing, local historical significance was not and remained woefully under-protected in policy and subsequent practice.

National interest and locality

As historic interest appears to be a shadowy concept on closer inspection, so too does national interest. In contrast to national respondents' ardent belief in the national taxonomy provided by EH and DCMS, at a local level national interest became an abstract concept which respondents found difficult to recognise. The main value of the grade II* listed building in the Square was its contribution to the Square; the building itself was not seen to have national status. Moreover, the definition of what constituted national interest in a feature appeared less objective than initially considered; instead it was defined by reference to other listed buildings across the region. Given that EH is regionally based, is it more accurate to contend that these standards are actually regional?

Despite the importance of improving the quality of the local environment, local familiarity fares little better. The lack of active public involvement in conservation may reflect the fact that features in the local environment are taken for granted. While it is evidently important to uphold local identity and character, everyday familiarity with these environments can lead to an under-appreciation of their qualities. When planning officers also question the credibility of some designated areas of local interest, the opportunities for exploring and working with undistinguished but equally important features of local value are further diminished. Most planning officers recognised that local knowledge and instinct helped appreciation of the attachment and identification felt locally, but these issues were not addressed in formal policy. Such an omission has led to charges of subjectivity, and more pointed criticisms, regarding local value. Indeed, it may lead to a situation in which local designations of value become irreversibly undermined and ignored.

Knowledge, professional and public appreciation

The strength of the approach taken by C&D may reflect wider shared principles with other conservation professionals. However, while this may be true, there were also significant variations in value interpretation among conservation professionals. While conservation inevitably requires discretion and flexibility, the Square highlighted two almost opposing interpretations of conservation interest between EH and the local authority. With other respondents complaining about individual officers imposing their own interpretations of conservation, there is a question over the conformity which national policy can promote. Divergence of opinion may be healthy and stimulate debate; however, it does question the consistency of opinions expressed.

It was notable that public contribution to the conservation debate in the town was lacking. Though the conservation adviser considered that the public interest in pursuing conservation was enshrined in PPG15's policies, he still believed that his conservation duties to be vigilant against unacceptable development in the town were important because of this responsibility to the public. Certainly it came across strongly from C&D that conservation can operate to enhance the quality of living and working in the town.

However, this is not to say that the local population neglected their environment or were blind to its features. Perhaps the lay interpretation of value simply did not enter the conservation debate as the language used to express local people's attachment was not compatible with, or indeed within the compass of, statutory land-use planning. Certainly in some cases the public took a much broader view of their environment, which included its function and use in addition to aesthetic qualities. For most lay respondents, function tended to define the character of areas as well as the value of particular buildings.

'Heritage' planning?

The temporal aspect of conservation, the significance of historic interest, appears to be a difficult quality to recognise and embrace. Historic interest was under-represented in assessing the value of features in the developments studied, but the reasons for this are unclear. Certainly a physical manifestation of historic interest is a policy prerequisite, otherwise the controls available to conservation and planning have nothing to act upon. However, orthodox historic interest – that is, a building's association with people or events – rarely leaves such tangible remains. Historic interest further suffers when people without any conservation training perceive significance by alighting on the visibility of physical features. Historic interest thus becomes too abstract an issue for DC practice to recognise and implement the necessary conservation measures.

While there were many views expressed about conservation contributing to a sense of place, this aspect rarely seemed to enter policy documents or decision-making arenas. The identity of a town is an accretion of cumulative development, providing contrasts and juxtapositions, yet the role of conservation, particularly in committee, appeared to be supported for its harmonising influence. Making features 'fit in' and respect their context, while commendable, was generally the over-riding requirement for new design. There can be an uncomfortable outcome when a committee without sufficient design training allows a poorly designed scheme to go ahead: it can lead to superficial reproductions of existing styles, thus actually reducing or flattening the diversity of the urban fabric's temporal collage. This is of particular concern given that planners' and the public's attention is focused on the grander buildings as carriers of meaning and symbolic value in the environment. The 'supporting cast', buildings of more meagre interest, while collectively contributing to a sense of place, are perceived individually to have very little meaning.

The influence of external pressures

The economic imperative

Economic factors have a profound effect on the potential contribution conservation can make. The general economic vitality of the region inevitably affects the uses and obsolescence of buildings and areas, and the town has been struggling against the restructuring of its industrial base. More precisely, in these marginal areas the financial viability of any particular development scheme often restricts the resources available to satisfy conservation objectives. However, it also affects practices within the authority, as reflected by the weight accorded to economic arguments in DC decision-making.

Given the political priority of encouraging local development, planning officers have been increasingly encouraged to satisfy applicants' (clients') development briefs. The political imperative contrasts with planning officers' perceptions of their own balancing of economic development with the wider needs of the community. However, balancing conservation against the economic pressures of development has proven particularly difficult, given the lack of a comparable basis for measurement. It is difficult to express the wider social and community benefits that conservation can contribute strictly in monetary terms. Thus the scales appear tipped heavily in favour of the more persuasive economic arguments for development.

More subtly, economics can also affect the perception of features' value. In the cases studied, certain features' conservation values were downplayed or elevated according to how these could support a particular economic argument for approving the development. The conservation value may be exploited for a particular commercial advantage, such as the building in the Square's impressive façade, or it may be under-played and relegated, such as the Yard's significant contribution to historical street form. It reflects the fact that identifiable values in features, while potentially intrinsic to the building, only carry as much weight as their utility in an economic argument.

Political support: people rather than buildings

It has been observed throughout that local statutory planning may have been eclipsed by a strong political imperative to encourage development and investment. The authority has seen the re-organisation of its planning and economic development services, and has created criticisms of planning's permissive attitude to development, which favours reducing conflict with the applicant. This has grave implications for conservation as it is further sidelined in the planning agenda.

Perhaps reinforced by the repercussions of several unfortunate cases, at the political level there has been a negative interpretation of conservation's aims. Politically, conservation has often been associated with the creation of obstructions for development and thus has suffered dwindling political support in the face of pressures to encourage development in the region. This orientation is quite in contrast to national respondents' assumption of society's (and by implication politicians') tacit approval of conservation. At the political coalface, it can appear that conservation's concern with the built fabric is necessarily at the expense of users' interests. This may explain a great deal of the political reaction against conservation since council members are arguably swayed to protect people's interests and livelihood rather more than inanimate architecture. The conservation-friendly initiatives of the then new chair of the Planning Committee tested the intransigence of political opposition.

In terms of any political preference for conservation, it is interesting to note officers' grievances. They considered that the committee does not place a great deal of significance on design issues and members have been happy to choose relatively safe, unchallenging schemes. Although applicants have exploited these easier routes to obtain planning permission, the result has been mediocre buildings which most architects loathe. Surely this is not a conscious decision by members to alienate architects, but must reflect personal, less design-based preferences for saving or making a particular image of the town. Successfully or otherwise, conscious or unconscious, these attitudes and preferences must be addressed if conservation is going to make any headway at all in local authorities' priorities.

Significant questions arising from the local culture of conservation planning

Before we examine the second case study, what are the salient points from observing conservation practice from this authority, particularly in relation to the attitudes found at the national level?

- Among planning officers the separateness of conservation controls and personnel from mainstream DC planning casework was not perceived to indicate or enhance any greater special status. If anything, conservation issues could be more easily marginalised by this distinction, to the detriment of conservation outputs.
- Although the reliance on PPG15 in development plan policies may create greater consistency between authorities, the local conservation culture is heavily influenced by the personal approach and priorities of key individual planning officers who can act as gatekeepers to conservation.
- The organisational structure of the planning service focuses meagre resources on conservation's treatment of buildings, which in turn influences perceptions across the authority of conservation's contribution. Broader environmental/area-based value is not well developed or supported in policy or practice to counter this effect.
- Historic interest suffers a diminution in value in contrast with architectural interest, which appears paramount, partly reflecting the commonly held view that the visibility of a feature dictates the degree of effort to be applied to its conservation.
- There is an expectation held by many people that listed buildings should possess stereotypical qualities, which in turn diminishes interest in buildings of more minor architectural interest and also undervalues concepts of valued areas and space.
- Local interest is poorly expressed but the national interest in features is equally intangible and difficult to recognise; it does not necessarily engender feelings of national status or responsibility.
- The public may consider the value of environmental features in broader terms than conservation professionals, exceeding the limits of what planning can legitimately address and control.
- The collegiality of conservation professionals is challenged by the significant distinctions in approach discovered between national and local experts.
- There appears to be a barrier to promoting conservation's contribution to local economic development. A diminished level of local political support appears to undermine national assumptions of a wide political consensus supporting conservation.

The extent to which these issues are contradicted or reinforced by conservation in a totally different local context is dealt with in the following chapter.

6   Conservation in a historic market town

Introduction

The second case study explores the conservation culture of a local planning authority but this time in the context of a historic market town. (The background to the case studies is given in the introduction to chapter 5.) Two different urban contexts were chosen in order to investigate whether the nature of the historic environment notably affects perceptions of the value, or contribution, of conservation in planning. A shire market town was chosen to represent the type of place that more actively promotes its historic identity, its image being more synonymous with that of the archetypal conservation town.

This chapter follows a similar structure to the previous one. First, an exploration of the structure and personnel involved in conservation within and around the authority illustrates the local conservation culture. Second, four planning applications, involving a range of conservation issues, illustrate the application of particular conservation approaches and also expose broader responses towards conservation in the locality

As with the previous case study, the time elapsed since the fieldwork will mean that operations, personnel and priorities inevitably will have changed and no doubt a slightly different picture would emerge if the town were revisited today. However, aside from the practical arrangements, the findings are of value because they illustrate more profound issues in the treatment of conservation planning.

An illustrative background

This market town in the Midlands represents a rich mix of architectural periods and boasts a proliferation of listed buildings, with some outstanding grade I and II* examples. Its urban morphology reflects centuries of continuous development from the medieval period onwards. However, as with the metropolitan authority, there are harsh realities facing the town. Following the deleterious effect of various recent food and agricultural scares within a weakened agricultural sector, the imperative for local economic diversification is all the more pressing. As with all medium-sized towns, competitiveness in the regional hierarchy is an issue and maintaining its local distinctiveness is a key priority.

A brief history of local conservation practice

The present borough council was created in 1974 following the reorganisation of local government. In contrast with the metropolitan case study, the planning

The Firestone factory, London: the cynical demolition of this art deco factory prompted Michael Heseltine, then Secretary of State for the Environment, to accelerate the listing resurveys service has not had a corps of long-serving planning officers, and although the scope for piecing together a historical narrative is slightly reduced, prominent themes do illustrate some of the changes to the authority's conservation practice.

Though the county council provides the strategic framework for planning, most active conservation responsibility has rested with the borough. The authority appointed its first specific conservation officer in the early 1970s following the introduction of the Civic Amenities Act. The original appointee, now a practising architect in the town, felt that those early years saw massive improvements in the town's fabric and the authority's attitude in encouraging applicants towards a conservation-oriented approach. Several initiatives, such as the instigation of a reclaimed materials depot, a survey of unused upper floors in the town centre, the reversal of slum clearance policies and the availability of grants to improve the properties, helped shape a positive view of conservation's contribution to the town's development.

Of this time, it was recalled that there was a greater level of debate regarding conservation's strategic role in raising the status of the town; generally, conservation was higher up the environmental agenda then than now. Satisfying the Historic Buildings Council criteria for grant funding in the early 1980s was seen as a vindication of these early achievements and reflected a measure of the local political commitment to conservation.

Following the original conservation officer's departure in the mid-1980s, two further conservation officers, both architects, took over the responsibility until the present officer's appointment in the mid-1990s. Attitudes and relationships between the conservation section and DC altered with the different officers.

Previously the town centre DC officer worked alongside the conservation section since most applications in the town centre involved conservation issues. The close working relationship illustrated an ethos whereby DC processed and ensured a high-quality treatment of the historic fabric. There appears to have been a tradition established for great attention to detail and a demand for high standards of workmanship in repairs to buildings which still characterises the authority's approach. Many working practices were introduced to maintain high quality, such as requiring 1:50 scale rather than the standard 1:200 scale drawings for applications and archaeological reports; such measures created definite and identifiable standards.

However, the committing of resources and officer time to a focus on the detail of planning applications was not always matched by the developing of longer-term, proactive conservation strategy. A 'buildings at risk' survey covering the entire borough was conducted in the early 1990s, though its effectiveness was reduced by a lack of monitoring of the state of these buildings. There is no local list either, as it was generally assumed that the listed buildings in the town provided a comprehensive coverage of all the features of interest – an extra level of identification would contribute little more.

In the town's listing resurveys in the early 1990s, it appeared that as many buildings were removed from the lists as were added. New listings tended to represent the town's Victorian legacy, which had been neglected in earlier architectural appraisals. Indeed, new conservation area designations over the past 10 years largely comprised Victorian residential areas adjacent to the town centre (which ironically had been saved from slum clearance 20 years earlier). New designations had not been problematic but some councillors had been wary of Article 4 Directions, which were viewed as an infringement on people's property rights.

It is clear that over the years the authority has improved the quality of the local environment and its historic buildings. This achievement is to be balanced against criticisms raised in the town that there has been a lack of vision for enhancing the urban environment generally and a perceived lack of sufficient mid- to long-term strategy for conservation.

While the local historic buildings annual repairs budget had gradually increased to £30,000, the budget for conservation area improvements was cut in the late 1990s from £15,000 to £3,000. More fundamentally, there were fears for the future within the conservation section following the termination of the £200,000 a year CAP funding in 2000. With EH's replacement HERS funding and the HLF's Townscape Heritage Initiative veering away from supporting the fabric of traditional historic areas, there was no longer the certainty instilled from 25 years of continuous national conservation funding in the town. It was an opportunity for the authority to respond to a changing national agenda.

Structure, operation and priorities

Conservation section

On the face of it, conservation planning was relatively easy for the authority compared to others' experiences. The town's venerable historic status added force to the requirement for applicants to comply with basic requirements such as the submission of better-quality drawings and archaeological site reports. Moreover, there appeared to be a strong contingent of local architectural practices in the town that by their nature contributed sympathetic new development.

The conservation section (figure 6.1) comprised four officers, with the conservation officer being appointed at senior officer level. It was a separate section and provided specialist advice throughout the planning service. DC officers consulted conservation as and when required; there was no compulsion, formal arrangement or framework to guide officers – the choice rested on individuals' discretion. A weekly case conference provided an opportunity for all senior planning officers to discuss the issues, implications and resolutions of particular applications received.

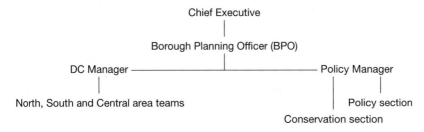

Figure 6.1 Structure in 1999 of the council planning service of the second town studied (a market town in the Midlands)

The conservation officer's view

All the authority's conservation officers trained as architects, not planners; the current officer straddled both disciplines. From this background, the officer appreciated the need for conservation to be flexible with the nature of design solutions for repairing and re-using historic buildings. He did not strictly consider himself to be a planner and believed that conservation contributed greatly to the discussion of the quality of developments, which was limited by the statutory eight-week deadline for processing planning applications.

In contrast with the reactive approach of the planning service, he viewed his role as more proactive. This approach could be based on informal lobbying and, to the occasional consternation of his colleagues, autonomously pursuing selected causes to champion. Furthermore, political manoeuvring was essential to the success of conservation: finding and creating support internally within the council and externally among prospective applicants, architects and residents. Similarly, he believed that an evangelical role – engendering conservation thinking – was as important as advising on the detail of statutory controls. Attempting to win hearts and minds bolstered support for conservation, attracted resources and investment interest, and, through heightening others' awareness, maximised the opportunities for external funding. Developing links with national organisations was a further priority, importing gravity and strength to local conservation arguments. He was critical that planning, as a profession, actually shied away from these more politicised tools despite their usefulness in promoting an agenda.

Though relations with DC were good, the discretionary consultation arrangement between conservation and DC highlighted the fact that some DC officers were more engaged with conservation than others. This raises two particular difficulties for the conservation section. First, if a particular DC officer made fewer consultations, this does not necessarily indicate that the officer concerned could suitably deal with the conservation implications of an application, for example by imposing standard conditions on a planning permission. Despite having redrafted them, the conservation officer still considered that conservation required a more intricate and sensitive approach than could be provided by standard conditions. Second, although DC officers may have believed that they could competently determine the case, imposing standard conditions could lead to instances where DC's interpretation of conservation was stricter than the conservation officer would have advised.

This can be particularly galling for the conservation officer, who wished to promote a more flexible position. The regenerative effects of good conservation – encouraging new uses for old buildings and revitalising areas – were his paramount concerns. Looking beyond the authority, he lambasted what he termed 'the rottweiler school' of conservation, which, by its treating of every single element of a building with insufficient discrimination, was counterproductive. He believed that elements of the historic fabric must be altered to reap much more substantial benefits in enabling the re-use of historic buildings.

Views of other officers in the section

The conservation grants officer considered the integrity of a building's structure and fabric to be the paramount consideration rather than its academic and historical aesthetic value. For him, the quality of craftsmanship and materials applied to a listed building provided both an objective standard for the regulation of the quality of workmanship, and inspiration for the craft of conservation. He demanded high standards and noted in comparison that some local developers considered the conservation officer to be 'a soft touch' over such detailing. While these two officers' approaches can complement one another well, their different priorities represent two interpretations of conservation, which might send mixed messages for DC to implement.

The conservation section as a whole felt frustrated by the general lack of design appreciation in the authority. Its personnel remarked that planning officers were generalists, and offering them a two-day design course did not make them experts in urban design. Yet planning officers felt comfortable with their own design competence. For instance, the authority's own architects' panel (offering independent design advice) had been gradually used less as it appeared that DC staff were more comfortable with their own design competence.

DC section

The borough council had a relatively small planning service employing around 20 officers. DC was answerable to two committees concerned with planning, the DC Subcommittee and the full Planning and Highways Committee, the former dealing with the more strategic and significant projects in the borough.

Conservation was viewed fairly consistently throughout the service as a priority for the town, with senior managers considering that they 'sang from the same songsheet'. All planning officers considered that the borough planning officer encouraged a robust adherence to the local plan and conservation contributed greatly to this ethos, providing a further means to control inappropriate development and enforce higher standards. Certainly the authority appeared more willing to defend local plan policies at appeal; in contrast, officers in the metropolitan council noted their lawyers' desire to avoid conflict at all costs.

Design training and regulation

DC officers considered themselves competent at dealing with most conservation issues as they involved similar design issues which percolated through planning applications. While DC officers' experience equipped them to deal with townscape and minor changes to buildings, their expertise did not extend to identifying the architectural and structural significance in features of special interest, for which they needed the support of the conservation section.

Referring applications for conservation advice had necessarily become a more *ad hoc* arrangement, given the conservation officer's preference for pursuing larger, higher-profile conservation projects over DC casework. While the quality of conservation advice had not deteriorated, such informal consultation must affect the consideration of complex issues and the comprehensiveness of conservation advice.

In strategic terms, DC saw conservation as a positive contribution to the service and town rather than simply a statutory responsibility. PPG15 and the local plan were seen as providing adequate conservation policy for most situations, so supplementary local conservation policy guidance was deemed unnecessary. In practical terms, conservation's additional controls and wider perspective of 'acceptable development' provided a convenient filter with which to reject unsuitable applications outright rather than attempt to negotiate them within the eight-week deadline. However, one DC officer commented that there could be an over-emphasis on conservation. Whereas government and Royal Town Planning Institute (RTPI) initiatives presented planning as a progressive tool of implementation, he felt he was operating 'a neighbourhood protection service'. The emphasis on this regulatory aspect appeared to emanate not only from the public but also from senior levels within the borough.

There were good reasons for this, specifically to ensure that applicants followed the correct planning procedures and channels through the Planning Committee, otherwise the planning service's ability to control inappropriate development in the town might be adversely affected. It is debatable to what extent a robust adherence to the policies in the local plan affected planning officers' discretion to negotiate and encourage partnerships with applicants.

Despite the BPO's insistence on planning delivering strong quality control, the planning service was not perceived to be a leading voice in the council *vis-à-vis* other services. While the council has no corporate structure and exists as separate services, without particular political appointees being responsible for each one, planning could be susceptible to being obscured by other agendas and priorities in council.

Wider influences and accountability

Policy and strategic initiative

At the time of fieldwork, the Local Development Plan was passing through the Inquiry stage. A specific chapter on the historic environment comprising some 20 pages was frequently cited to illustrate the significant local political commitment to conservation. The Local Plan ought to be read in conjunction with the County Structure Plan, completed in 1989. A special section on conservation provided a cursory strategic framework and highlighted the borough's additional responsibilities and powers to protect the market town's historic core.

While there is a Historic Environment team within the county council, its interaction with the borough regarding the built environment has diminished considerably, though the team remained statutory advisers to the borough on archaeological matters. Indeed, this concern has fostered a partnership with the borough over the preparation of an archaeological database of the town, not only to assist DC decision-making, but also to provide a wider resource for local tourist, educational and academic uses. However, at a county level, it appeared that the political emphasis on developing and fostering sustainability and Local Agenda 21, with its concern for sustainable development, has pushed building conservation out of the picture in favour of a concern for the natural environment. In addition, central government rate-capping and the loss of rate revenue from the creation of a new unitary authority within former county boundaries further reduced the resources available to the county council. The team's general retreat from built environment conservation created further difficulties for the borough, especially as it is a small planning service and may struggle to free resources to realise broader strategic goals.

In contrast with the county's environmental management strategies, members of the county team considered that the borough had a compartmentalised conservation operation and chose to focus on specific buildings and not wider environmental factors such as flood risk. To the county team there appeared to be less guiding vision from the borough for the town's development and the proper treatment of sustainable development.

Perspectives of and from members

The concerns of borough council members were wide-ranging but notably focused on the threat posed by a neighbouring town to attract businesses away from this town centre, thereby undermining the local economy. One or two councillors considered that planning restricted the town's economic vitality, particularly the measures to reduce traffic in the town centre (although these were also Highways' responsibility). In general, a consensus prevailed in support of conservation, though this was equally expressed as existing to protect the users of these buildings, who were often small independent retailers, and to maintain residential property in the town centre. Conservation was perceived to be as much about protecting a way or quality of life as about protecting the buildings themselves.

Many in the authority noted a slight tension between members and officers. Some attributed this to a parochial mentality in which councillors favoured their intimate local knowledge over officers' detached professional advice. In relation to conservation, many considered this to reflect past developments in the town, whereby certain planning decisions in the 1960s saw the destruction of several significant historic buildings. While many of the members were of a generation to recall the pre-1960s townscape, the hangover of the modernist surge into the town appears to have cast a long shadow over subsequent attitudes concerning new buildings: the Planning Committee chair noted, '[W]e are very possessive about conservation here.'

Officers (and also many applicants) could be frustrated by the Planning Committee's preference for traditional, safe designs which were familiar to the town. Considering the sheer diversity of buildings spanning a six-hundred-year period, the concentration and proliferation of a homogeneous Georgian pastiche was quite abhorrent to design professionals working in the town. Professionals were critical of members' ability to appreciate contemporary design and worried about the longer-term repercussions of the notable lack of late-twentieth-century buildings in the town.

Perceptions of and from the public

The established channel for involving the public was through the Planning Liaison Group, which comprised representatives of various local resident groups, the Civic Society, the Council for the Protection of Rural England, the chamber of commerce, the police and others. It was intended to be a forum for discussion and dissemination rather than active canvassing and participatory consultation. However, as with all representative bodies, it is debatable how far its members' views can ever represent the public at large. Individual officers characterised a section of the town's residents as having a 'drawbridge mentality', in that they wished to preserve the centre of the town almost as a museum piece. It was fine to have a prosperous centre so long as it was prosperous only from 9 a.m. until 5 p.m.

On the other hand, in promoting the town's economic and cultural vitality, the local Civic Society saw itself as encompassing wider concerns than just planning. Relatively prosperous and enjoying a membership of around 800, the society was in a strong position to lobby the council. It was particularly critical of the council's treatment of many landmark buildings in the town, especially those under its own stewardship. These buildings not only were missed opportunities to promote their re-use as heritage attractions, but, more fundamentally, they were threatened by structural dilapidation. Partly these results were seen as endemic of the borough's 'planning by the rule book' culture – the authority was perceived to lack 'flair and imagination'. One Civic Society member noted that while the authority remained committed to conservation, the constructive dialogue previously characterising planning application negotiations had passed by. In fact, this member considered that the authority was abrogating its public responsibility of ensuring quality new development in the town.

Table 6.1 An outline of development cases' attributes

The Terrace
- A significant new residential development within the central conservation area, affecting the setting of a prominent grade II listed building and involving the demolition of an unlisted building
- Site purchased by a local firm of specialist residential developers

The Bank
- The final phase of a site's development, introducing new office accommodation and two smaller units: development in the central conservation area affecting the setting of two listed buildings
- Site owned by an established local business

The Annexe
- A series of unsuccessful applications to erect additional hotel accommodation in the rear garden of a grade II* listed building in the central conservation area
- Listed building owned by local hotelier

The Gardens
- Renovation of a private house in a grade II listed terrace in a conservation area
- Local land agent privately purchased and renovated the house

Development cases

The second tier of investigating the conservation culture in the local planning authority involved in-depth studies of four separate development control cases. Invaluably, this tested the rhetoric surrounding policy statements and also identified a range of parties with differing experiences and values relating to conservation in the town. It was essential to identify a range of developments and parties involving different aspects of conservation control. The list set out in table 6.1 outlines their correlation with the selection criteria specified in table 5.3. The names of the cases have been changed to respect respondents' anonymity.

The Terrace

A summary of the development

A prominent town centre site

The town centre falls sharply down to the river on the eastern side, making for a prominent and uninterrupted skyline. The site, on the approach to the centre over East Bridge, comprised such a characteristic view of the town that any new building here demanded a sensitive approach. The new development in question was proposed in the heart of this area, and while only the latter stages of the scheme are related here, a brief explanation of the whole site's recent history is required.

The former hospital had occupied the site until its relocation in the early 1980s to the outskirts of town. Following its move, the local health authority had sold the site, covering an extensive area running down to the river, to a local developer. Two principal buildings remained, the hospital itself and the adjacent staff house, though both were in a poor state of repair. After several years of vacancy and dereliction and extensive negotiation with the local planning authority, the first renovations were completed in the late 1980s.

The hospital, a Georgian grade II listed building, formed a monumental neo-classical crown atop the town's skyline. It was restored, respecting its rigorous symmetry, and converted into retail units on the ground floor with residential accommodation occupying its five upper floors. However, the scheme for the whole site was not completed as the recession and development delays forced the original developer into receivership in 1992, leaving the former staff home still vacant and the rest of the site undeveloped. Though suffering a fire in the intervening years, it was purchased by an established local firm of housebuilders in 1995. Despite the fire damage, its Victorian red-brick construction was still structurally sound and the new owners converted this grade II listed building into 28 flats. Both conversion schemes won local conservation awards, as did the same firm of local architects, who were again used for the final phase of development studied here.

Following these conversions, the firm acquired the final undeveloped plot on the site from the receivers. Though planning permission already existed for 20 large detached town houses, the slump in the housing market made such a scheme unviable. With both the developers and the planning authority wanting to revise the density and design of any new development, negotiations started in earnest. However, the demolition of an existing building on-site and the style of any new development proved to be contentious issues all round.

The prefab block

From the outset of discussions in the summer of 1995, the prominence of this site was stressed by planning officers: '[It] is essential that this classic view of the town is enhanced and not harmed by any development.' In the original outline permission, the council had demanded a comprehensive development scheme for the whole site and attached a condition requiring the demolition of a three-storey 1940s pre-fabricated building located at the top of the site in front of the former infirmary on the river side.

However, the developers considered that this building was still structurally sound and, following local planning policy on retaining buildings in conservation areas, they wanted to convert it for residential use. After muted initial support in principle, by early 1996 the authority was vigorously opposed to the idea. The architects submitted various designs and styles to improve the building's appearance, but the authority stood by its requirement that it be demolished, despite the developers' suggestion of a formal review of the condition. The prefab was becoming such an obstacle to the whole site's redevelopment that the council proposed a breach of condition notice.

Public opposition to the building's presence was particularly vocal and the authority received many letters of objection, mainly from the local Civic Society, which had galvanised its members to lobby for its removal. Many members who lived in the recently converted staff home were particularly incensed as they had received reassurances given by the developers when purchasing their flats that the prefab's removal would provide them with uninterrupted views over the river. The local Friends of the Earth group stated that the building was 'a considerable blemish on the riverside environment'. Similarly, the Town Centre Residents' Association (TCRA) objected to any compromise short of removal. One eulogising resident was 'horrified to note how the very ugly, seemingly temporary and derelict building ruins the fine view of the listed buildings around it. No renovation can improve it . . . any modern "dolling up" . . . would make it even more of an eyesore.' EH did not object to the prefab's demolition since it was 'not listed and appears to us to make little, if any, contribution to the character and appearance of the conservation area'. Yet, equivocally, EH did not oppose its retention either, 'particularly if its harsh utilitarian character can be softened by the application of appropriate features'.

Increasing political interest clamoured for the building's demolition. The developers considered that such politicisation had made the view from East Bridge sacrosanct, leaving little room for its retention. Despite revisions over the summer to reduce the height of any conversion scheme and various architectural makeovers, the results were aesthetically unsatisfactory. In October 1996 the applicants finally agreed to demolish the building to assist the progress of the overall development of the site.

The new development

Parallel negotiations concerning the design of the new buildings on-site courted their own friction. The layout of the approved scheme of 20 houses from 1991 had intended to replicate the haphazard arrangement of much older properties built on the slopes from the town centre down to the river. The new scheme, instead, presented two apartment blocks running parallel to the contours of the site. However, EH recited its earlier comments from the 1991 scheme:

> While a traditional approach to their design may seem appropriate within the wider historic context of this part of [the town], the contours of the site tend to undermine the classic forms attempted. By opting for traditional forms the architects have set themselves considerable design problems. In view of the difficult terrain and the importance of the setting, English Heritage considers that . . . a modern design solution might be more appropriate on this part of the site.

But although the developers wanted to design a modern building, neither their architects nor the planning authority were particularly enthusiastic. Their architects were locally respected for their traditional designs, and planning officers had emphasised that committee members were extremely cautious in approving non-familiar styles.

By August 1996, EH reviewed the revised scheme comprising two parallel apartment blocks of four to five storeys and considered that they conflicted with the 'monumental' style of the former hospital. EH was critical of the architects' 'traditional approach' as this was producing neither a new, modern building nor a historically correct copy. Instead, this combination 'has resulted in squat proportions which help to give much of the development a heavy, ponderous character'. The architects rebuked EH for its approach, claiming that the building had to feel right in this context and not pursue a statement of design purity for its own sake. As project architects for the other phases of development on the site, they had already contributed to the retention of much of the historic skyline along this stretch and were not willing to sacrifice its integrity to a passing fashion for 'modern' design.

As the neo-classical design was not well supported, a safer option was suggested to appease all parties: a Georgian design that would be more sympathetic to the rest of the town. By November, new drawings were submitted, again showing two blocks parallel to the contours of the site 'designed in a plain, though hopefully not unattractive, Georgian manner incorporating where possible local detailing'. Planning officers felt such a design was necessary in the light of continuing vocal opposition to change in the town. Despite a safer design premise, the authority still received letters of objection from the public concerning not only the 'excessive' height of the blocks but also the higher density of dwelling units and the ensuing access and traffic problems.

At a Planning Committee meeting in March 1997, officers recommended approval of the scheme to demolish the prefab and allow a more spacious setting for two Georgian-style terraces:

> [T]he overall design approach to this sensitive site is correct. The buildings need to be on a grand scale to complement, rather than compete against, the surrounding buildings. The chosen style of architecture again is complementary to the site and its surroundings. The detailed design is well considered and studied and would enhance this part of the town centre.

In granting permission, members commented on the importance of protecting the impressive skyline and historic surroundings. That the whole scheme 'fitted in', that people didn't even recognise that it was brand new, was considered a major achievement, its lack of impact being a positive measure of success. One councillor noted that it was irrelevant if it was criticised as 'pastiche', so long as it did not ruin this important view of the town.

After protracted negotiations, the scheme was finished in 1999 and the first home-owners moved in. The development was considered such a success by the planning authority that it was proposed for an RTPI award and also a Civic Trust award. One planning officer noted the developers' thanks for the authority's guidance: 'I'd say it's a total success, the best scheme that we've got in the town centre, in my opinion anyway. In terms of its impact on a conservation area, its detail, its quality of work, it's spot on.'

Despite its potential awards, it is not the ideal solution for either the developers or the architects, nor the progressive conservationism wanted by EH, but represents the best compromise on which all parties could agree.

Attitudes to conservation illustrated in this case

Change and continuity in urban planning

Surprisingly, the developer and some DC officers believed there were no particular conservation issues raised by the development; rather, the context and setting
demanded a sensitive approach to urban design. Such an attitude may indicate
a particular interpretation of conservation: that it is relevant only where existing
historic fabric is directly threatened.

The context of the new development was the paramount concern. Though
respondents considered this a quintessentially English town, as compared with
other local historic towns, the prevailing local attitude was perceived as being
less appreciative of contemporary building in the town centre. The emphasis
appeared to be on ensuring continuity and minimising contrasts with the existing
surroundings. This may be due to a general apprehension, possibly even fear, of
repeating unsympathetic developments, such as 1960s replacements for many
historic buildings in the town centre. Despite DC wanting to encourage modern
architecture, this attitude did affect them:

> I think in all honesty we'd have ended up being criticised for a modern
> building in that location. I think that Georgian approach is very successful
> in that location and people are saying to us now, 'Oh, it looks like it's been
> there for ever', which is exactly the approach we [thought] it should be.

'Sympathetic' development effectively excluded a contemporary design
approach despite sustained objections from EH over attempts to ape traditional
styles. Some local cynicism arose over EH's advice because nationally EH had
to be seen to champion contemporary architecture and adopt the regeneration-
based initiatives of central government; but sometimes this approach was just
not appropriate.

Local interest in the proposed changes was potent, vocal and well organised.
However, the authority was a little sceptical about the public spirit of some objectors' motives since a significant proportion resided in the recently converted
hospital buildings; retaining the prefab obstructed the view from their windows,
thus the enjoyment of private property fuelled their angst. While opposition was
vocal, it represented a minority of the townspeople: predominantly those who
could afford to live centrally – the educated, wealthier and slightly older middle
classes – and who could express their dissent most influentially.

New design: fitting in or juxtaposition – an image of the town

The demolition and new scheme question design distinctions between tradition
and modernity. The conservation officer noted how the profession divided into

architects who preferred a traditional and those who preferred a contemporary architectural vocabulary. He noted that working to local architects' strengths is essential; asking a traditional practice to produce a contemporary design is totally inappropriate.

The authority was adamant that this site was 'one of the most important views of the town'. While the local plan contained a policy protecting important views, most people were galvanised by the look of the scheme. The conservation section principally cited the need to respect views into and out of the town centre because these gaps and vantage points illustrated the morphological development of the urban fabric. Protecting the opportunities to see these views was as important as the quality of the views themselves. The prospect from East Bridge catalysed much local sentiment, revealing people's identification of the view as in some way symbolic of the town, though this may have involved a certain romanticism. The stark utility and brutal outline of the prefab made the blemish on this 'historic' scene all the more obvious. While it was structurally sound, its ugliness subsumed any perceived attachment to it despite its having been a familiar element of this view for the past 60 years.

In contrast, the adopted Georgian style of the new development proved sufficiently familiar to be acceptable, as the developer noted:

> [I]t became clear that the only way that the planners would grant consent was if we used pastiche style, Georgian style, a replica, a style that they were familiar with so that councillors on their planning committee would say, 'I've seen that before, I've seen one of those in Bath, I want one of those', and they're happy.

Planning officers did not consider it was pastiche, since it meticulously followed original Georgian proportions and detailing as far as commercially viable. However, the developers and architects held widely differing views on the appropriateness of the design. The latter considered that this debate on authenticity was fraudulent, describing EH's advice as overly dogmatic:

> [W]hat is considered modern or not is a completely false distinction in my view. . . . It doesn't matter what you do, it doesn't matter how carefully you make your most beautiful repair or copy or reproduction, it will have 1999 written all over it and the honest response is to do what you feel is best at the time rather than say, 'I feel like a bit of Gothic coming on or I feel like a bit of 1930s.'

A committee member also warmed to this perspective: 'I think they've kept a feel of the place, I think the buildings do blend in quite nicely and quite well. . . . I don't mind what people call it.' However, while such contextualisation is admirable, in the wrong hands there can be a tendency to emphasise homogeni-sation. The developers felt constrained by the prevailing local ethos, which shied away from embracing contemporary, late-twentieth-century contributions to the town: 'I'm afraid that in [this town] we'll never see a modern classic.'

In attempting to maintain a particular character, there can be a tendency to stereotype. Many respondents picked out the large, neo-classical buildings along the skyline, effectively those features that stand out, to define the town's char-acter. The preference to harmonise development, to make it fit in, may actually be reducing the scope for contemporary buildings to be distinct and similarly contribute to evolving perceptions of the town's identity.

Economic and political pressures

From the developer's perspective, it was evidently worth pursuing a variety of approaches to maximise the site's development potential, including all manner of conversion schemes for the prefab. It was not the conservation value of these buildings which had originally interested them, but the sound construction of the staff home, which permitted a conversion scheme. Their town centre loca-tion would also prove saleable; listed status and the buildings' place in the central conservation area were merely coincidental.

Despite the developer's wishes to follow a contemporary treatment for the site, the authority remained in a strong position throughout the case and would not permit a development that was not worthy of winning an award. It is debatable whose vision the finalised design more closely represents – the developer's or the authority's.

Evidently, pressure from local residents had increased the political profile of this case but the view over the town itself proved to be a powerful and emotive force politically. While the developer considered that this irreversibly restricted negotiations over the prefab, its demolition had changed the issue from one of planning or design to a political one, with the Borough Planning Officer becoming increasingly involved. Retaining an unadulterated view of the town supported members' inclinations towards a safe architectural treatment which complemented their interpretation of the town's character.

The Bank

A summary of the development

Background

The Bank is a new building, part of a new development scheme next to West Bridge on the opposite side of the town centre from the Terrace. Latterly the area's retailing has suffered competition from two new shopping malls in the town centre; the closure of the adjacent main bus station and multi-storey car park has increased this disparity. Local businesses, including the applicants, have been lobbying the council to produce a regeneration strategy for the area.

The site is owned by the applicants, a local family business established in the town over a century ago. Originally based in wholesale grocery distribution, they have a tradition of local property development in their portfolio of commercial activities. While their long-standing contribution to the town's development and economy has placed the applicants in an influential position *vis-à-vis* the council, planning officers characterised their applications as being of a consistently high quality.

The site had originally housed the applicants' business and goods distribution, but, following the relocation of this function, the applicants submitted a radical master plan to develop the whole site at the start of the 1990s. Though only loosely defined in design terms and its specific uses, it initiated the largest single investment in this part of town for 30 years. By 1998, three phases of development were complete. Along the riverside, two dilapidated red-brick warehouses, albeit grade II listed, had been converted into smart café bars. An unlisted warehouse on the far corner had been demolished to little public or local authority objection and replaced with a 'restrained modern' building echoing the vernacular style of the adjacent Victorian warehouses. It is now an established restaurant. These developments were praised, locally and nationally, as good examples of urban regeneration.

The applicants' head office is located on the corner of the site, adjacent to West Bridge. Built by the firm in the 1920s, it is a copy of a William and Mary-style building. However, the symmetry of its design is only three-quarters complete, its completion being prevented by a small adjacent grade II listed building. This now vacant building is the last remnant of a local primary school demolished in the 1960s to make way for the inner circle road scheme. Intending to complete the extension of their main office, the applicants had recently acquired the listed building from the council, which had last used it as a hostel.

The application and wider concerns

In January 1998 a planning application was submitted for the final phase of development, the most significant element being a new three-storey office block on the town side of the site.

The application also contained measures affecting two other grade II buildings on-site. The former hostel was to be completely relocated to be next to two other listed properties on the southern side of the site. These buildings were the only two remaining examples of a previous Victorian artisans' terrace, and although currently vacant, they had been in residential use until 15 years previously. Initial plans to demolish them partially were later changed to a repair scheme providing further office accommodation with the former hostel.

Planning officers rejected this part of the application outright, since 'essentially the majority of the character and fabric of the listed building[s], and a part of [the town's] history, will be lost'. DC noted that the applicants argued a very poor case for removing the former hostel and had not proved its necessity on grounds of structural obsolescence, a view reinforced by a belated EH response. Though the building was omitted from a later, amended application at the end of February, it still obstructed the applicants' long-standing desire to extend their main office block. Though most parties acknowledged the architectural and townscape benefits of this extension, the authority considered that PPG15 prevented the removal of this listed building. However, the applicants remained undeterred, preparing the relevant appeal files. Agreeing with their local firm of architects, they saw little merit in the former hostel to justify its listed status and considered that their scheme would dramatically enhance the conservation area.

A landmark new building

Given its location at the bottom of the slope rising up to the town centre, the proposed new office block would be all the more visible, and ensuring its contextual fit was vital. This was a flagship project for both the applicants and the authority. The applicants wanted a striking contemporary design to attract a major tenant to use the whole building. The authority wanted to encourage a high-quality modern design in contrast to the ubiquitous Georgian pastiche of much new development in the town centre.

From an archaeological perspective, the site was considered 'highly' significant since an earlier county council archaeological investigation in 1997 had discovered the remains of the medieval town wall underneath it. The intrusion of new foundations was potentially very damaging, although EH experts ultimately considered that rafting over the deposits would constitute sufficient protection.

Initially, the conservation officer had suggested reflecting this archaeological significance in the new building's design by the use of a curved wall and corner turret or rotunda. The local architects noted this element too and also had tried working aspects of the surrounding area, specifically the changes in roof lines and pitches and the variety of building materials, into their design. Their proposal, presenting a curved sheet-glass façade to the street, supported by a white render finish, was a conscious deviation from the red-brick vernacular characterising other buildings on the site and attempted to reflect the many small arcs and crescents in properties along the town walls.

However, the authority considered the first submission quite unsuitable, especially in this sensitive location. To anyone looking down on the building from further up the rising street, the height, bulk and roof line became all the more intrusive. The authority attempted to negotiate a reduction in its height by a storey, and though the architects objected, by June a compromise was achieved, with the building's height being reduced by 2 m to achieve a more harmonious balance with surrounding roof levels. According to the architects, the massing, and especially the roof detailing, had been 'jumbled up' and made more characteristic of the town.

A contrasting or complementary design?

The design of the new building polarised opinion between professionals and what may be loosely termed 'the lay view', which included most committee members, who considered that the design was incongruous in terms of its surroundings.

Members were not the only ones objecting to the new scheme: it attracted adverse comments from several local bodies. The TCRA considered that the concrete and glass style was 'totally alien . . . more appropriate for an out-of-town motorway setting rather than in the middle of our historic town'. Similarly, they objected to its scale, which 'dwarfs all the adjacent buildings'. The Civic Society shared some of these views, feeling that it was 'grossly out of scale and character with its surroundings and would be seriously detrimental to the visual amenity'.

Members considered that the modern white render finish was not in keeping with that area of town, providing too stark a contrast with the many red-brick buildings surrounding it. Brick constructions appeared uppermost in members' definitions of the area's character, and, contrary to officers' advice, they asked the applicants to reconsider a brick finish for the new building.

In contrast, the authority's own advisory panel of local architects returned a fairly positive approval of the building, even noting that the scaling was largely appropriate for the area. It seemed that the professionals liked the design yet lay opinion did not. Alternative schemes were produced, but the architects expressed severe misgivings over the loss of the original design's ethos and integrity, reducing a contemporary building with dramatic impact to a 'missed opportunity'. However, at this late stage obtaining the planning permission was of paramount concern.

Several planning officers, in retrospect, considered that members did not understand the principles and vocabulary of this modern design. Following another deferral, the committee finally approved the application yet insisted that the exterior design should be partly in brick, and they should choose the finish.

At the time of the study, the building remained in model form since the possible tenant withdrew their interest. A couple of firms had expressed interest but subsequently rescinded their offers. Given this delay, the applicants were considering returning to the planning officers once the construction of the new building was under way to reverse or revise the committee's insistence on brick facing in the permission's conditions.

Attitudes to conservation illustrated in this case

Conservation, urban design and planning

While there were several contentious issues – demolishing a listed building and constructing a new building in a conservation area – again there did not appear to be a great distinction between the DC's and conservation sections' approaches. In fact, it would be difficult to separate conservation and planning concerns as they were perceived in terms of townscape, scale and massing – issues in which both sections claimed complete competency. However, technically the only officers in the authority with a formal design training were in the conservation section.

Regarding the former hostel, the authority considered that 'it's a nonsense to demolish a listed building no matter how carefully you move it somewhere else – it loses its listed status, you can't have a brand new listed building'. A particular DC officer could not recall any approvals for the total demolition of a listed building in the town over the past 20 years – it was simply 'bad practice'. Though anecdotal, this may reflect a percolation of conservation sensitivity through the DC section.

Great difficulty was encountered in judging how the new development would enhance the conservation area. DC considered that any new development was an improvement, given the site's previous neglect. The applicant, while personally supporting conservation, believed the authority was unduly rigid in approach, attempting to preserve everything. Rather than reflecting quality, the high number of listed buildings in the town implied that conservation had been spread too thinly, obscuring the few truly valuable features within a haze of ill-informed preservationist attitudes. The architect described general public attitudes to the town as 'precious', sentiments that equated with those of many committee members, who were perhaps the most preservation-oriented group in this case:

> [T]he message from the planning officers, the Chief Planning Officer, the conservation officer and even English Heritage was very much contemporary development and not sort of twee pastiche. I think the committee members, as [are] many members of the public, are very nervous about [the] design; I think that's a general cultural issue which is prevalent within a town such as this.

Certainly a desire for harmony and continuity in the town's appearance seemed to stimulate most public objections over this design.

Replication and over-familiarity?

The listed buildings on-site were perceived by the applicant and architect to possess little of interest. While the poor state of repair was influential, they questioned these features' architectural justification for listing: the former hostel was seen as one of many standard Victorian designs – the minor interest in its carved stonework alone was not sufficiently impressive to retain the whole.

Visually these properties were considered very ordinary, maybe expendable, especially in the applicants' vision to complete their William and Mary-style head office. In terms of townscape, most people considered that this extension would provide a more impressive gateway for approaching the town from West Bridge. Even the TCRA considered that the former hostel's relocation from 'an incongruous site' to a more suitable setting on a quieter street was an improvement. Anomalously, one local group noted that because the building was 'early Victorian rather than anything older', its relocation was of minor significance. Support for the aesthetic merits of its relocation contrasted sharply with retaining its authentic value *in situ*.

The historical value of the listed buildings was also open to question. Few people expressed any interest in their history. This is surprising, considering that they were the last remnants reflecting the previous character of the area, one being a former school. In fact, the development parties viewed such historical aspects pejoratively, perceiving that conservation areas protected things simply 'because they are old'. One planning officer noted the historic interest of the former residential properties illustrating the town's development and the previous inhabitants' living conditions. However, this was a lone opinion in contrast with the predominant view in the planning service, which considered that these features' value lay mainly in their contribution to the street scene.

Admittedly, these grade II buildings are not significant landmarks, but their familiarity, rather than fostering ties of attachment and identity with the town, appeared to count against their positive evaluation. The relative ubiquity of such small Victorian buildings in the town seemed to undermine the significance people attached to them. The grander, older listed buildings overshadowed appreciation of these minor ones, outstripping any consideration of their 'national interest'; for these buildings that phrase appeared vacuous and derisory.

As mentioned above, DC was eager to encourage contemporary design in the town; officers were 'fed up with dealing with pastiche buildings':

> [O]nce you get a modern building sitting next to [those listed buildings] I think there will be an interesting juxtaposition between the two. It's an interesting record of the sort of scale: that's what was there and this is what we've allowed – bigger, bolder – that's important, I think.

Whereas the architects attempted to contextualise the design by taking cues from forms and materials further up this street, most lay observers objected to these inappropriate aspects. A local residents' association member noted of the design:

> [T]here's an awful lot of glass; the fenestration doesn't make sense to me, it's totally out of keeping with any of the buildings in [the town]. . . . Everybody who has any feelings about [the town] agrees that it's wrong, it doesn't look right.

He maintained that the other developments on-site along the riverfront had all blended nicely into the fabric of the town (despite two of the three being conversions of existing buildings):

> The style of them, the fenestration, is not so far removed from eighteenth- and nineteenth-century buildings, nice proportions that we like, that are acceptable. . . . You can argue, "Oh we must have some modern buildings", but I don't see why.

Not only did lay comments concern its design but they also concerned the materials and scale. The building stuck out, not only physically but also in its perceived character. Members were concerned that the building's white render finish was not in keeping with the predominantly 'red-brick' character of the area. Although there were concessions over these points and the committee chair considered that they had got the balance about right, other members believed that just tweaking minor details and changing its external finish did little to mitigate the building's overall impact.

Driving their objections was a notable concern among committee members not to replicate the mistakes made in the 1960s in allowing stark new designs. Though members felt a moral compulsion to protect the town, their unease also revealed a notable humility about their competence to evaluate design issues. As officers noted, the design was 'far too adventurous for the members. It was clear at an early stage that we were going to have problems with the members and we did: they just totally failed to grasp it at all.' Parties outside the authority were particularly disgruntled by members' extensive involvement:

> You end up with a number of schoolteachers, shoe shop owners, retired people, choosing the bricks without any architectural training at all. . . . I mean, that has to be an argument for requiring professional councillors' advice . . . that's conservation area planning gone berserk.

The fact that there are conflicting opinions about the design highlights two things: first, from the professionals' point of view, it challenges the compatibility of public participation in design matters; second, from the public's perspective, it illustrates that there is a gulf between lay appreciation and the perceived esoteric world of architectural debate. The accumulation of these factors means that new design becomes harder to pass through committee. The potential for juxtaposition and contrast within the urban context is reduced as a more familiar and established aesthetic is preferred, to co-ordinate elements.

Local political and economic factors

While the local planning authority retains statutory responsibility for conservation, the development parties viewed a conservation ethos as essential to their operations, albeit for different reasons. The applicant appreciated working with the craftsmanship and good-quality materials in historic buildings, qualities frequently absent in contemporary buildings. These inherent qualities, in terms of design and construction, meant not only that building professionals respected the building, but also that these qualities added value to the product. Any market operator would wish to enhance these qualities irrespective of local authority intervention. In contrast, the architect noted that conservation regulation was essential, since otherwise 'everybody would be just block building with no windows because it's nice and cheap with lots of space'. The brief for this new building was no exception, requiring a certain amount of floor space irrespective of specifying a particular look.

That office vacancy rates in the town centre were particularly high and set to increase made the applicants' search for a tenant all the more challenging. They felt hampered by the council's alleged lack of a long-term economic vision for the town. The architect too noted that the town's future rested entirely on developers' unilateral proposals rather than the authority's strategic vision for the town's economy. To external parties, the local plan was not perceived to perform this role. Time and again the town was compared to its larger urban neighbours, whose authorities appeared more dynamic in pursuing specific enhancement strategies. The authority was parodied for believing development was something that happened elsewhere, not in its historic centre.

Similarly, it was apparent to parties outside the authority that there was no corporate approach to conservation in the council. The preferences of the Planning Committee tended towards 'prettiness', and conservation appeared restricted by this orientation. Most respondents, bar those holding political posts, observed a small-town, parochial mentality prevalent in local politics: '[W]e find that it's not the local authority which leads, which sets the parameters, which sets the style if you like – it tends to be the Planning Committee members.' However, members gave the impression that they were willing to be led through design issues as they were conscious of their own lack of design training. Generally, they would defer to greater architectural knowledge unless they were emphatically opposed to an application – probably those cases of a more progressive or modern design. Here, lessening the visual impact of the new development was considered paramount. The conservation section found this particularly frustrating:

> I would have had it referred [to CABE] because I do think it is difficult in a parochial situation to make judgements about buildings like this because you've got members who don't understand the architectural philosophy and you do need a third opinion, a better opinion from outside the town rather than from in-house because the political lobbying and so on tends to cloud aesthetic impact and knocks the edge off the design.

But is it just a case of political lobbying diluting the design or does it reveal greater unease about how the council wishes to use conservation resources to portray the town? The tendency towards 'safer' architecture provides a template which is easier for developers to exploit in driving through quick planning permissions. It is precisely this conformity that the professionals wish to move away from.

The Annexe

A summary of the development

Background

The Annexe is a large, three-storey Georgian town house, grade II* listed. A fairly inauspicious-looking building from the road, it has suffered a series of unsympathetic alterations over the years, the most recent being a side extension with an uncharacteristic mansard roof. In contrast, the garden elevation has retained most of its original character and charm. The interior is the real star and the reason for its grade II* status, exhibiting exquisite eighteenth-century decorative plasterwork throughout the reception rooms. The property has been a hotel for the past 25 years and the current owner purchased it in 1995; it is also his home.

Because it has only 11 rooms, the current owner wanted to expand the accommodation, which, judging by the number of previously approved extensions, would not appear to be a problem. Some planning permissions remained unimplemented, such as a still active permission from 1993 allowing a two-storey rear extension on to the hotel. Though this was unsuitable for his business vision, his plans were dramatically influenced by an impending regeneration scheme for the area around the hotel.

The hotel is located on a narrow street off one of the main roads through the town centre, leading down to the river. However, despite the presence of other listed buildings nearby and the fact that it is within the central conservation area, the immediate vicinity appears quite down at heel, largely following the relocation of a local car firm, which still owns most of the surrounding land, complete with deteriorating warehouses and garages.

The car firm had entered into partnership with the council with a view to implementing a regeneration scheme for the area, providing 90 new houses and flats. A new road would serve the development and relieve a congested section of the road approaching East Bridge. The authority was hoping to blend in the new buildings with the surrounding historic fabric, maintaining a distinctly urban feel by utilising a three-storey terrace design.

The hotelier supported this long-overdue improvement to the area, though he only became aware of its scale and proximity when he approached the authority to discuss building further hotel accommodation in his rear garden. The proposed new two- and three-storey terraces of the regeneration scheme would surround the hotel on three sides, coming to within 1.5 m of its gables. The prospect of being so overlooked robbed the hotel garden of its amenity and so he considered a more intensive development at the rear.

Pre-submission negotiations

In May 1997 the hotelier submitted a proposal for new accommodation comprising 40 bedrooms in a four-storey block. The footprint covered the entire garden and was actually larger than the main listed building. While the designer did not respect the hotel's exterior, because he saw the 'importance of the building [as lying] in the internal plasterwork', unsurprisingly the planning officer considered that the style, size and scale were gravely flawed. Despite a swift revision to a scaled-down 24-bedroom annexe over three floors, the authority responded similarly:

> [T]he unanimous opinion is that there would be a presumption against any large-scale extension to the property. It is considered that ideally there should be no development within the rear gardens as this space is of great significance to the setting of the listed building and offers a pleasant green space within the conservation area. You are at liberty to consider a minor small-scale, single-storey extension.

Relations between the applicant and the authority appeared soured by the scale of these initial proposals, and the applicant instructed new agents, a local private planning consultant. Ironically, the consultant was formerly a planning officer in the authority and had recommended the hotel's previous permissions.

A series of down-sized applications

By late 1997 the proposed design comprised 21 rooms on three storeys. Planning officers considered it still too large and its mansard roof detailing wholly inappropriate. Undeterred, the applicant canvassed widespread support for the scheme from the local MP, the Chamber of Commerce, the ward councillor and the Civic Society (though the latter subsequently withdrew its support). The authority's own Director of Tourism welcomed the scheme for its provision of budget hotel accommodation in the town centre.

In opposition there were some equally powerful objectors to the scheme. First, the architects commissioned by the car firm to design the regeneration scheme were concerned by the loss of the hotel garden, as their new terrace accommodation 'is carefully grouped to enable the continued benefit to the surrounding occupiers' of a view on to this open green space. This angered the applicant since his own privacy and amenity had not been considered when the authority permitted the regeneration scheme to envelop his hotel. His agent was similarly infuriated as it was treating the hotel's private garden as if it were public space. Second, the Environment Agency was concerned that the new annexe, being so close to the river, was at severe risk of flooding. While the Agency had also objected to the surrounding regeneration scheme on similar grounds, the council considered that the scheme's provision of a relief road through the town was in the public interest and outweighed the flooding concerns.

In January 1998 the Planning Committee rejected the application. The applicant was considering legal action because the council had effectively blighted the enjoyment of his land with its regeneration scheme. Instead, he proposed a smaller design and, following on-site discussions, conservation officers from the authority and EH supported a small-scale development, in principle, to ensure the hotel's commercial survival. A small mews building was suggested as an appropriate historical design precedent.

The new design comprised a two-storey free-standing coach house with 16 bedrooms. The applicant maintained that the development would not be detrimental to the setting of the listed building because the hotel's exterior had already been extensively altered. Despite his impassioned letter to all committee members, the application was refused in April. Planning officers had emphatically stated that 'the erection of any free-standing structure in the rear garden for extra hotel facilities would not be supported in this instance'.

The appeal against refusal

The applicant was perplexed – he had addressed all the authority's concerns and followed EH's advice – yet he considered that the authority remained closed to negotiation. In response to the appeal, the council restated its reasons for refusal:

[I]t is unsatisfactory in that the location, scale, height and design of the proposed building are detrimental to the character and appearance of the [central] conservation area and the character and setting of this important grade II* listed building. . . .

[I]t is unsatisfactory in that it is located in an area liable to flooding and will have an adverse effect on flood storage capacity in the area. . . .

[I]t would represent an incursion into the new urban space created by the new development approved on the adjoining land, constituting an obtrusive feature within that space, and harming the outlook from the residential properties within that development.

The council contended that the central conservation area was 'outstanding' and that the grade II* hotel, though externally altered, still possessed significant interest to over-ride the uncomplimentary style of the proposed annexe. The council also argued that it was desirable to retain the open garden space to offset the density of the surrounding regeneration development. The flooding argument was further emphasised since the Environment Agency had become more agitated following serious flooding throughout the Midlands that year.

The agents argued that the setting had been compromised already by dereliction in the surrounding area. Furthermore, since the regeneration scheme itself would dramatically affect the setting of the listed building and character of the area, neither the existing nor the anticipated 'setting' or 'character' could be used to gauge the annexe's impact. Similarly, to refuse the application on a flood risk argument seemed disproportionate in comparison with the greater flood risk waived for the regeneration scheme's 90 dwelling units.

The inspector found in favour of the council, mainly because the development would adversely affect the setting of a listed building and the character of the conservation area. The design was not of a sufficiently high quality; its styling paid 'little respect to the traditional detailing of the listed building and would have the appearance of a large structure unrelated to the character and appearance of the hotel'. Although local plan policy favoured the retention of open space in the town centre, the inspector noted that the loss of the garden and its effect on prospective neighbours' amenity could not be a legitimate consideration because the regeneration scheme had not been approved. The inspector supported council policy on the flooding issue: there was no ulterior benefit in this application to deflect strong environmental objections.

Despite the applicant's losing the appeal, the inspector had given the applicant some grounds for believing that a smaller development and more appropriate design respecting the listed building and conservation area might be possible under local planning policy. At the time of fieldwork, a smaller 10-bedroom, two-storey mews-type development was on the drawing board.

Attitudes to conservation illustrated in this case

Planning or conservation priorities for regeneration?

While there was a difference of opinion between conservation and DC sections in this case, surprisingly the latter was the more conservationist of the two. DC wished to restrict further building in this vicinity for fear of over-development: '[N]one of us thought there should be a building in the back garden.' Conservation policy provided a convenient justification for this restriction, but in the light of the surrounding regeneration scheme, were conservation issues being manipulated to ensure the success of that scheme? The conservation section was more willing to compromise to enable the hotelier to continue in business, but personal circumstances cannot be legitimate planning considerations.

Despite the immediate area's run-down appearance – one officer described it as 'bloody awful' – the authority appeared to consider its amenity and the annexe's impact on the conservation area almost as if the regeneration scheme was physically complete. The authority stated that the viability of this scheme was not the main reason for refusing the annexe, but it seems anomalous.

The contrast between the arguments for the protection of either the setting or the intrinsic merit of the listed building also raised questions. Although it was grade II* listed for its impressive interior, DC officers were correct to follow PPG15, treating it as an integral whole: '[I]t doesn't matter why it's II* – it is grade II*; that's it. Anything that took away from the character or setting or fabric of the listed building was not going to be acceptable.' Protecting the building irrespective of the variation between its fabulous interior and mediocre exterior proved difficult for the applicant to accept. He did not mind the physical proximity of the regeneration scheme's new terraces as they did not actually touch the hotel. However, he could not comprehend how the authority could consider that the setting of his listed building was not affected by this regeneration scheme, yet his own annexe 16 m from the hotel was considered so detrimental to the same setting. Similarly, he could not understand why the authority had granted previous applications for extensions to the hotel building itself which had radically altered its appearance, yet his wholly separate annexe was considered too intrusive.

A further contradiction arises between regeneration and preservation objectives. The applicant considered that although there were several neglected listed buildings in town, the majority were so evidently valuable that no one would consider demolishing them. Conservation areas in contrast he saw as a superfluous imposition which served only to restrict development, particularly in the run-down areas of town which needed improving.

Inside out: appreciating interest and value

The hotel itself forces an examination of the conventional perspective of listing value; externally it is unremarkable, yet the internal features are a revelation. Those with access to the property or who know about the decorative plasterwork may have a totally different affection for the building. Indeed, the owner considered that he was merely looking after these features and could never contemplate altering them.

Although planning officers considered that respect for the setting of the listed building was more important than the character of the conservation area, most respondents did not consider the building externally to be anything special and certainly not a grade II*. If the building lacked such external aesthetic merit, the validity of protecting its setting is questionable.

Such feelings towards the building may reflect the notion that conservation requires special qualities to gain people's support. Familiarity in this instance counted for little; it was not a landmark building like many other grade II* features in the town. Certainly the building received little wider attention, the agent noting, '[I]t's got to be something major before the [public] start jumping up and down.'

The design of the new annexe proved unacceptable to all officers. However, it may be no surprise when the applicant was more concerned about obtaining the planning permission than about satisfying a particular aesthetic. He believed that if the planning authority was so concerned about its appearance, it should have stipulated a satisfactory design from the outset – a hypothetical requirement that would infuriate private architects!

The agent lamented a further wasted opportunity to make a contemporary contribution to the urban fabric with the surrounding scheme. In contrast to the preference of the authority and EH for a small mews development, the agent considered this totally inappropriate:

> I still think that we do tend to take the easy option and copy rather than innovate or design. . . . I think it's more difficult to be innovative in a conservation situation . . . all right, it fits in but . . . the system I suppose forces [planners] to go for the simple route.

In attempting to replicate features of the surrounding area, the details of the building were far from true to its functions. Even in the new, post-appeal design, a DC officer had suggested an arch detail in the brickwork, which the agent thought illustrated how:

> conservation has become just really a copying of the best of the past and not relating it to its proper function. There's no need for that arch. You know

in three hundred years' time somebody looking at that building is going to be thinking, 'what's that arch there for?'

The main criticism levelled at local conservation practice was that the authority had no courage in 'imposing our particular stamp' on the town. In contrast with the progression of historical styles characterising the central conservation area, even with many contributions from the 1960s and 1970s, there is no representation of contemporary buildings over the past 20 years. As the agent noted, '[W]e are leaving it to the next generation to decide what they want to do with it.'

The regeneration scheme: a larger economic and political picture

The pressure to redevelop this particular area and the council's interest in securing a regeneration partnership were perceived by some respondents to influence the council's approach and cast a shadow over the way it dealt with the proposals for the hotel annexe. The local car firm behind the regeneration scheme might be relatively stronger from a commercial point of view, but, irrespective of this, the applicant did not enjoy particularly warm relations with the authority. His initial attempt to maximise the development's size and the disregard of conservation constraints appeared to set a negative framework for the ensuing discussions. He believed that the council's restrictive interpretation of conservation was not operating in such a way as to attract further investment in the town centre.

The case certainly highlighted tensions in applying council policy regarding town centre investment and retaining historic fabric. Some respondents noted that the refusal of the annexe application had become a politicised matter as the development could disrupt the regeneration scheme, to which the authority had significant commitment. Unfortunately, this led to accusations that the authority lacked impartiality in considering the application. There appeared to be different standards applied regarding the flood risk to the regeneration scheme on the one hand and the annexe application on the other, but the planning inspector vindicated the authority's approach.

As regards representing the democratic interest, the applicant believed the committee members were weak and ineffectual in this case, providing little critical scrutiny or opposition to the authority's officers. Members were not very progressive when it came to new development in the town centre and criticisms of advocating neo-Georgian pastiche designs were encountered once again. For parties outside the authority, the case seemed to occlude any transparency in local decision-making; '[T]hey just shelter behind the local plan because it's simpler, making the local plan the material consideration.'

The Gardens

A summary of the development

Background

The property lies in the middle of a grade II listed Georgian terrace in a quiet residential street. While lying outside the river loop of the town centre, the street still falls within the central conservation area, which has been extended to encompass the nearby abbey and its former grounds.

Although the house in question had lain empty for some time and was in need of extensive modernisation, it still proved an attractive purchase for a local estate agent, who privately renovated and resold the property. Its poor state of repair provided an opportunity for the agent to remove the old extension and enlarge the ground-floor living space. He proposed removing the existing external rear wall, containing a Georgian sash window, and building a new, larger extension across the whole width of the rear yard.

This would not be so controversial but for the fact that each property in the terrace has an outrigger extension at the rear which covers half the rear yard and gives a symmetry along the length of the terrace while visually separating the individual properties. Those adjacent to the property in question have single-storey extensions, rising to two-storey extensions further up the street. Although the majority are contemporaneous with the terrace, one or two are post-war additions.

Initially the authority was reluctant to grant listed building consent since the scheme involved too great a loss of historic fabric. Neighbours were also concerned and several wrote letters to the authority:

> The proposed development would not conform to this pattern [of outriggers in the terrace]. It would fill this adjacent yard and would, I believe, alter the nature of the terrace when viewed from the rear. I am unaware of the reason for the designation of the conservation area but I believe that the form and scale of the proposed development would be out of sympathy with the existing property and the appearance of the listed terrace.

Other neighbours were concerned about the adverse effects of such minor changes in the area: '[O]ne only has to walk around the corner . . . to see how an unsympathetic extension to the side of the terrace will offend discerning eyes for generations'. Other sentiments highlighted how the proposal contradicted the convention of respecting the whole terrace:

> As the terrace is grade II listed it would be true to say that the existing resi-dents have all tried to keep any changes to their properties within the keeping

and spirit of the original design. . . . For those of us who have tried to remain faithful to keeping the houses as near as possible to their original intent, this proposal is a poor piece of design which we feel would not do justice to this fine Georgian terrace.

Though the authority was considering refusing the application, the applicant revised the design following negotiations with the conservation section. Minimising alterations to the rear wall and retaining the original window would satisfy the authority over the loss of historic fabric. Introducing glazing into the new roof over the former yard below could reflect the fact that it had previously been an open space, but the proposal still built across the whole yard. The neighbours did not share the authority's placability and felt that none of their previous objections had been answered:

It remains a substantial brick-built extension covering the full width of the property and with a substantial roof, albeit with a skylight. If the original proposal was not in keeping with the dwelling's listed building status for these reasons, then the revised plans do not address this concern.

However, in recommending approval to committee, DC stated that because the site was not visible from the road, '[t]he proposed extension is not considered detrimental to the character of the listed building. Other properties in this terrace have extensions in the rear yards, less sympathetic than this one now proposed.' The street façade was considered the 'most important' elevation and the authority did not concur with the neighbours' continuing objections. After approval in July 1998, the building works were completed and the property sold by the end of the year. Seeing the finished article, neighbours felt that their objections were well founded. Although the extension is competently executed in the correct materials, it breaks the scale and symmetry of the terrace's rear elevation, thereby setting a precedent for further disruptions to the historic pattern.

Attitudes to conservation illustrated in this case

Planning for conservation areas and neighbourhood protection

Most of the applicant's dealings with the authority were through the conservation section. While an expert is required to consider the proposals to a listed building, there is a risk that other planning officers perceive conservation as just dealing with issues concerning small-scale, minor developments in highly specific circumstances.

The scope of the external alterations polarised opinion. As it was located in a listed terrace, respecting the building's fabric was essential, yet various parties held different interpretations of the qualities of the surrounding area. The applicant considered that it was a desirable area in which to live, though this was largely due to the impressive façades of the terrace's elegant streetscape. However, local residents offered a more holistic view, considering that protecting the rear of the properties was equally important in respecting the character of the conservation area.

The negotiations between the authority and the applicant led to accusations of the conservation section being incredibly 'wishy-washy' in protecting the terrace and conservation area. One local resident commented on their previous experience dealing with the authority: '[W]e could have built Disneyland out the back there and they would have never come back to check.' He also noted that there appeared to be little urgency or coercion used to support the essential conservation controls in the area. In fact, most parties, even the applicant, were surprised about how far the extension was permitted to encroach over the rear yard, thus disrupting the historic pattern.

This upset neighbours, who had retained period features and detailing on their own properties out of a sense of respect not only for their present enjoyment but also for the buildings and their future occupiers. From their letters to the council it is apparent that they had a good command of the relevant planning terms, which surely strengthened their arguments. Although conservation controls had not restricted their household improvements, conservation appeared to possess insufficient mettle to subject a commercial developer to the same controls, when required. In contrast, the applicant stated his support for conservation; however, he railed against the 'fanatical' preservation lobby in contrast with the more 'practical' and realistic approach he encountered at the authority.

A significant local attachment to historic features

All respondents considered that the need to protect the front of the terrace was incontrovertible. For the applicant, the street elevation was the main selling point of the property and it clearly had architectural merit, which alone generated a sense of responsibility for its protection.

Neighbours stressed that they were not against a modern extension to the rear of the house. In fact, they had liked a modern extension built further up the terrace, but the proposal in question was a hybrid of traditional materials in a bland, functional design. The applicant admitted that his interest focused on the internal rather than the external aesthetics. He believed that the rear elevation 'was not something that people would be particularly concerned about; it's not something people sit and look at'.

It would appear that the extent and accessibility of the public gaze does influence, or at least can be used to justify or deflect criticisms of, these more extensive works. Neighbours were frustrated with the authority because they felt that the symmetry of the backs was an essential part of the terrace and, moreover, the character of the conservation area. Despite its not being visible from the street, they argued that conservation area protection ought to encompass all aspects of the area.

Local residents' opinions contrasted with the professionals' not only over the contribution of the terrace to the conservation area but also in the higher level of quality they wished to apply to alterations in the area. They were disappointed by the official line, noting that there was no encouragement from the authorities to become interested in conservation: '[M]aybe we're our own worst enemies in a way as we're so passive about it [the historic environment] and take a lot of it for granted.'

While the applicant considered conservation to be related solely to the architectural interest of buildings, the neighbours perceived their properties rather more as reflections of previous users and uses. They highlighted tiny features in the buildings, for example a name and nineteenth-century date scratched on the window: 'I mean it's neither here nor there but in a sense it gives a connection with history.' Equally, the historic interest of the buildings in the town's development provided a tangible and visible 'passage through time' which interested them. Moreover, they felt that the local authority had not respected these qualities in recent developments in the town. Concentrating on the economic functioning of the town had left the town's unique historical qualities neglected and underappreciated. In contrast, the applicant was less persuaded by the temporal value of the features and dismissed the argument of respecting the fabric for posterity as being too abstract for building practice.

The price of conformity

The economic incentive to obtain the house and renovate it is testament to the desirability and the proven saleability of listed property in this residential area. The period features, while perhaps worth maintaining for their intrinsic value, lend status, character and individualism and can add to the house price. However, the features must look impressive and aesthetically pleasing to have this effect; their historic authenticity is less vital.

Concluding observations from the case study

The nature of conservation planning

Consolidated conservation activity within planning practice planning

Conservation appears to enjoy a good standing within the planning service – its ethos evidently having percolated through DC operations and officers' attitudes.

Indeed, most officers perceive conservation to be more than a statutory responsibility – though in this sense conservation is not 'separate' or 'special': it is viewed as an essential planning activity in the town. This climate of formal policy and practitioners' support for conservation (and applicants' realisation of this culture) engenders greater acceptance of the higher standards demanded by the authority over development in the town.

However, despite general support and frequent convergence of officers' views, the conservation culture of the authority is distinctly influenced by the personalities involved and their interpretations of conservation's role. The conservation officer's independence reflects personal priorities but does it also reveal a more significant disparity with planners' perceptions of conservation's role?

Perhaps because the borough is operationally a smaller planning service, the differences of approach between successive conservation officers become more significant. The former conservation officer was more concerned with DC applications and listed building consent work. In contrast, the current officer has a passion for larger restoration and regeneration projects. This approach has to be fitted within the authority's emphasis on ensuring that new development conforms to the policies in the local plan.

This use of conservation perhaps reveals more about the authority's DC section than about conservation itself. Officers in the conservation section considered themselves to be the more proactive of the two sections, whereas DC was arguably seen as an administrative function efficiently processing applications but content to let developers set the agenda.

The difference is reflected in the working relations between DC and conservation. The day-to-day arrangements for obtaining conservation advice were relatively dependent on the discretion of individual DC officers. However, the current conservation officer's autonomy has contributed to a more casual interaction between sections; thus DC officers may have inadvertently found themselves with greater responsibility for determining conservation issues. They may not have considered consultation over smaller issues worthwhile, in which case the conservation section considered it dangerous for planning officers, with only minimal design training, to attempt to second-guess the conservation professionals' response. This created unacceptable situations whereby DC officers might pursue preservationist arguments more dogmatically than conservation principles can sustain.

Environmental context of conservation controls

Several professionals within and outside the authority noted that the borough operated a very traditional approach to conservation of the built environment. Because of the town's 'recognised' historic status, the authority was perceived as perhaps resting on its laurels. Though conservation was considered a 'given', the emphasis in practice was seen to concentrate on attending to listed buildings, with less attention being paid to other components in the urban fabric.

However, developing the role of wider environmental protection was inhibited largely by resource constraints. There are a few conservation area character appraisals covering the town but there are few authority staff with the formal design qualifications to undertake this work. While many planning officers characterised urban design as the uniting discipline between DC and conservation, conservation staff believed they themselves did not have the influence outside their small sphere to promote the need to respect urban design across the council. The prominence of ensuring quality urban design was illustrated in the Terrace and Bank cases. Generally, as with many local authority practices, design training could be more widely encouraged. Conservation and DC are equally concerned with the quality of buildings and places; although urban design could provide a bridging point, it seemed to fall into a gap of recognition between conservation and DC.

In contrast, the county's Environment team was pursuing conservation in the form of environmental management strategies. If there is a preference in the authority for a more traditional conservation role, how far does this inhibit developing a broader perspective to tessellate with this revision in strategic environmental priorities?

Who defines 'acceptable' change

The conservation officer's more flexible approach to determining acceptable change created some tension with other planning officers, who were more familiar with conservation providing definite standards of control – regulating rather than encouraging change in the historic fabric.

The conservation officer distinguished between the 'rottweiler school' of conservation whose confrontational approach towards applicants extended to scrutinising minor details in applications, and his own self-labelled 'progressive', or partnership approach. His flexibility, while achieving success in promoting the re-use of buildings, created some uncertainty for both other planning officers and applicants, who felt that the goalposts were continually shifting in response to specific development pressures.

Within the conservation section itself there were mixed views: some maintained a more principled, traditional approach; others advocated the revitalisation of buildings as their principal goal. Repairing buildings was commendable but finding suitable users for them would ensure their longer-term contribution to the town. This required a more permissive attitude when dealing with more extensive alterations to the historic fabric to accommodate such new uses and users.

Thus although respondents claimed widespread support for conservation in the authority, they were actually promoting distinctly different strands of conservation under the same name, such as in the Annexe case. This split can result in planning officers' reinforcing a restrictive interpretation of conservation in the majority of planning applications where they believe that they can handle the conservation issues themselves.

Perhaps this preference for a more traditional conservation role is reflected in a planning officer's comment that while the RTPI emphasised planning as an 'enabling' service, he felt the local DC function had turned into 'a neighbourhood protection service'. Perhaps planning is just satisfying wider public perceptions of what role conservation ought play in the town?

The basis of conservation's support and legitimacy

Many local residents appear supportive of conservation's contribution to the town, though the reasons usually cited were the maintenance of a particular way of life provided in the centre of town, encouraging high-quality retailing and residential uses. Aside from the evident landmark value of the town's historic buildings, many members supported conservation because the town's historic image was a valuable backdrop attracting residential and commercial users.

A popular concern cited was the perceived 'mistakes' of the 1960s when many prominent old buildings in the town centre were demolished to make way for modern replacements. The shadow of modernism's aspirations for progress appears to hang over the conscience of those residents who remember these changes. For members, this fear of 'improvement' via radical or contemporary designs led many to advocate a conservative approach to conservation's role. Some members viewed planners with a little scepticism; officers were not necessarily local and thus did not care so much about the continuity of the town. Although applicants described this predilection as 'precious' and 'possessive', generally respondents noted that the public did not appear to care a great deal about the built environment and would express an interest only if some important building was demolished. Even in a historic town, the consensus supporting conservation has its limits.

The interpretation of value in the built environment

The interpretation of features' interest

The four development cases predominantly involved the introduction of new elements into the historic townscape, rather than alterations to the historic fabric *per se*. Thus the inferences that can be drawn relate more to existing features' interest in the broader environment, but it is significant that context, over fabric, proved such an emotive factor.

In terms of the balance between architectural and historic interest, most respondents distinguished the town by its mixture of properties from different ages. Generally, the older properties were perceived as the most valued for their age and their survival. Thus the medieval remains were more prized than the Georgian properties, while the value of the 'more recent' Victorian buildings remained a little eclipsed. Buildings' superficial appearance of age, rather than their detailed history, was the more significant factor to those outside the conservation planning discipline.

Generally, the appearance of the town rather than its structural fabric was the paramount concern. The views of the town, while comprising buildings, involved more than simply acknowledging the architecture of its constituent parts. The more that protecting views is emphasised over protecting buildings, the less adequately do individual listed building consents appear to address this more holistic idea of conserving the town. While conservation area character appraisals would have assisted enormously in this exposition of value, not enough had been undertaken.

However, there is a tension between protecting the appearance of the town and the interpretation of character in this process. Ironically, some DC officers considered that certain areas' character was so obvious that it obviated the need for any formal appraisal. For them, an area's character was defined by the predominant style of buildings within a defined location. While architecture does contribute to character, there is a gamut of wider factors contributing to the broader environmental context. The development cases in particular showed that acceptable new design had reflected a preference for Georgian architecture – it fitted in with the predominant building style but neglected the areas' character, which includes not only a diversity of building styles, but urban spaces, functions and general morphology.

This is particularly difficult given DC officers' enthusiasm for promoting new architecture in the town, but this enthusiasm did not seem to be particularly well communicated to the wider world, as some local architects remained sceptical of the authority's ability to ensure high-quality new development in the town.

Local interest appears to create the national interest

Local interest in the town is perceived as sufficient to warrant the town's attention nationally as one of *the* historic towns. Local character is highly regarded by many respondents, in contrast to the industrial town studied in chapter 5, where the inherent quality of local interest was viewed with some scepticism. Structure Plan policies to protect the significant views and skyline of the town (rather than any specific buildings) emphasise the regional significance of the town's character. In fact, it is difficult to perceive a distinction in attitudes towards the more prominent listed buildings since the widespread local interest in them is taken as evidence that these features ought to be nationally respected.

The physical presence of more modest listed buildings appears to carry little public appreciation. In a town with such a wealth of truly impressive buildings, the listed buildings of less obvious quality, even though they may have fine interiors such as the hotel in the Annexe case, are more likely to remain unrecognised and, like the former hostel in the Bank case, taken for granted. Features require special and distinctive aspects, usually aesthetic ones, to raise awareness among the public and to alter the attitude of those parties involved with that building.

An inversion of norms in professionals' values

In the authority there can be as significant a distinction between officers' professional views as there is between the professionals' view and that of the lay public. A loose distinction between professional approaches could be described as one being an academic interest largely concerned with the formal aesthetic and architectural value of buildings, contrasting with one seeing conservation as a 'craft', oriented to the integrity of the structure and its technical construction.

Evidently, personal interpretations are highly influential, especially given the small size of the planning service. It is curious that with an apparent increase of conservation specialisation, professionals' advice became more tolerant of change. The DC officers maintained a fairly traditional interpretation of the values which conservation should be protecting, the conservation officer took a more tolerant view of change and, further still, EH had actively encouraged change in the environment. Expectations of professional opinions had almost become wholly inverted.

Turning to the public's expressions of value, from the development cases there was certainly no shortage of opinions expressed, albeit by a vociferous minority. However, while members of the public may have considered that they were contributing their popular interest in conservation, many professionals bemoaned the lack of public debate over conservation's contribution to the town's future. It was generally perceived that to the public, conservation meant replication, whereas the professionals involved with conservation were attempting more innovative approaches to development.

Public comments tended to display a broader consideration of conservation as a means to retain particular uses and functions in the town by maintaining the buildings which housed them. Thus rather than a design matter, conservation was only a means to an end. In contrast, there was a general sentiment from the planning authority that the value of consultation was undermined when unrepresentative swathes of the public responded with idealistic comments. This has grave implications if the public's comments are considered to be irrelevant.

Contrast and replication: aspects of heritage valuation

Perhaps most significant was the distinction between the design preferences of professionals, who wished to encourage a move away from new developments' ubiquitous historicist design, and the lay public, who preferred this style since it fitted into the town better than strident contemporary design.

Professionals cited the variety and contrast of the different architectural periods as one of the town's main defining characteristics: it was a quality in itself worth recognising. However, it is incongruous that one of the strongest criticisms levelled at the authority was its tendency to permit homogeneous new design in the town. The prevalence of a particular retrospective style for many new additions in the town would appear contradictory and counterproductive. The nature of contextual design as interpreted by council members, rather than planning officers, was a preference for familiar, usually Georgian, aspects of the town.

However, the reason for this preference constantly returns to the town's experience of 1960s development. Many timber-frame buildings, and neo-classical and Victorian public buildings were replaced with examples of modern architecture that produced a stark contrast in the town centre. Despite winning recommendations and awards at the time, today these buildings are loathed and cited as the worst abuses to the urban fabric. The fear of repeating such mistakes in the name of progress appears to have paralysed debate over contemporary design in the town. Many design professionals consider that their generation has contributed nothing to the town centre and several consider that caution will prevent the town ever being able to boast any future listed buildings from the late twentieth century.

Furthermore, there would appear to be a generational aspect to this concern. Those over 50, who are more likely to have witnessed the 1960s alterations, were profoundly affected by memories of the features that had been lost; those under 45, with no recollection of the previous townscape, were less hesitant to endorse overtly contemporary additions.

The influence of external pressures

Economic trading on the historic imagery

There was a perception among respondents outside the authority that the planning service was not particularly dynamic in encouraging or influencing economic/

business development in the town. In the face of competition from other local towns, there were concerns that the town could lose essential retailing and commercial services. Conservation was not necessarily an obstacle in itself, though in contrast with other historic towns, for instance Chester, conservation was not perceived as contributing to a more progressive vision for investment in the town. To local businesses, the authority appeared to have failed to generate coherence between important functions – namely planning, economic development, tourism and leisure – which are all closely linked in a historic town.

In the development cases, historic features represented a very saleable asset. However, conflict arises when applicants or users only need to retain a few, more visible historic features to realise the economic value of the heritage. Yet despite the capacity to trade off historic status, many respondents felt that the authority could learn from other historic towns which maintained an almost recession-proof reliance on tourism and high-value, small-volume retailers. Neither the town's economy nor the authority's budget could support the current level of conservation measures without external assistance. It was a worry that EH's HERS funding may no longer be available as its priorities were targeted at improving problems of economic stagnation, which did not really occur to any great extent in a traditional historic town. With a relatively small local authority conservation budget, it was feared that conservation funding from national sources would fall through the gaps left in the absence of grant subsidy and the town's economic buoyancy.

Conservation on the political wane

While the political support for a traditional conservation role appeared to be reasonably healthy among members, it would appear that conservation had lost ground over the past 15 years to other policy priorities. This could be explained by the authority's relatively early boom in conservation activity having targeted the main priorities. Subsequent politicians had seen these tasks accomplished and the impetus had naturally waned. However, many respondents noted that the borough was resting on its laurels.

Certainly this effect was reflected in county council priorities, which had retreated to the margins of built environment conservation, their focus now predominantly being driven by sustainability and Local Agenda 21 policies. With less strategic lead from the county, the borough upheld the local plan policies and responded to development proposals accordingly. However, in parochial small-town politics, if formal support is not necessarily forthcoming, then conservation cannot afford to pass by opportunities to win friends and influence as wide a circle as possible. Indeed, one of the conservation officer's roles was attempting to lobby for greater influence.

Significant issues raised by this case study

The two local planning authority case studies purposely contrasted two urban contexts for the implementation of national conservation policy. Some of the tentative conclusions from the study of the metropolitan borough council are replicated in the experiences highlighted here, while other aspects provide a distinct contrast.

- Conservation's moral weight appeared to be endemic in thinking throughout the planning service and also among most external respondents.
- Conservation was essential to planning largely because of the town's historic status, rather than because of any special awareness created by the presence of a distinct administrative arrangement for conservation controls.
- The duty to respect the context of this historic town often meant there was a greater correspondence between the views of the DC officers and the conservation officer.
- There were a variety of interpretations of the role conservation should play, depending on the beliefs of certain influential individuals.
- The conservation officer was attempting to encourage a more regeneration-oriented approach to conservation, entertaining a flexible approach to allowing change in buildings' fabric.
- In contrast, the DC section could argue a more preservationist line, fulfilling the authority's and public's expectations of a more traditional role of protecting the historic fabric in the town.
- While the service lacks area-based management strategies, conservation arguments are most incisive over the protection of the general appearance of the town in terms of townscape; the public certainly backed these arguments.
- Unpicking local interest from the national interest proved particularly difficult as those features of greater local renown, by virtue of the town's historic status, were also considered of importance to the nation.
- In contrast to the intensity of grade I and II* historic buildings, more recent or modest local/familiar grade II listed buildings appear relatively unloved.
- There was a general public preference for new development to fit in and harmonise with the existing surroundings, for fear of replicating the contrasting developments of the 1960s.
- While harmony of style was seen as a characteristic by lay observers, most design professionals in the town lamented the proliferation of new buildings' historicist designs; they saw the town's diversity of buildings as a positive characteristic in itself.
- Conservation activities were more closely linked to satisfying economic development objectives for the town, thus fulfilling the authority's wider goals and potentially achieving more political support.

- A perception remained that conservation was losing out at a strategic level to the increasing emphasis on sustainability and LA21 initiatives.

Part II has presented all the evidence from the national interview survey and the two case studies. So far, each sphere has been treated almost as a separate entity but the real interest lies in their comparison, looking at where there is overlap and agreement or tensions and divergence. Part III collates and dissects the findings in detail, analysing the salient issues on the basis of themes identified in chapter 3.

PART III

Challenges to conservation

'[S]ocial science is afflicted by double jeopardy – damned for stating the obvious when its findings support conventional wisdom, condemned for being political when they do not.'

Gordon Marshall, Chief Executive of the ESRC
(quoted in Richards 2000)

7 Making the connections

Introduction

Much of the literature on conservation planning suffers from not having linked the minutiae of practice with broader issues in terms of either wider social agendas or longer-term strategic objectives. In response, this study has specifically addressed these criticisms by investigating policy and practice at both the national and the local level. This chapter dissects the evidence from the national interview survey and the two local planning authority case studies and discusses the findings in relation to the thematic framework. The emerging outcomes challenge many of the existing assumptions made about conservation practice and the justificatory norms supporting it.

Before embarking on this analysis, two caveats ought to be raised. Throughout the study the thematic framework has provided a robust, and yet flexible, theoretical and methodological tool to approach a diversity of issues in conservation. But as the framework is dependent on those issues raised in the conservation literature, there is a risk of reinforcing these themes without being fully aware of others that are important in practice.

Few other studies have attempted this comparison between national and local policy and practice. While the three areas of qualitative investigation will not necessarily represent the whole of conservation practice, the relationships highlighted will have broader application. The important issue is to identify issues rather than clarifying their definition across a much broader substantive base. It is recognised that with a shifting policy culture and continual revisions to the structure of local governance, the findings can only ever attempt to convey a snapshot of the values underpinning conservation. The empirical evidence does now represent a more historical than wholly contemporaneous picture of how these fields, people, practices and organisations have subsequently evolved, but as so few studies have attempted to compare these relationships, the accumulated material paints a rare picture.

The relationship between conservation and statutory planning

Summary of findings

The national interview survey reveals contradictory perceptions of the relationship between conservation and statutory planning. In principle, conservation was perceived as being central to any system of land-use regulation. However, this perception was not accompanied by a corresponding desire to further integrate

No. 1 Poultry, London: years of legal wrangling concluded in a new James Stirling building rising from the rubble of the former eight listed buildings conservation controls into the planning process. Rather, the majority view, particularly in regard to listing, was that the separate identification and management systems highlighted the special, and almost morally superior, qualities of conservation. Without such distinction, conservation would be lost in a medley of 'mere' planning issues. By implication, planning was an inappropriate mechanism in terms of the extent and scale of available controls and the shorter timescale over which it considered land-use changes.

Most respondents said it was preferable for local authorities to have a dedicated team of conservation specialists, though it was widely noted that this too created potential marginalisation and conflict with other officers. In contrast, the representatives of more planning-oriented organisations emphasised that conservation was one of planning's 'key roles' as it concerned townscape and urban design and, more generally, environmental protection.

Neither local planning authority had made conservation wholly central in its planning service. In the metropolitan council (chapter 5), it appeared that the separate conservation section was becoming marginalised: the diminishing C&D staff meant fewer conservation contributions at a strategic level and increased responsibility on the part of the DC officers for conservation decision-making, particularly for developments in conservation areas. For DC officers, conservation was not seen as any more 'special' than any other issue. These changes follow the political view of conservation as restricting vital economic redevelopment in the town itself. Although C&D's standing in the planning service may have been reduced, the section was often described by other planning officers as the 'authority's conscience'. This statement is important, since many planning officers characterised planning as a mechanism to balance competing issues with efficiency; there was no particular moral ethic to planning's framework.

The borough (chapter 6) too had a separate conservation section that could be consulted by the DC section, though – perhaps inevitably in a traditional historic town – recognition of conservation's importance was prevalent throughout the planning service generally. Curiously, there was some scope for inconsistency between conservation and DC sections. In contrast with previous appointees, the current conservation officer was eager to pursue regeneration-oriented project work, encouraging the funding of larger restoration works. Responsibility for handling planning applications involving minor conservation issues and some listed building consent work was left with DC officers. This had the potential for creating anomalies in consent cases whereby DC had inadvertently advocated a more preservationist approach than the conservation officer would have. This potential disparity, with the conservation officer devoting time to priority projects, can affect the time and resources devoted to consent casework.

Discussion and implications

While PPG15 and many of the national respondents emphasised the close rela-tionship between conservation and planning, it appears that those at a local level did not necessarily share this view of proximity. Admittedly, many national respondents were expressing an opinion about the ideal location of conservation within practice and noted that this was often not realised. Significantly, there appeared to be few corresponding initiatives and no great desire to centralise conservation in this way within local authorities' statutory planning practice.

National respondents considered that the separate system for listed building consents emphasised conservation as a special consideration, but local DC officers saw conservation as just one of many competing issues. This is vital since in both authorities, conservation's involvement in a case was often deter-mined by individual DC officers' discretion. Indeed, the extent to which the local planning service must be seen to operate efficiently in applicants' interests could preclude officers from consulting the conservation section, especially as the case could be processed more quickly without their doing so.

Conservation issues, such as altering external features in conservation areas or carrying out minor works to listed buildings, were dealt with by DC officers. Evidently, major works and all applications affecting grade I and II* buildings would still involve the conservation officer, but increasingly DC officers were facing greater responsibility to determine conservation area cases. This was defin-itely the trend in the metropolitan council, where senior managers were encouraging conservation to move towards the type of regeneration-oriented projects which the borough's conservation officer was already pursuing.

It is ironic that in both local authorities control over the minor changes – which cumulatively erode areas' character and kill listed buildings 'by a thou-sand cuts' – was passing out of the hands of the specialist, despite this being the area in which conservation protection was felt to be weakest. If planning officers have the necessary urban design skills and townscape awareness to deal with these concerns, then no problem arises. However, the case studies high-lighted that planning officers referred applications for specialist conservation advice when they approached the limit of their own architectural or historical knowledge. Unfortunately, this reinforces a perception of statutory conserva-tion as being solely concerned with significant architectural history, usually with regard to a building's physical structure. This relationship will be discussed in the following section. It is restricting the role of conservation in planning to a particularly traditional one, contrary to the contribution envisaged in most recent guidance addressing the impact of both the sustainability and urban renaissance agendas on planning.

The spatial focus of conservation controls

Summary of findings

It is to be expected that at a national level respondents would be more concerned with listing, since the administrative hierarchy pre-determines this focus. The bias is interesting for the relative strength, legitimacy and thus defensibility which listing is perceived to have over conservation areas. Protecting the actual historic fabric of a building and ensuring the high quality of repairs and renewals were of paramount concern – facets which, as outlined above, respondents considered planning could not address. Despite this prime concern, a significant minority considered that the weighting of the protection systems was slightly anomalous. Ideally, areas should receive the most attention, as buildings were only ever components of wider living historic environments. The potential clash between priorities is illustrated in responses to the increasing numbers of listed buildings and conservation areas. The former was universally welcomed as appreciating more recent architecture, while most viewed the latter as local authorities' mis-application of the original concept of the conservation area. Notably, respondents from planning-oriented bodies emphasised conservation areas as an under-appreciated vehicle for townscape and environmental management strategies to complement planning. The question for the case studies was to explore whether the different focus – on protecting buildings or areas – created distinctions in professionals' practice and results.

In the metropolitan council, the organisation of the statutory conservation responsibilities directed C&D's concerns towards advising on listed building consents and the relatively building-oriented work of DC applications. Concentrating on structural detailing appeared to suit the conservation adviser's technical expertise and personal preference. An area approach to conservation tended to be the province of the Implementation section, which operated parallel to the statutory planning process. Cuts in C&D's budget had reduced its capacity to produce supplementary guidance in the form of specific design guides. More importantly, there were few character appraisals across the authority's 50 or so conservation areas. With such incomplete identification of areas' character and DC officers handling all minor conservation applications, there was often a lack of recognition for concepts of area value. A telling illustration was the Yard case, where only EH's support for C&D lent any credibility to upholding the building's legitimate contribution to the area's character. In the case of the Lodge, the surrounding area was considered so bad that many DC officers questioned the value of saving a listed building in this context.

The borough's conservation section was attempting to move away from concentrating on the details of buildings in isolation which neglected the vitality of the wider area. Despite this move, the borough planning service was still viewed externally by some as taking a traditional approach to building conservation. At the time there were only a few comprehensive character appraisals on which to base conservation responses or strategies. Within the authority, there appeared to be complementing professional competencies between conservation and DC. In the Bank and Terrace cases, the over-riding concern was the look of the schemes in context. Such an approach emphasised the link which urban design provides between conservation and planning; however, those few officers with design training considered that the discipline was woefully under-represented within the planning service.

Discussion and implications

It was noted earlier that different countries' approaches to conservation are most readily distinguishable by the relative importance attached to protecting isolated fragments or, alternatively, broader environments. In professionals' perception of the merit and contribution of the English control processes, the listing system appears superior at all levels. The distinct superiority of listing expressed at a national level was not countered in local practice by support for the local control, autonomy and flexibility offered by conservation areas. Indeed, most respondents operating at the local level did not praise the conservation area framework, despite assumptions of the mechanism's popularity with the public.

Given this bias towards listing, does the case-study evidence address whether conservation activity is limited by the parameters defined by listing's treatment of features as independent artefacts? If conservation is mainly dealing with specific buildings objectively as individual components, does this conflict with or even preclude addressing the value of local areas and aspects of the historic environment which are not necessarily derived from a historic building *per se*? Furthermore, does the difference between the two regimes create professional distinctions in the interpretation of conservation's contribution?

To answer the first question, it would be difficult to conclude that listing is the comprehensively dominant approach. However, the concepts which distinguish conservation areas from listing – that is, character, morphology, place identity – appear less well developed in these local authorities' planning practice. Some DC officers considered that the character of particular areas was 'so obvious' as to render a formal assessment of it quite superfluous. Yet in contrast, those same officers considered that further guidance in relation to the architectural or structural details of a building was essential. There also appears to be some residual cynicism, even among planning officers, about the added value which conservation area status bestows on an environment. It certainly does not command the same respect as listing. This evidence would tend to contradict assertions that conservation and 'place-making' are synonymous, despite the best intentions to make them so. The evidence suggests that conservation in these two local authorities is not well positioned to achieve this. Obviously this depends on what constitutes 'place-making'; for example, in the borough, the concern to respect the views of the town does constitute an attempt to work to protect a vision of 'place'.

One notable legacy of the development of conservation planning is local authorities' freedom to identify local areas of character on an autonomous basis. In 1967, conservation areas were introduced with little prescriptive guidance and this has ultimately backfired, since, nationally and locally, insufficient attention has been given subsequently to developing the strategic and abstract concepts for area-based conservation. For example, the work of Conzen (cited in Larkham 1996) addressing precisely this field, while intense, has influenced a select group of academics but has struggled in its application to planning practice.

The freedom of local authorities to designate conservation areas has also excused central government from providing directions as to how to interpret areas' value. With significant budget cuts in local government, the resources have not always been available to pursue such initiatives and local planning authorities have struggled independently to develop these concepts in a systematic way. In the study authorities, DC officers appraise character sporadically, reacting to planning applications; conservation sections with meagre resources were too stretched to develop area-based evaluation strategies. Instead of providing a possible bridge between conservation and planning disciplines, awareness and analysis of area-based concepts fall into a gaping chasm between them, thus only increasing the need for better national guidance. However, of the national organisations concerned with conservation of the built environment, most are principally concerned with the architecture of specific buildings. EH has attempted to champion a process of developing the contributions of area-based concepts of value in conservation planning but such initiatives take time to percolate through.

The extent of acceptable change

Summary of findings

When national respondents were surveyed, the emphasis was firmly placed on conservation's concern to ensure 'organic change'; as one respondent noted, conservation is 'the art of intelligent change'. Indeed, the national amenity societies (NAS) in particular seemed eager to distance themselves from being portrayed as opposing change. Notably, those in senior positions within EH reinforced the view that conservation was spearheading the regeneration of many urban areas. Respondents concerned with more direct management of historic features noted a schism between these politically motivated proclamations and their own professional passion for the country's historic buildings.

Defining 'acceptable change' also depended on the regime of protection. Respondents noted that scheduled ancient monuments required strict preservation for their inherent didactic interest, while listed buildings and conservation areas were able to accommodate increasingly greater changes respectively. However, some respondents, particularly though not exclusively the NAS, considered local planning authorities' management of change to be far too liberal. Conservation demanded a longer timescale in which to consider change, one that many politicians and planners, bound by expediency, appeared incapable of realising. Despite celebrated rare occurrences of bold architectural vision for contemporary buildings across the country, their design was felt to be of too low a quality. Respondents were divided over whether or not commenting on new design was within the competence of conservation professionals. This distinction reflects difficulties in attempting to define good modern design which respects context, yet simultaneously avoids merely replicating it. Several respondents considered that the public actually contributed to the problem through their preference for traditional built forms, motivated by the type of preservationist attitudes which professionals themselves claimed they had left behind.

Planning practice in the mill town (chapter 5) evidently displayed operational conflicts between the competing policy presumptions in favour of development and retention in PPG1 and PPG15. While senior managers favoured moving towards a regenerative approach to conservation based on projects in the Implementation section, C&D remained passionately committed to protecting the architecture of the region against inappropriate development. Perhaps this division reflects the same type of split between professionals and senior managers within the national level. For most DC officers, acceptable change was determined by the situation and function of the individual building, subject to conservation control. This is a different consideration of acceptable changed than that of the conservation adviser who believed that conservation provided objective standards. It is not right to say who is correct but it begs a further question: when does conservation stop being 'conservation' in accepting a transition from the repair to the re-creation of a building? The Lodge, although listed, was effectively an entire new building following its reconstruction. Most of the interior of the grade II* listed building in the Square was removed, with EH's approval. In both instances, the degree of change was wholly unacceptable to the C&D section.

In the borough (chapter 6), the views of the conservation officer and DC officers did not follow this pattern in determining 'acceptable' change. The historic context of the town might create more resistance to change; certainly the application of the local plan policies provided a robust framework for controlling inappropriate development, but the conservation officer wished to promote a flexible approach. This meant that DC officers had to maintain close links with the conservation section to ensure they shared the same view within the authority.

If they did not, then there was the potential that officers would express differing views, a point which had not gone unnoticed by some applicants. The conservation officer determined acceptable change in relation to the outcome of the overall project rather than whether it was acceptable *per se* to change specific features of the building. Ironically, if DC officers did not maintain a close conversation, there was the risk of inadvertently advocating a more traditional interpretation of acceptable change than the conservation officer would. Though one planning officer thought the borough provided more of a 'neighbourhood protection service', local residents in the Garden case did not share this view.

Discussion and implications

It is clear from the conservation literature that there is no place for a strictly preservationist approach to listed buildings and conservation areas. Recently the debate appears to have moved on apace as national agendas place an increasing emphasis on the regenerative aspects of urban development and conservation's place therein. Although sustainability has been similarly introduced into national policy statements, it has yet to influence fully these local authorities' building conservation practices. Perhaps a more appropriate debate is the relationship between conservation and regeneration. While these are closely linked in the recent literature and certainly in the responses of many national respondents, the evidence among those more directly involved 'at the coalface' of conservation reveals that not all professionals share this direction or inclination. Indeed, there are some significant conflicts between the means and the ends, especially if the priority for conservation is moving towards encouraging re-use over the treatment of form and fabric.

Though their conservation responsibilities are roughly similar, the conservation approaches in the two local planning authorities are the exact opposite of those anticipated. The mill town's planning service is politically driven towards encouraging development and senior managers wish to orient conservation towards a similar regeneration emphasis. However, the conservation officer wishes to achieve this by promoting the identity of the town, ensuring a high-quality treatment of the historic fabric, despite the town's non-traditional conservation image. In the historic market town, it would appear that one of the conservation officer's priorities is to ensure that historic buildings remain in use. The difference between the consistency of objective standards and allowing greater flexibility in relation to the historic fabric illustrates the influence of the officers' personal attitudes and principles. Their own professional outlook and interpretation of policy has a significant influence on the perceived orientation of conservation across the whole authority.

The development cases illustrate the breadth of definition of the 'enhancement' of conservation areas, which allows almost any issue, economic or aesthetic, to be argued in an application. In the absence of character appraisals and enhancement strategies, it is easier to avoid contesting 'enhancement' by arguing that the application does not preserve the character or appearance of the area. Thus the absence of a conservation strategy can further reinforce a perception of controls being applied restrictively. The introduction of new architecture is a particularly difficult field, since in both authorities it is mainly officers in the respective conservation sections who hold any formal design qualifications. In both, though notably more so in the borough, planning officers were frustrated by conservative attitudes in the town and particularly in their planning committees in trying to encourage new design. Thus despite officers' attempts, promoting contemporary design still inflamed prejudices residual from the unpopularity of new development in the 1960s and 1970s. With this in mind, it is debatable whether conservation can be wholly aligned with regeneration as a positive process of enhancement.

The basis of conservation's support and legitimacy

Summary of findings

At a national level, respondents saw conservation as enjoying immense popular support. The prolific degree of public interest was reflected at a political level by an underlying cross-party consensus. The mandate of such firm public interest and political acquiescence was seen to justify the development of practice by conservation professionals on the public's behalf. The popularity of conservation was seen to add weight and legitimacy to this executive model, especially for the NAS respondents who considered that they were representing 'a public position'. However, some respondents also acknowledged that despite conservation's popularity, the public perception of the conservationist conjured up associations with the 'slightly cuckoo brigade'.

Significantly, public support for conservation was dependent on respondents' perception of the public. Generally, support was seen as emanating from those possessing an appreciation of the artistic and historical objects of conservation. It was also noted that much of the active support for and interest in conservation came from the residential owners of old buildings. More generally, among the public at large a degree of apathy, rather than action, characterised their response to conservation. However, all sections of the public were seen to react negatively when conservation restricted their ability to alter their own private property. Generally the restrictive use of conservation prevailed: they wanted to prevent damage to their own property or amenity from a neighbour's development.

The general socio-economic composition of the two case-study towns may reflect divisions in the public's interest. In chapter 5 the metropolitan council's planners considered that generally the level and quality of public contributions to planning were low, thus perhaps it is not surprising that conservation suffered a corresponding diminution of interest, despite the presence of a local Civic Society. The comments received by the authority were mostly objections to particular incursions or development threats. The lack of positive contributions reinforced the view for C&D that it was their responsibility to protect those features which members of the public, if they possessed the relevant skills to appreciate them, would want conserved. However, in the development cases the reasons for conservation cited by members of the public were often outside the grounds permitted within conservation (and in some cases, planning) legislation. This can work against conservation, as in the Lodge case, where the public viewed conserving the listed building as an inappropriate solution which did not address the wider social problems.

In contrast, planning officers in the borough (and several applicants) noted that some local residents in the town centre made a highly vocal contribution to local planning debates. High property prices in the town centre would indicate that residents were the professional middle classes whose active enthusiasm for conservation was largely recognised by national respondents. The local Civic Society was far more active than its counterpart in the mill town, scrutinising and lobbying the planning authority; it also had a significantly larger membership. There does appear to be a general cynicism among the public following the uncompromisingly modern architecture of the 1960s and 1970s which replaced many historic buildings in the town centre. Certainly these attitudes characterised public reaction to the Terrace and Bank developments, where the fitting of new design into context was fiercely contested. More significantly, though, there would appear to be strong public interest expressed by several committee members in protecting a way or quality of life in the town. The role of conservation in the authority was supported not just for art-historical reasons but for wider objectives to protect the town's identity and livelihood.

Discussion and implications

Given that respondents at a national level place such reliance on the legitimacy that widespread public support confers on conservation, it is vital to address two questions. First, does this widespread support actually exist? Second, does the support correspond to the scope and nature of legitimate conservation interest perceived by professionals? If there is a negative answer to either question, does this undermine conservation professionals' exclusive definition of conservation as justified by upholding the public interest? Need there be a correspondence with broader public interpretations?

Certainly the popular political consensus supporting conservation claimed of national politics becomes far less tangible in local politics. The case-study towns differ tremendously: in the metropolitan council, conservation is perceived as something of a hindrance; in the borough, it is perceived far more positively. In both authorities, planning officers invited public participation but noted that the comments received were often of a low quality and, with the greatest will in the world, did not relate to matters that constitute legitimate planning issues. Attitudes towards public involvement unconsciously followed a liberal model whereby officers assumed that relevant interest groups would coalesce and participate. Often the public's contributions were partisan and not necessarily representative of the general public. Despite the introduction of the Civic Amenities Act in an era of participatory planning it would appear that the potential for such inclusion has not been realised.

If one is ascertaining the public's interest, people's contributions can only be indicative rather than definitive of lay appreciation or public sentiment; further research may wish to address this specifically. On the evidence gathered, it is difficult to say categorically that conservation is of widespread public concern. It is debatable whether the public interest in conservation is actually just a coalition of shared private property interests. Those public comments deemed admissible tend to share the same language as used by the conservation professionals, reinforcing a notion that conservation does connect with the public, though this tends to be the property-owning, well-educated middle class. This is just one section of the public. Other sections may well be excluded, especially if measures to involve the public continue to follow existing practices.

A lack of comments does not necessarily mean that the public are not interested, just that the language, access and the pre-determined scope of what constitutes a legitimate contribution may inhibit certain sections of the public. These distinctions will be considered later, though the potential for disparity can undermine the position of conservation or planning professionals, both at local and at national levels. If they claim to be acting on behalf on the public, then it is only appropriate that they ought consider the diversity of public support, rather than limit concern to those who already share their values.

The interpretation of features' interest

Summary of findings

Certain commentators highlighted the lack of scrutiny and policy reviews regarding the statutory criteria of special architectural or historic interest but respondents at the national level enthusiastically supported the term; the flexibility and comprehensiveness of the phrase obviated the need to formally review it. Respondents noted some definite boundaries to its scope, essentially distinguishing a formal objective evaluation from wider cultural value. Only the former approach could be quantified in a rigorous system of protection dependent on a 'rolling consensus' of objectivity among professionals. These professionals' ability to identify and judge features' inherent interest was instilled through a similar education, training and professional culture, producing a particular confluence of opinion. However, respondents noted their own considerable discretion in forming, even leading, the definition of these objective phrases. For example, some noted that in the 1980s listing resurveys they performed a 'virtual U-turn' in broadening historic interest to include features reflecting social and economic history in addition to those of formal, national history which previously dominated the term's interpretation.

In contrast, while the cultural importance of the built environment was a prime justification for conservation, the subjectivity of wider cultural interpretations of environmental value was seen as a reason for preventing their inclusion in any formal administrative appraisal of value. Indeed, the suggestion of broadening concepts any further encountered considerable resistance. A minority of res- pondents recognised identifying cultural value as a particularly weak area of English practice, partly as planning law is focused on physical elements connected with land use. Defining and protecting historical value can encounter this problem too, since even significant historical factors may not leave physical traces. However, amorphous concepts such as character and place identity floun- dered against the more obvious and ascendant value of features' architectural value. Such associations lying outside architectural assessment were generally dismissed as nostalgic and sentimental despite the fact that they reflected strong cultural and personal attachment.

In the metropolitan council (chapter 5), one of the conservation adviser's main concerns was to protect the architectural integrity of buildings, particularly their technical construction. Respecting the fabric's authenticity, treating the building as an integral whole, stood in stark contrast to most other planning officers' opin- ions, which were based on the visible quality of a feature. Visibility seemed to provide a rule of thumb with which to gauge the appropriate conservation response: those which were more prominent were more likely to be conserved. Visibility also affected attitudes to new contextual development; as long as they looked reasonable, the authenticity or accuracy of new insertions was less of a consideration.

Many planning officers inadvertently expressed preconceived notions, stereo- types even, about the qualities a listed building ought to possess. Where the physical state of the building did not correspond to the *image* of a listed build- ing, as in the Lodge or the Square case, it did not command the respect listing status ought to convey, and this influenced attitudes regarding how these features were treated. In balancing architectural and historic interest, a further distinc- tion was the extent to which local historical value, in contrast with vernacular architecture, was under-represented in both listing policy and local conser- vation strategies. For example, the contribution of the Yard to the town's morphology proved very difficult to defend in the absence of any assessment of historic character.

In the market town, different issues flowed from the development cases as they mostly concerned new buildings in the historic context. There appeared to be less distinction between the conservation officers' and the planning officers' interpretation of value, perhaps because the predominant concerns throughout were the views and image of the town generally. However, not all areas of the town had character appraisals and accompanying guidance. Planning officers often considered that character was so obvious that it did not require formal appraisal. But this was largely based on equating character with recognising the most obvious architectural elements in an area. Ironically, for a town with a wealth of historic features, historic interest appeared to be regarded more passively. Several respondents, notably developers, commented that features were protected simply because of their age rather than for any discernible value. But perhaps more interesting was a feeling that the Victorian buildings were eclipsed in importance by the Georgian buildings in the town. The image and stereotype of the town may be seen as invoking antiquarian prejudices.

Discussion and implications

Evidently the responses across the fieldwork show that the statutory criteria are very flexible, though despite a firm belief in their strength at a national level, the diversity of value interpretations at a local level may suggest some weaknesses.

A belief in the universal recognition of features' inherent architectural value in contrast with their extrinsic social or cultural value is severely tested. The comparative subjectivity of listing professionals' rolling consensus may be sufficient to undermine a whole-hearted belief in its seeing intrinsic interest in a building. This is dealt with in greater detail in the section 'The influence and variety of knowledge and experience' (p. 32) but suffice it to say that if the objectivity of professional evaluation is undermined, then this weakens the argument for excluding extrinsic interest on the grounds that it is over-subjective. If this is the case, then what is the objection to at least acknowledging and further exploring interpretations of extrinsic, cultural value?

One manifestation of the division between intrinsic value and extrinsic value is highlighted in relation to historic interest. A lack of physical evidence means that discovering historic interest requires greater effort, thus often inhibiting its contribution either to policy formation or in the expediency of determining a specific application. Such omissions further emphasise the relative strength of architectural value in defining conservation value. It is also difficult to generalise standards for historic interest since by definition each feature is unique because of the cumulative historical events that have shaped its existence.

Another restriction, illustrated by attitudes in the Lodge and the Yard cases, is a subconscious architectural stereotyping of listed buildings which can inhibit the consideration of value in other ways, such as cultural or social value. The stereotype is often of polite architecture, of superior ornamentation or scale that may be worthy of attention. If a listed feature does not appear to meet this standard stereotype or image, it can be more easily dismissed as not being a worthy listed building and consequently treated less favourably. The apparent reliance on features' superficial visible qualities contributes to this perception. This is particularly acute in relation to concepts that are ill served by an orthodox reliance on intrinsic value, such as character and place identity, which equally reside in extrinsic cultural attachment and valuation. It partly explains why conservation areas, in which value extends far beyond architectural terms, suffer such significant under-appreciation. Problems of measuring and accessing these values should not prevent an attempt to do so, otherwise, as Jones (1993) notes, the system of recognising value becomes merely a self-serving activity. Relying on the authenticity of fabric as the benchmark may not wholly correspond to the socio-aesthetic aims for conservation control.

The hierarchy of significance

Summary of findings

The survey of national organisations highlighted their inevitable disposition towards the 'national interest'. Most respondents commented that recognising and managing conservation resources requires a strict taxonomy, a set of criteria by which features are identified and defended. However, contrary to this resolute defence of national interest, respondents noted several exceptions which may undermine it as a coherent benchmark. First, in identifying listed buildings, only thematic twentieth-century listings involved comparing features on a national scale of interest. The majority of listed buildings were surveyed by individuals operating under various committees' national auspices. Second, the different routes of survey, thematic listing and also spot-listing created different pressures and motives for recognising interest. Third, there were no explicit reasons given in list descriptions defining the qualities that make the feature of national interest. Lastly, there was no corresponding national commitment to monitoring controls or ensuring the direct financial support for features of value; only a tiny minority of buildings receive such national attention.

In contrast, while national interest was ardently defended, local interest was less highly regarded. Although national interest is acknowledged by national respondents as an important foundation of conservation, its weaker basis and susceptibility to subjectivity in local policy and practice created much scepticism. The incursion of emotive and intangible factors was considered too difficult to measure and accommodate in any system of recognition, particularly as private property interests often motivated them. Thus the concept of local significance as a means by which to support and define conservation areas remained undervalued.

In the case studies, local significance was a difficult concept to identify, though not necessarily because of clouded subjective emotions. It was difficult to distinguish local interest from national interest, partly because national interest was itself a fairly difficult concept to recognise. In the development cases studied in the mill town, (chapter 5), for example, the awareness and respect for the national interest in a listed building was relatively low even in the case of the impressive grade II* listed building in the Square. In this case, EH's officer defined 'national interest' as being judged against comparable buildings across the region. Familiarity with the local built environment for many respondents, especially those further removed from any specific involvement with conservation, appeared to engender apathy rather than affection; familiar components were taken for granted, with little further cognition of their value until they were under threat.

In the market town's locality, the perception of the town as a quintessentially English historic town seemed to blur people's distinctions between local interest and national interest. However, the presence of such important listed buildings in the town had some unfortunate consequences for modest features and areas which were perceived by many in the town as less worthy in comparison. In contrast with the metropolitan council, there was perhaps a greater willingness among borough planning officers to uphold a listed building's national interest rather than question its listed status. Despite local interest's subordinate position to national interest, features still required distinguishing aspects to mark them out from the familiar and ordinary in people's conscious appreciation. Responses to familiarity were more evidently expressed in terms of a general favouring of a particular style or feeling of the town, rather than specific individual features. One notable exception was the Gardens case, in which residents felt aggrieved by the conservation officer's alleged oversight of the more modest qualities of their grade II listed terrace.

Discussion and implications

While national interest evidently provides a benchmark for the national respondents, in local practice it appears to suffer from some obfuscation and false assumptions. Although it defines the extent of the state's responsibilities regarding listed buildings, the cumulative evidence from all respondents suggests it is not a concept which provides a definite and credible indication in all cases.

There is too much variety in defining national significance among the different national and local conservation experts. The division of listed buildings into grade I, II* and II buildings, taken with the state's financial involvement in supporting only a handful of these, does not necessarily reflect a consistent national interest, if interest is manifest by actions as well as by abstract evaluations. Most of the responsibility falls on local authorities, in which case the concept of national interest may suffer from a lack of recognition. The practical assessment of national interest is arbitrated through the regional offices and officers of EH, which, despite contrary contentions, reinforces the fact that these assessments more closely represent a regional contextualisation of interest.

If national interest is not as cogent as is portrayed, then what additional contribution does local interest play? Criticisms of it as weak and subjective are perhaps fair, given the lack of formal guidance in local authority practice generally and officers' consequent reliance on their personal discretion and intuition in its definition. The present state of statutory planning appears to offer little scope to realise its contribution. Although familiarity is viewed positively by the literature, the evidence would suggest that the ubiquity of familiar features undermines any consideration of their particular interest. In relation to views and the general townscape, experiences in the market town do illustrate some 'familiar and cherished local scenes'; however, this is still a passive and often unconscious evaluation until the scene is threatened. It appears to require an external force or recognition to catalyse a consideration of local interest. As seen in the mill town with the devolved listing resurvey, the external recognition of a national value in the local environment which had been hitherto taken for granted raised the conservation profile of local interest. Perhaps this role could be played by an external agent, possibly EH, providing a framework in which to highlight and develop appreciation of the local interest already present.

The influence and variety of knowledge and experience

Summary of findings

Reflecting opinions similar to those regarding 'special' interest, national respondents set great store by their professional rigour in maintaining the standards and boundaries of conservation; this set them aside from the enthusiastic amateur. The cogency of having general conservation principles was considered to be of only marginal assistance because conservation involved a sensitive balancing of issues, requiring an astute exercise of professional discretion and judgement. Thus the professional craft of the conservationist, having an 'eye' for value honed through experience, was paramount.

National respondents noted that as the professional discipline became more complex, so the onus on them increased to ensure that the public continued to understand the professionals' work. In addressing the public there appeared to be a subconscious division of the public into, on the one hand, those who had some knowledge and interest in conservation and, on the other, the majority who were not as well informed, who had less aesthetic sensibility. To address this, EH promoted various initiatives through general education programmes and specific issue campaigns to win hearts and minds. These campaigns were to inform the public but also to promote discussion and awareness of conservation issues to consolidate public support. But these campaigns seemed to define the extent of involving the public in conservation planning. Most respondents considered that the planning system already offered the public sufficient access to contribute to local authorities' conservation decision-making and no extension of process or initiative was required. Several respondents referred to the public's contributions as 'pure unalloyed nostalgia' or sentimentality. These emotive responses were seen as excellent support for conservation when buttressing a more legitimate architectural reason but there was little willingness to explore alternative perceptions of interest that these sentiments may represent beyond the architectural association.

The local authority case studies revealed discrepancies between the respective local authorities' conservation officers and EH officers over the interpretation of features' value and appropriate treatment. While individuals are bound to have differences of opinion, the extent of these differences, for instance regarding the Square in the mill town and the Terrace in the market town, questions national respondents' reliance on a professional collegiality.

In the metropolitan council, planning officers considered that there was little local debate and minimal public interest in conservation; the public's contribution was infrequent and often related to issues which were not valid on planning grounds. The conservation adviser considered he was protecting features on behalf of a 'non-visual' public who, despite not having a design education, would nevertheless appreciate and support his professional judgement because of the overall improvement to the quality of the environment which conservation could deliver. However, in the development cases the public's response reflected wider concerns and values. For example, the Yard case illustrated the extent to which public reaction to the loss of a local restaurant far outstripped any expression of attachment to the building. Similarly, where a building was unoccupied, as in the Lodge and the Square cases, the public perception of these buildings' worth declined dramatically. Although the conservation adviser considered that this reflected an inability to visualise renewal potential, in these cases public attention was centred on the buildings' use and external appearance.

Public reaction in the market town was oriented towards the general view and appearance of the town. In the cases studied, the contribution of the public may represent a particular section of the public, essentially those who could afford to live in the centre of the town. As in the mill town, lay perceptions appeared to attach significant weight to buildings' use in defining their conservation value.

Several committee members reiterated this, that conservation was another means to ensure the quality of life in the town by helping to retain local commercial and other users. Similarly, in the development cases, vacant listed buildings, such as the former hostel in the Bank case, suffered under-appreciation. Interestingly, members were acutely aware of their own lack of design training, especially in contrast with their officers. Members' preference was for development to 'fit in' organically to the town irrespective of criticisms concerning the possibility of pastiche architecture.

Discussion and implications

As discussed previously, Fowler (1981) noted the overlapping intensity of interest in the past from experts to lay observers; the evidence here reflects a similar arrangement.

Notably, a distinction not particularly highlighted in the existing conservation literature is difference of opinion among conservation experts. While this is inevitable, given the impracticality of hard-and-fast rules, such disparities surely question the projected hegemony of conservation's professional culture. This is also highly significant for the internal relations in local authorities. As planning officers are reliant on the conservation officer for advice, perceptions across any one authority of how conservation can operate will be influenced by that person's approach and values.

National respondents may be happy to broaden the appreciation of value relating to architecture, but do by implication exclude a significant public response that falls beyond their professional consideration. It is evident that many members of the public do not possess the language or rigour to express their feelings about the local environment in acceptable conservation terms. However, the case studies show that, aside from emotional responses, lay interpretations of value often fall outside what professionals would consider 'legitimate' conservation values. To highlight this point, to a professional the function and use of a building are peripheral and ephemeral in assessing its conservation value, but in lay perceptions the utility and role of the building appear to be a critical influence in defining the 'character' of areas and buildings. The significance of use is poignantly illustrated when vacant listed buildings are seen as lacking any value precisely because they are unused.

Lay perceptions also appear to place greater value on considering the general environment – the context of buildings rather than the buildings themselves. This may be due to the simple fact that a building's exterior is generally the only aspect on show. Even if a building has a wonderful interior of listable quality, what access and therefore what interest can the public be expected to have if that building is privately owned? Paradoxically, the professional is left to value the interior on the public's behalf, but the professional has fewer tools with which to evaluate and uphold area-based value, which is what the public are most interested in. This anomaly increases the potential to exclude the lay view from conservation outputs.

These issues are important for the relationship between professional and lay perspectives because they affect initiatives to involve and educate the public. While national organisations seek public support for their campaigns, without due care this can be a one-way transfer of information to legitimate the profession's consideration of value. A contradiction arises between requiring this indirect popular support and encouraging the public to have more direct influence in conservation issues. National respondents considered public participation to be a local authority responsibility, but, as shown, local authorities are hard-pressed to encourage such initiatives in respect of conservation, partly through existing cynicism arising from meagre public involvement in statutory planning processes. While access for the public remains reliant on statutory planning mechanisms, the potential appears limited for encouraging a two-way exchange of information to contribute a lay appreciation of the historic environment.

Aspects of heritage valuation

Summary of findings

The widening interest in the past was welcomed by all respondents in the national interview survey as evidence of the public's appreciation of and support for conserving these features. The listing of buildings less than 30 years old was seen to exemplify conservation's correspondence with this interest: conservation is not limited to the ancient and archaic. When widening appeal was presented in terms of acknowledging different types of reaction or appreciation for these features, most respondents' enthusiasm notably diminished. In this sense, 'heritage' became viewed pejoratively, as a debasing influence undermining the legitimacy of conservation. Many considered it to be an abused and retrograde term which could be hijacked by disparate groups to sanction their naïve, irrational nostalgia in defending some obscure and eccentric interest. The side effects of heritage's commodification of the past, obscuring authentic features and confusing the real with the fake and tawdry, was considered to be a destructive influence on conservation. Such tweeness was seen as a 'dumbing down' of the past's rich diversity in favour of synthetic, homogeneous pastiche and reproduction imagery.

At a local level, evidence of the widening heritage influence was more difficult to identify directly because it is a particularly abstract concept. The impact of heritage in the metropolitan council appeared somewhat muted, despite the then new Planning chair, who wished to use the area's heritage potential for developing its tourism and cultural industries. Certainly the number of listed industrial buildings reflected the inclusion of 'less polite' architectural value. The conservation adviser believed that conserving the built environment satisfied a human need for orientation in time and space. Many respondents reflected on their own personal ties with an area to really appreciate its value – and some from outside the area felt somewhat excluded for not having a local or insider's perspective. These expressions did not appear to depend on concepts of authenticity or criticised aspects such as nostalgia. Indeed, the concern over the visibility of protected features even among planning officers proved of greater concern than features' authenticity.

In the market town there appeared to be a belief, contrary to professional opinion in the authority, that the town was characterised by a particular period, the Georgian, and that ensuring sympathetic new development was of paramount importance. The majority of building or planning professionals interviewed (inside and outside the authority) considered that focusing on the visual and not the temporal continuity of the town's development was a fundamental flaw in expressing its character. Most believed that the established diversity of buildings over hundreds of years created a responsibility to ensure that the twentieth century was equally represented. Without contemporary architecture there would be a distinct gap in the continuity of the town's evolution, a characteristic that was important to maintain. However, many people in the town did not consider this continuity of contrasting styles a quality of the town *per se*. As mentioned previously, the legacy of several 1960s buildings in the town centre created unease over the impact of brazen new design. Of the Terrace case, most people believed that the authenticity of this design did not matter; criticisms of it as pastiche were irrelevant because it fitted the spatial context. Thus rather than highlighting a contrast in the temporal collage, it was consciously smoothed over. While it may be appropriate in certain contexts, neglecting the diversity of the temporal collage could be wholly counterproductive.

Discussion and implications

In the development cases, the expression of socio-aesthetic values highlighted the limitations of conservation practice. How can conservation acknowledge fundamentally intangible qualities which require the examination of people's experience of and associations with these features instead of, necessarily, the features themselves?

While national respondents had a favourable attitude towards more progressive architectural value, any broadening of the type of appreciation of value in features was seen by them as undermining conservation's legitimacy. However, the local planning authority case studies indicated that in contrast with recognition of the best modern architecture in listing, some respondents, particularly those belonging to the general public, considered that modern architecture was the reason why conservation controls were needed. This was not necessarily a reaction to architectural form but a reaction to experiences of built environments in which a sense of place, identity and attachment had been profoundly disturbed by new development. This strength of reaction would suggest that people's experiences of the built environment, rather than an appreciation of architecture, contain potent types of valuation which could benefit conservation.

The centrality of the concept of authenticity to justify conservation was also challenged. In the national survey, heritage was seen as a threat since it was not considered genuine, but many respondents in the local case studies were not concerned about the academic authenticity of features. Authenticity relies on an assumption that researching under-valued aspects of the built heritage extracts self-evident values from these features and brings this knowledge to the surface. This was the language used by many national respondents in relation to protecting unloved architecture. But this view assumes that values await discovery when really each successive generation creates these values anew, reflecting specific currents in society which will themselves mutate over time. It is a contemporary cultural value, not an objective and neutral assessment. If this argument is accepted, then opposition to widening the scope of legitimate interpretation surely ought to be lessened. Conservation then becomes a framework for various parties to explore value rather than an imposition of one particular group's interpretation.

The preference for buildings to 'fit in' while presenting an aesthetic challenge has more profound implications. If contemporary buildings are blended in to the extent that they are indistinguishable from what is already there, this minimises the impact of the early twenty-first century on the continuity of a town's identity. It means that the qualities of scale, ornamentation or function which mark out existing buildings in people's perceptions of the urban environment are downplayed. The preference for 'fitting in' can create a bland, homogeneous environment filled with new buildings that will potentially not attract any attachment or recognition in the future. By pursuing poor contextual development, badly applied conservation may be making the built environment less stimulating and diverse when these are precisely the qualities it should be enhancing.

Rather than pillory heritage, it would appear that there are three ways in which a heritage perspective could benefit conservation's objectives. First, heritage encompasses a broader range of subjects for protection, which can be equated to a wider environmental appreciation of context. Second, heritage studies focus on the experience of users of the subject matter, the extrinsic rather than intrinsic value of features. Third, heritage provides a reconceptualisation of conservation interest which is equally concerned with temporal relations – an orientation with time being as important as an identity with place.

237

Economic pressures and their impact on conservation

Summary of findings

Respondents at both national and local levels considered that economic viability defined the circumstances in which conservation could make a contribution. However, there were significant discrepancies among national respondents over whether economic considerations presented an obstacle for conservation, or whether harnessing economic vitality could ensure that historic buildings were maintained in active use. Most considered these to be delicate questions more appropriate for local authorities because of the individual circumstances of each planning application which required a sensitive balancing of economic value against policy and non-monetary values. Respondents perceived EH to have changed drastically over a short period in its direction towards revitalising urban areas. Within EH, senior respondents especially promoted conservation's economic contributions, thus integrating it within the wider urban regeneration agenda. An emphasis on persuading property developers to consider conservation positively helped ensure that historic buildings paid their own way rather than being 'state pensioners'. However, a significant number of respondents were perturbed by this emphasis, seeing the drive for change as a threat to historic fabric rather than an opportunity. They considered that this regeneration emphasis was not necessarily the most appropriate leading message for local planning authorities, many of whom were characterised as ever willing to sacrifice conservation and historic buildings to applicants' arguments based on the economic necessity of development.

National respondents noted that the economic obsolescence of building types created circumstances in which conservation required greater vigilance to protect them. The decline of the UK's traditional manufacturing base means that much industrial architecture would have been demolished had conservation initiatives not raised interest in its protection. Thus despite working with markets, conservation was also seen to consider the longer timescale, providing a stop gap to protect features. Portraying the value of these features contributed to raising economic interest in their retention. Though development markets were now more inclined to revitalise historic buildings, some respondents noted that this was attributable to exploiting an easier route to obtain planning permission than a genuine concern for the features.

While the economic situation in the case-study towns is markedly different, and perhaps it is unfair to make comparisons, it did have a significant influence on the priorities of the respective councils. It evidently determined the development pressures in the region but it also affected the authorities' internal resource allocation. The metropolitan council's planning service operated to encourage and facilitate local development and the management ethos directed conservation towards a promotion of local economic regeneration. However, an emphasis on prioritising a business-friendly approach pushed conservation and design issues to the margins and put them at greater risk of exclusion. Certainly in the Yard case the economic reasons for redevelopment were paramount. The location of the Lodge created a ceiling on its redevelopment potential and a disregard for its conservation value. In the Square, the applicant considered that his business would benefit immensely from the kudos and associated value bestowed by the building's impressive façade. However, since the rest of the grade II* building made little economic contribution, he saw no point in its retention. In these cases, economics had a profound influence on planning officers' relative balancing of conservation and economic issues.

In the market town there was not the same political imperative to encourage investment opportunities as felt by the planning service in the mill town. The ascendancy of a neighbouring town did pose a threat to the market town's commercial and service functions, though conservation was seen to bolster the local economy through the ability of leisure, tourism and retailing to trade on the town's historic image. While conservation was not a marginal issue, the borough was viewed by some outside the authority as falling behind the success of other historic towns in promoting its identity commercially.

Notably, the general context and ethos of this market town's historic centre did appear to engender a sense of respect from local developers in approaching new build. Perhaps such commercial recognition was equally due to the sale-ability of conserved and period features, providing some guarantee of recouping the extra costs of their conservation. In the Bank case the applicants were willing to move the grade II listed former hostel rather than demolish it. Such acceptance did reduce the need formally to enforce conservation controls, though the message was not universally received. A local architect noted that conservation controls were still needed to stop developers building windowless blocks to maximise profit.

Discussion and implications

The history of urban development in the UK has illustrated that property markets have been incapable of respecting conservation, or perhaps unwilling or not to be trusted to respect it, therefore state regulation was required to ensure that important elements of the built environment were not changed without due consideration.

The economic viability of development has a profound effect on conservation, and not merely in determining the opportunities for its contribution. It divided professional opinion at all levels, forcing professionals to question whether rushing to embrace the urban regeneration agenda presented a threat or a lifeline for historic buildings. In the development cases, economic viability also influenced the interpretation of value of a particular feature in question, increasing or diminishing the weight accorded to its interest to fit in with acceptable development proposals. These issues go to the root of the planning system: whether it is a tool of regulation (illustrated by listed building consents) operating to uphold principles or whether is it a service to facilitate the market in land development, thus requiring flexibility and expedience. To ensure the maximum success in regulation, a priority must be encouraging endemic conservation thinking so that markets perceive conservation as producing economically attractive results. However, a stumbling block is the disparity in timescales and measurement of value between property development and conservation disciplines.

Conservation professionals appear to pride themselves on their consideration of the built environment on a much longer timescale than that demanded by property development pressures. Thus one acute problem for conservation is highlighting the value of particular types of buildings (e.g. mills and factories) as they undergo an inevitable period of low economic viability following the loss of their original use. But balancing economic benefits against conservation benefits is an uphill struggle for conservation, as illustrated in the local development cases. They cannot be measured on the same scales and, as Larkham (1996) noted, the hard facts and figures of economic assessment will always prevail over the relatively weaker and less tangible conservation benefits. The difficulty in comparing conservation and economic value has further implications for decision-making because conservation issues appear to be among the first to be sacrificed if the local planning service is oriented to prioritising local economic development.

What is required is a robust framework in which to present the wider benefits of conservation to the community and weigh against the more closed argument of the economic viability of applications. Conservation professionals must address this shortfall in the same way that the architecture and urban design disciplines have started to demonstrate that investing in good design pays social and financial dividends over the lifetime of a building.

Admittedly few have attempted this – Lichfield (1988, 1997) classified a scheme implemented by UNESCO for management guidance – but there was little evidence in either local authority that conservation was supported by such a full analysis as this. This flag-waving is also required to emphasise conservation's wider socio-economic benefits to local authority decision-makers both in DC committee decisions and in determining political internal funding priorities in which conservation often loses out, despite its indirect contributions to many other local authority activities such as tourism, leisure and community regeneration.

The influence of political agendas

Summary of findings

Respondents in the national interview survey emphasised the cross-party political consensus supporting conservation. Many noted the general acceptance of conservation, as illustrated by the fact that it remained relatively unscathed during the period of the Thatcher administration. Political non-intervention also reflected respondents' belief that conservation is apolitical; for example, civil servants considered that the socio-economic side effects of conservation were separate matters for planners or politicians. However, several respondents noted that conservation does create its own political value by protecting certain types of features which can embody certain political messages such as those related to the 'national heritage'. At the time of interview, the political consensus was about to face a potential revision through the UTF report, then unpublished. Concerns were mounting over the possible exclusion of conservation in the drive to encourage an urban renaissance.

In terms of policy direction, some confusion arose from the 'dysfunctional' split of conservation between DCMS and the then DETR, although respondents within these departments considered that the division was immaterial. Some EH officers noted the partial knee-jerk reaction of policy-making to political currents. Though conservation was generally considered to sidestep politics, several respondents noted that their decision-making was inevitably a political balancing act, particularly in advising the distribution of limited grant funds. Although politics remained understated at the national level, respondents were frustrated by the inevitable autonomy of local politics, which often compromised the conservation initiative. Implementing the mere statutory minimum of their conservation responsibilities, a proportion of local authorities were seen as abrogating the positive spirit of PPG15, without which conservation's wider relevance could be more easily dismissed.

The two case studies display a striking resemblance in certain aspects, notably a perceptible weakening in conservation's contribution to the authorities' wider activities and the consequent slippage of conservation down the political agenda. These trends are more evident in the mill town, where the local political priority of encouraging investment and economic development dictated the planning service's goals, particularly under the previous local Conservative council. Several unfortunate cases seemed to cast aspersions on C&D for allegedly obstructing this programme; members supported conservation as long as it did not inhibit development. It may be that in political terms the users and uses of these buildings are more important to the council than the inanimate architecture *per se*. These perceptions have influenced internal funding arrangements – a series of reductions in the conservation budget reflecting a political distribution of limited resources. A similar political will is illustrated in development control decisions such as the Square and the Lodge cases, where accommodating users' requirements for these buildings took precedence over conserving their fabric. Planning officers lamented the committee's preference for safe, traditional architecture, which in turn has the unfortunate consequence of providing a slightly easier route for developers to obtain planning permission. Perhaps the then new chair of the planning committee could transform political thinking to harness the investment potential of the area's local heritage.

In the market town, the strategic policies of the county council were notably moving away from historic building and area conservation to LA21 and the sustainability agenda. The borough had enjoyed success in terms of conservation results and had been considered (by external and some internal respondents) to be resting on its laurels. There was wider political support for the results of conservation planning since it was perceived as contributing across several spheres of socio-economic activity to improve the general livelihood of the town. However, the absence of a corporate structure within the borough was a handicap in ensuring integrated planning, and therefore conservation, strategies across all the council's services. Planning was a relatively small service within the council, though in contrast the conservation officer was active in lobbying behind the scenes.

The relationship with members surfaces throughout the developments studied, particularly concerning the introduction of new design elements into the town, as regards which similar reactions to those of the mill town's councillors are evident. The Planning Committee forced an unprecedented change of materials regarding the Bank development; officers welcomed a safer design for the Terrace, but it was necessary in order to ease members' concerns. Curiously, officers were simultaneously offering safer architectural schemes to satisfy members while grieving over the lack of contemporary design in the town. Surely, allowing an easier design route to planning permission will tempt the most ardent of conservation-minded developers to sacrifice some architectural form.

Discussion and implications

Political issues inevitably affect conservation at a multitude of levels – formally in the national and local political party agendas and informally in the power relationships between and within organisations. Even though the literature unconsciously follows an assumption of political support for conservation, the research evidence suggests that it remains to be proven whether conservation is supported by a political consensus.

In terms of national conservation policy, there is no particular distinction between Labour and Conservative; PPG15 has spanned two administrations without upset, though this is possibly indicative of the general drift to the middle ground in politics. This consistency is perhaps more indicative of the different political ends to which conservation can be subtly used while maintaining the neutrality and apolitical nature of the activity – for instance, protecting national heritage and private amenity and then promoting urban regeneration and a civic renaissance. It is the use and political capital which conservation can generate that retain politicians' interest rather than a concern for conserved buildings *per se*. In the segregation of responsibilities between government departments, conservation seemingly has a very low status in the larger and more influential ODPM. It is perhaps more accurate to describe conservation's latent consensus as a lack of active political interest.

The impression from the local authorities studied was that conservation was waning in terms of political impetus. Though conservation had once enjoyed greater political kudos, and while both councils still supported the idea of conservation, its status was losing ground to that of other agendas such as sustainability, LA21 and urban regeneration to which conservation ought to be making a significant contribution. Instead, conservation was often politically pigeon-holed, performing a traditional role of controlling design, which further restricted its opportunity to contribute to these emerging priorities. It seemed that conservation was taken for granted in political circles.

It is personal conjecture but this may reflect the nature of the threats facing conservation. The demolition of listed buildings in the 1960s and to some extent 1970s which caused much public sabre-rattling is no longer tolerated. Perhaps conservation has won the day? Development threats are now more subtle and, in occurring on a smaller scale, are less evident to the public. For the public, and politicians responding to their concerns, the conservation problem largely appears to have been solved. The EHTF asked, 'Has built environment conservation been left behind?' (1992: 5). The answer is yes – arguably it has been supplanted by other political priorities.

Respondents' fears over the UTF report highlight the problem of the urban regeneration agenda espousing a preference for the modern over the historic, the new over the old; indeed, listed buildings were mentioned briefly, but only in so far as they should not be seen to obstruct progress (1999: 251). The writing would appear to be on the wall for conservation; it requires repackaging if its political support is not that strong. EH is portraying itself as a regeneration body; the question is to what extent this stance can be successful for conservation at the local level too.

Fundamentally, conservation needs to highlight its contribution to local councils' wider socio-economic aims. The status of conservation was politically higher in the borough (chapter 6) since its wider contribution was more evident. However, although conservation may be moving in this direction nationally, acknowledging the wider contributions of conservation would necessarily require a more open admission of the political issues involved in identifying and protecting features of 'special' interest. It would mean exposing conservation's claim of apolitical neutrality and necessarily require greater consideration of its cultural and socio-economic bias and effects in using finite state resources.

Concluding reflections

This chapter has comprehensively compared material from the three areas of fieldwork and it is apparent that several pervasive issues are recurrent. There do appear to be differences between the way that conservation is perceived to make a contribution and its actual contribution. This is not just a distinction between the national and the local levels as two separate realms but is equally apparent within local authorities and also in individuals' own responses. Generally, the comparison challenges rather than reinforces existing assumptions about the values used to justify conservation policy and practice. The more significant findings, which transcend the 10 themes of the thematic framework, are identified below.

- Conservation's relationship with planning is at risk of greater marginalisation than is perhaps currently recognised, despite an accompanying belief in its integral contribution. This is evident in many ways, from the policy division between DCMS and now ODPM, to the treatment of conservation advice in the local planning authority practice.
- A professional's own attitude towards and perception of conservation's role is highly significant because of the extent of possible differences between individuals' interpretations. The differences are not necessarily simply between national and local levels or between the planning and conservation professions; they exist between *and within* individuals' own views.
- A culture of professional conservation, formed by similar training and education, has the unfortunate consequence of working as a filter on value interpretation, inhibiting the development of alternative value perspectives.
- The interpretation of special interest focuses on features' intrinsic architectural interest, which is portrayed as self-evident. Valuations lying outside this sphere are treated less favourably, and even historical interest has struggled for recognition.
- National and local conservation practices demonstrate a predominant bias towards treating features as independent artefacts rather than primarily considering the discipline as one of contextual environmentalism.
- Local interest is under-developed as a concept, partly through a lack of central support and guidance. However, national interest, portrayed as a more robust concept, is similarly intangible in practice.
- The public's support for conservation and its consideration of value, on perhaps a less 'informed' basis, places much greater weight on conserva-

tion as a means to an end – that is, contributing to a broader social, cultural and environmental context.

- While a political consensus may support conservation in so far as demolishing historic buildings is morally abhorrent, a lack of real active political support, reflected in meagre grant-financing for conservation, would indicate more apathy towards it than a live interest.
- In local practice, conservation can suffer from being stereotyped. It does not appear to have the conceptual ability to emphasise its relevance to the agendas now capturing the political initiative.

It cannot be claimed that these are *the* issues affecting the whole of conservation practice as the evidence provided is from a limited base. However, their pervasiveness does suggest that they are very real concerns for the longer-term existence and relationship of conservation with statutory land-use planning. The concluding chapter will look at the implications of these issues and discuss the broader lessons to be drawn from this study.

8 Conclusions

Introduction

This book has aimed to profile the orientation of values underpinning UK conservation policy and practice towards the built environment. At a time of rapid policy change around conservation, as efforts are focused on urban design and regeneration, it has exposed conservation as attempting to ride a number of horses, some more successfully than others, in an attempt to stay the course.

The study has shown a greater tendency for diversity than consensus in the values underlying conservation so it would be naïve to think that this chapter could ever comprise a conclusion to the bigger questions. However, the use of the thematic framework to consider and analyse the evidence can address the research issues posed earlier in the book:

- How does conservation relate to planning in principle and practice?
- How is value in the built environment perceived and interpreted for conservation purposes?
- How do economic and political pressures contribute to or undermine conservation?

The qualitative approach used in the study has permitted a deeper analysis than would be possible with surveys or other quantitative methods. It has permitted an examination of why decisions are made in certain ways and the influences on and attitudes towards conservation. However, the findings do need to be treated with an element of caution as the qualitative methods used cannot be expected to produce definitive or comprehensive answers. The extent to which the conclusions are generally applicable is also debatable as approaching different interviewees and local planning authorities could have revealed different concerns. In some respects, qualitative research is distinct to the time it is conducted. Certainly personnel and practices may be different now from when the study was undertaken, and revisiting the case studies and resurveying the national organisations could paint a different picture, but there remain cogent arguments borne out in the analysis which retain their relevance.

While the thematic framework has proved robust and flexible, it was constructed from tensions identified in the existing literature. In the analysis this may have pre-determined an emphasis on reporting conflict rather than consensus. On the other hand, it is possible that these tensions are inherent and unresolvable, and to consider them as being transient obstacles in the path of planning reform would be imprudent.

The Tate Modern, London: an iconic result of the conservation ethos, although, ironically, it is an unlisted building
© Rachel Royse/CORBIS

The nature of conservation planning: integration or marginalisation?

At the heart of the relationship between conservation and planning lies a paradox between principle and practice. It is a confusion of ideas about conservation's role in planning, arising partly from a succession of threats which have influenced conservation's development, partly because of a dilemma concerning planning's function either to regulate or to facilitate land development. Put simply, conservation is vaunted as a fundamental to development considerations, in this sense originating from Geddes' early vision of surveying and enhancing the qualities of the existing environment. However, in attempting to reinforce this notion of centrality in planning, an accompanying belief in conservation's moral weight holds conservation as superior to and purer than a 'mere' planning issue. Herein lies the paradox. While many people believe that conservation is central to planning, the processes and constrained practice of conservation reinforce the 'separateness' and 'specialness' of conservation as a positive value in itself. This 'specialness' is reflected in all aspects of policy and practice, in relationships among professionals and also externally with the public. It undoubtedly casts a different light on the future relationship of conservation, with planning subject to the proposals in the government's Planning Green Paper for reform.

Principles

Many practitioners have been attempting to squeeze conservation to the centre of the planning mind-set, but the stronger economic and political forces competing for this position have easily pushed conservation up and out of this plane. Conservation seems to float above planning, certainly in perceptions of the moral compulsion to undertake its responsibilities, while below, planning continues more or less oblivious, occasionally glancing up to conservation for guidance when other pressures recede.

Conservation's attraction does stem from a moral undertaking not to see historic buildings needlessly destroyed, but this is a culturally determined attitude and in no sense can be taken for granted. Planning paradigms of the post-war era evidently took a different view towards conserving the old and attitudes may change again. In contrast to this conscience of conservation, there did not appear to be a similar response concerning a social, moral or conscionable purpose for the planning system. Planning was perceived as an administrative framework with which to consider applications as efficiently as possible. Conservation was one factor to balance against a range of competing issues. Despite there being separate consent systems, in practice conservation was not as 'special' as national respondents and policy would suggest.

Though PPG15 emphasises conservation's integration, evidence from practice suggests that conservation suffers a significant degree of marginalisation in planning. The pressure to review the separate conservation consent procedures highlighted a fundamental disparity in attitudes concerning listed buildings and conservation areas. Suggestions to integrate listed building consent into the planning permission were rejected by many for further displacing conservation issues in an application. However, following the *Shimizu* decision reducing the scope of effective control over development in conservation areas, EH preferred closer control over development via the GPDO – that is, regular planning provisions. It believed this would not subsume area-based conservation issues but actually provide greater strength and legitimacy. This 'double-think' and the will to retain listing's complete exclusivity illustrate listing's predominance in the conservation field. To what extent do the process and attitudes involved in listing embody, orient or determine the extent of conservation's contributions to planning? Are conservation areas to be allowed to wither on the vine or can planning provide the expertise to deal with the protection of areas? Certainly conservation areas have not received a great deal of policy support or development in proposed revisions to the planning system.

Professionalism

The different professional perspectives between planning and conservation provide a further level at which to explore this relationship of integration or marginalisation. The widespread claim that conservation is 'the art of intelligent change' is well founded. However, is not planning also the art of intelligent change? Does this suggest that there is greater unity between the two professions' aims than is commonly believed to be the case? Or is conservation required because planning has deserted this aim and planners lack the competence to deal with change 'intelligently'?

Though to perceive professions as homogeneous groups is potentially misleading, planners appear to share a culture characterised by relatively limited architectural knowledge and design awareness. Practical experience rather than education and training furnishes their competence to deal with these issues. A lack of confidence or acknowledgement of the limit of their own knowledge defines when planning officers consult conservation staff for specific architectural, structural and technical advice on buildings. However, conservationists recognise a more comprehensive deficit – in planners' ability to consider urban design *per se*. In contrast, matters of scale and massing, townscape and the appearance of areas are fields in which planners consider themselves sufficiently adept to reduce the need to resort to specialist advice. There appears to be a conscious professional distinction between competencies relating to the specifics of buildings' architecture and the general character of areas. This is particularly worrying in itself, given the widespread concern over the low levels of design skills throughout all local authorities, levels inadequate to ensure the delivery of high-quality new design. It is not therefore a matter merely of providing better training, as is called for in the report of the Urban Design Skills Working Group (2001), but of actively changing attitudes across authorities about competencies as well.

In both the local authorities studied in this book, conservation was a consultee to the DC section, frequently invoked through DC officers' discretion rather than by robust formal policy or guidelines. Planners' perception of conservation as contributing mainly specific architectural or structural advice restricts conservation in realising the integral role emphasised by PPG15. It also illustrates a more substantial problem. Planning officers consider that much of their DC work involves design considerations, and conservation is one aspect of these. But many applications – such as minor works to listed buildings, or small-scale changes in conservation areas – may not raise a distinct conservation issue and are consequently not referred for specialist advice. In the authorities studied, working arrangements increasingly placed more responsibility on DC officers for these aspects. Ironically, it is precisely the effects of cumulative small-scale changes which conservationists consider pose the greatest threat to the protection of areas' character. On the evidence of these case studies, they are also the aspects over which the conservation specialist is losing control to the generalist planning officer.

Despite differences of opinion between planning and conservation officers, a further distinction barely mentioned in the existing literature is the extent to which conservation professionals' personal interpretations of conservation differ. While the local development plans often paraphrased PPG15, ensuring central policy compatibility, the professional outlooks of the two authorities' conservation officers differed appreciably. Both were fiercely enthusiastic and shared a resolute individualism in the face of corporate compliance: their personal philosophies appeared to be highly significant when giving conservation advice. This is important, because in most local authorities this officer/adviser often provides the sole interpretation of conservation policy. Thus it leads to the surprising contrast whereby the conservation officer in the market town was more tolerant of new development there than his counterpart in the mill town, despite the fact that the council in the latter wished to encourage new development.

Scale

Two aspects relating to the scale of conservation have become apparent through the study. The first is regulating change spatially: whether conservation is more concerned with buildings as specific, independent artefacts or whether the environmental context as a functioning whole is more important. The former receives far more attention at both local and national levels. National bodies' (beyond EH) main interests are protecting the fabric of listed buildings, with areas being secondary; the structure of local authorities' DC processing and conservation referrals reinforces the consideration of a building and its fabric as taking precedence over consideration of the *area*. In both authorities, reductions in the number of conservation staff meant that resources were redirected to fulfil the statutory responsibility of determining listed building consent referrals from DC.

Many national respondents argued that listed building consent was necessary because general planning measures were too blunt to address the intricate level of detail required. By implication, if their scales are incompatible, this ought to mean that planning is more appropriate to ensure areas' protection and a contextual appreciation of conservation. However, the developing of an area-based conservation approach in these local authorities' practice was led neither by planners nor by conservationists. Area character appraisals have been a lesser priority; indeed, they were often considered a luxury as resources were not available. The concepts available to define and explore areas' character are weak and underdeveloped, partly because legal definitions limit planning issues to the physical use of the land, thus excluding a whole array of valid interpretations of character. However, it is also an important consequence of a prolonged period when national policy neglected these concepts under the guise of allowing local authorities to develop them autonomously. A rejuvenated urban design discipline would appear to embrace both aspects of conservation and development control, but instead of bridging a gap within these authorities, it currently falls into a gaping chasm in professional attitudes and practice between the two. Simply investing in training to improve design skills will reap only modest rewards if it is not accompanied by a change in planning processes and culture to recognise the value of visually literate planners. Elected members equally need to be better instructed not only in the value of design, but also in the value to the local environment of having officers who understand urban design.

The second aspect of scale is the different timescales on which conservation and planning operate. On a superficial level, this encompasses the eight-week planning application target, which stands in contrast to the lengthier negotiations that seem to characterise processing conservation applications. On a more abstract level, conservation measures change on a far longer timescale (perhaps hundreds of years) than that of planning, which is more concerned with meeting the needs of the present. Evidently conservation coincides with sustainability: meeting the needs of the present without compromising the inheritance for future generations, though, as noted throughout, there are more profound aspects to these temporal relationships in interpreting value.

Timescale also determines what is considered an acceptable rate of change. The rapidity of new development is perhaps more disorienting than its scale, though the preservation–conservation–regeneration debate is not discussed as frequently in relation to time. There would appear to be a distinction in views regarding the relative temporal rates of change between conservation and planning professionals and the general public. The latter wish to see change happen at a slower pace, allowing for the assimilation of new development within the existing environment. However, nationally, conservation policy is moving away from restricting change, to become an agent of change through regeneration. While conservation has been portrayed as one of many approaches to development, it may be more accurate to state that conservation itself contains many diverse approaches to delivering development. The difference of opinion between the public and professional interpretations of conservation's role is significant, especially if the public wish conservation to take a more preservationist stance, in contrast to the emphasis on allowing change and encouraging new architecture. For many members of the public, new architecture is still the threat which conservation ought to counter.

Support

The conservation conscience, its moral weight, is a widely appreciated sentiment shared by most of the groups studied. In this sense, interest in conservation has moved a long way from being an elitist concern; indeed, planning draws on public support for conservation in a similar way as over green-belt policy. However, there is a huge difference between active and passive support and the motivations behind them. National political interest could be described as apathetic, and certainly in local politics the importance of the conservation agenda has slipped from the elevated position it enjoyed 30 years ago. The political situation is in part a reflection of the public's interest in conservation, which perceives that conservation has largely accomplished its task, given that the scale of comprehensive town centre development of the 1960s and 1970s is now unusual, or, if it happens, at least it is now better integrated into the existing urban fabric.

Although access to conservation decision-making in local planning authorities is as open for conservation as any other planning issue, the public response is generally modest until specific property rights or the immediate quality of amenity are detrimentally affected. Property concerns are a significant motivating factor behind much 'conservation' interest, which prompts questions about whether the public interest in conservation is just a coalition of private property concerns. The approach of the local planning authorities to involve the public in conservation appears to assume that interested groups will always make their interests known. Although this liberalism creates distinctly partisan contributions, there appears to be little active compensation to address the apparent lack of interest among other sections of the community. This is possibly reflective of attitudes welcoming the public's contribution to conservation decision-making when it supports professional opinions yet disregarding it as irrational and sentimental when it highlights other values in protection. This question of a shared understanding and interpretation of value is explored further in the next section.

Concluding remarks

Conservation is currently at risk of being marginalised in the planning process by competing policy principles, through practical procedures and also by different professional competencies and attitudes. With limited resources in each authority, the most significant perceived conservation contribution is made in response to DC applications rather than policy or strategy.

The study illustrates that there are different types of conservation hidden within the structures of these local authorities. While conservation involves a flexible approach, these distinctions reveal more than just professional discretion; they address separate concerns and priorities.

- Minor works within conservation areas or to modest listed buildings are dealt with almost exclusively by planning officers, with few references being made to conservation officers. Often these are seen as design, rather than 'conservation', issues and are determined by external, superficial appearance.
- Significant works in conservation areas or to listed buildings involve the conservation officer to a greater extent; he or she offers advice on architectural and structural aspects of the buildings. This involvement characterises perceptions across the authority of what comprises 'conservation'.
- Project works can be initiated and developed outside or in parallel to the statutory planning process and are determined more by the external funding grant criteria than by local conservation issues *per se*. The regeneration of areas and the re-use of buildings are paramount.

There is no denying that conservation has benefited from its relationship with planning. The question that arises now is whether this relationship can continue to develop. Although sustainability has re-invigorated planning to some extent, in terms of conscionable goals *Modernising Planning* (DETR 1998) indicates that planning is to provide an efficient administrative service to facilitate development rather than a proactive tool with which to intervene and redress development imbalances.

With the proposed Local Development Frameworks of the *Planning Green Paper* (DETR 2001), conservation may find a new opportunity to develop a more strategic approach at the local level. However, the resource commitments illustrated in the local authorities studied show that there is little chance of this happening, as meagre resources are already stretched. The accompanying proposal to have a single planning consent further affects the way that conservation will be perceived. The treatment of listed building consent does define what conservation is at a local level, and in terms of perceptions; removing this explicit consent could undermine conservation significantly as a special consideration. On the other hand, it might be precisely the move that is needed to free conservation from the margins as the mechanics of separate consents create perceived distinctions between conservation and urban design issues. Supporting a single consent might not be the unacceptable sacrifice that many conservation bodies fear.

The interpretation of value in the built environment: value in features, value from context

The essence of conservation is determining those features considered worth saving; not only are the types of features important, but also the attitudes which support these choices. Although intellectual and policy unity are provided by the statutory criteria of 'special architectural or historic interest', the robust defence of the term encountered during the study obscures significant collisions of value in these concepts' application. One conflict is the distinction between the treatment of buildings as independent artefacts or as components of a complex, interwoven urban fabric in which physical evidence is but one aspect. Practice and policy are oriented towards the intrinsic value of features and are considered self-evident by professionals. However, emphasising the intrinsic value of the features portrays value as more objectively determinable, thus removing the valuer from the picture. The interpretation of value is culturally determined, influenced by contemporary circumstances and significantly created anew by each successive generation. Moreover, the interpretation is also a very personal process shaped by education and experience, preferences and idiosyncrasies. The lay view sees features' value more in terms of context, place and associations connected with its use. Thus while the extrinsic or experiential value is not accommodated within conservation parameters, there is a further distinction between the professional and public interpretations of value. If the former is to rely on the latter's support, then ought there to be a closer correspondence between their interpretations of what is considered important in the environment?

Intrinsic interest

In terms of intrinsic interest, PPG15 notes the prominence of architectural over historic interest. Certainly the evidence has shown professionals' preferences to rely on the more quantifiable and identifiable aesthetic qualities of features. Architectural interest provides a relatively universal benchmark with which to gauge value. This becomes a problem when the relationship wholly obscures historic interest. The study shows that a rough hierarchy of priorities may be illustrated as follows:

1   *aesthetic*: architectural integrity, appearance, contribution to townscape;
2   *structural*: construction, technology;
3   *historical*: architectural history and more widely reflecting the passage of time.

The first two concentrate on the physical fabric of a feature; the historical is much the weaker, utilised when it supports the above two considerations, but ineffective independently. Historic interest is a less quantifiable concept since every feature reflects the influence of historically unique factors. It involves a greater political selection in identifying features as particular reflections of past socio-economic circumstances. It requires greater effort in terms of research and access, as historical importance is not necessarily as evident as architectural interest. Furthermore, historic interest starts to stray into extrinsic interest, revealing a difficulty for conservation. The law requires planning issues to relate to land use; thus the extent to which broader, more intangible historiographic qualities can be accommodated and defended is severely limited.

This dilemma of planning law, limiting the interpretation of value, is most poignantly reflected in attempting to define the 'character' of a conservation area. The development of area-based concepts in practice has been inhibited by a number of factors. The first is the autonomy and lack of support given to local authorities to perform this task; the second the diversion of resources away from conservation in local planning authorities. A third reason is an attitude shown by many planning officers that character can be expressed simply in terms of building types. Assessing area-based value by the same principles by which individual components are assessed excludes a host of broader social, cultural and environment factors. Although urban design physically addresses the value of spaces between buildings, it still falls short of this broader realisation of value. Despite the availability of approaches to investigate character, such as urban morphological analysis or conservation plans, statutory planning appears ill equipped to develop these as fundamental guiding principles, yet they are still invoked in phrases like 'the sense of place' in both local and national planning policy.

Standards

The objectivity in evaluating buildings is a justification for the respect given to listing over conservation areas. The banner of national, as opposed to local, interest provides the conservation standard. However, it has been noted that 'national interest' is an abstraction created by the conservation profession. It has been difficult to recognise what actually makes a feature of national interest in the cases studied, aside from the obvious examples of grander or more ornate architecture. This has several detrimental consequences, the first being the listing stereotype.

Most people outside the conservation profession expect a listed building to be an impressive or significant piece of architecture, either in scale or in ornamentation. The visual quality of a feature is paramount: if a listed feature does not fit the stereotype, then ensuing cynicism undermines its credibility. This is particularly grave for modern listed buildings, or for buildings of specific socio-historical interest. A preconceived notion of a building of 'interest' also undermines credence in conservation areas as they encompass a wide range of buildings which will not necessarily fit this stereotype. Seeing the value of a conservation area in terms of buildings alone thus undermines the area-based concept and does not reflect the endemic conservation thinking which many respondents at EH were eager to encourage among the wider population.

Second, the importance of 'national' interest also appears to subjugate local interest, to the extent that the latter has become relegated to the status of, and pejoratively referred to, as a subjective valuation. However, national interest is only a professional tool which, when examined, is a subjective creation of this group. Only in relation to twentieth-century schematic listing can a national standard be realistically identified; the majority of listed buildings are not monitored nationally, nor do national funding opportunities ensure their upkeep. National interest appears to rely on the discretion of individuals to determine importance in the light of particular local circumstances. Indeed, it may even be more accurate to suggest that features' importance is determined by reference to regional, rather than national, interest. It was suggested in the fieldwork that local conservation interest is more tightly interwoven with historical interest in the development of a town, whereas national conservation interest is more concerned with architecture. If true, this is a further reason why local interest has struggled for recognition since the revelation of historical interest has been the poorer cousin of architectural interest.

Third, local interest remains dogged by the problem of being taken for granted. Whereas the phrase 'familiar and cherished local scene' may portray attraction and affection, it would appear that familiarity is widely undervalued because of its common occurrence. In the cases studied, only a threat to or an external identification of this quality raised awareness to a level whereby local interest became a sufficiently cogent force to be considered. It would suggest that national organisations ought to become more proactive in creating a framework to raise awareness, engagement and development of local qualities.

Informed opinion

The contrast of professional with lay interpretations of value has been a significant theme. It requires specific attention here as it involves further distinctions between conservation and planning professionals, and differences within the conservation profession too.

A 'professional' can be defined as a person possessing exclusive knowledge and skills relating to an identifiable area, participating in a culture and socialisation within a group of similar individuals. For conservation, the evidence would suggest that a shared rigour and consensus distinguish the professional's interpretation of value from the lay person's. In the absence of suitable hard-and-fast rules on which to apply conservation knowledge, an essential quality was the sensitivity of the professional craft or 'eye', a judgement born of years of expertise. It is the rigour and strength of this 'rolling consensus' which underpins the interpretation of 'national' interest and defines 'special architectural or historic interest'. 'Legitimate' values are interpreted by a group of individuals who through a common background and training share certain attitudes to recognise particular types of value. However, the study highlighted a significant diversity of interpretation not only between the two conservation officers in the two local authorities, but also within the scope of interpretation from EH officers. While the contrasts did not outweigh the consensus of professional interpretation, they were significant enough to question it. This is notable since professionals use their consensus of objectivity to defend their legitimacy over a lay interpretation of value which they consider too subjective and diverse to recognise.

In terms of informing, consulting and educating the public, a further contrast is raised in professional attitudes. The profession requires, and believes there is, widespread support for conservation, which justifies applying its expertise on behalf of the public. There are campaigns specifically to raise public awareness of conservation and there is ample opportunity to become involved 'at the coalface' through participation in the planning system. A particular section of the public sharing the professionals' framework for assessing value will avail itself of these means. However, a greater section of the public are excluded, partly through their own apathy towards being involved in local governance, but more fundamentally because their perception of value is incompatible with the professional determination of legitimate conservation value. This focus on intrinsic interest excludes many factors from consideration which the cases illustrated to be central in lay interpretations of value.

As the study did not attempt to canvass public opinion comprehensively, this evidence is only indicative, but it would suggest that conservation is perceived in far broader terms than the building-specific orientation of professional practice. In one sense, lay perception sees the environment as a whole; appearance and views are just as important as, if not more important than, the specific details of buildings. The spaces between buildings, context, topography and uses of buildings are all aspects of character which are significant issues in lay opinion. Features' use or function is particularly important, as is demonstrated by the disregard for vacant buildings. Avoiding vacancy is crucial in maintaining public perceptions of buildings as being worth conserving. In many respects this is seeing conservation as a process supporting the continuity of an urban environment's uses and vitality. When viewed as a means to an end rather than an end in itself, conservation becomes more flexible in tolerating changes. However, this may create further professional difficulties, shifting the focus from a feature's intrinsic value to its potential use value.

To continue this point: a significant exclusion persists between professional and lay interpretations. Knowledge of a locality, experience of environmental changes, intimacy and intuitive reactions to familiar elements and activities which contribute to 'place' were professionally dismissed as sentimental, nostalgic or irrational emotions. Yet these are precisely the types of reactions identified by a host of writers as the basis for conservation's appeal. These interpretations suffer a dual exclusion in the mechanisms to encompass public interest in conservation. In campaigns by EH or other bodies, the process is generally a one-way transfer of information explaining intrinsic interest; there is less scope to accommodate the public's returning interpretations which lie beyond specific features' interest. Similarly, contributions made through the planning process suffer the legal limitation of statutory planning to physical features and their use; the present opportunities for exploring value remain limited.

Reconceptualising value

Heritage is a chimera of interpretations, attracting criticism and support in equal measure. The arguments concerning commodification, misrepresentation, tenuous authenticity and 'dumbing down' are well established. Despite its vagaries, heritage's re-orientation of value perceptions may benefit conservation in resolving a fundamental discrepancy between principle and practice. This was illustrated during the fieldwork when one conservation officer noted that the main reason for having conservation was helping people to place themselves in an environment relative to their existence in time and space. While other conservation professionals may not universally share this justification, this author finds it a most persuasive exposition. However, the officer then proceeded to criticise unsympathetic new window frames in buildings in the town centre. At the time, this appeared to reflect his zeal for detail, but in retrospect it illustrates the inappropriateness of narrow, building-oriented controls ultimately to pursue an aspiration founded in human cognition. Heritage re-orients interpretations of value by placing as much significance in the value experience of the user as in that vested in the inanimate object. This is not to say that one orientation is supreme, or that they can be easily identified as two distinct spheres of value. The philosophy of aesthetics continues to struggle with this question and is no nearer resolution as a result of this study. The significant point is that both aspects, intrinsic and extrinsic, are required to reflect the wider purposes of conservation planning.

From the evidence collected, the wider experience of users of the urban environment appears oriented to recognising continuity. Phrases such as 'the connection with history' and 'the patina of history' expose support for conservation in terms of identifying temporal relationships. As noted above, it is possible that historical interest may be a more cogent force in local conservation since the urban form reflects the unique development and identity of a settlement through time.

It is the author's personal view that the attraction and moral support for conservation is not wholly accounted for by a respect for aesthetics and craftsmanship. Conservation allows a virtual extension of an individual's lifetime by the creation of personal and societal connections with evidence of the past woven into the contemporary built environment. The maligned concept of 'authenticity', rather than reflecting the genuine aged material in a building, is arguably a more valuable concept in terms of representing continuity through time. A feature's attraction is in its connection with a longer timescale than people can physically experience, not particularly the fact that the physical entity remains in an 'authentic' state. If sections of it are replaced, this contributes to the process of evolution, rather than undermining its originality.

The preference for familiarity is not just a desire to see existing features retained. Indeed, threats to familiar scenes or appearances provoked a stronger public reaction than threats to specific familiar features, which were often taken for granted. Familiarity was a prevalent consideration over the introduction of new features in the environment. This may be natural conservatism but it illustrates the desire for continuity in the new. New development had to harmonise with the existing surroundings and historicist design was more acceptable to members of the public than to those professionals involved in the development and planning processes in the towns studied. While this reflects a desire for continuity, if misapplied it can lead to a pastiche 'national vernacular', specifically contradicting the point of conservation, which should be to address and enhance local distinctiveness.

While this may reflect different design preferences, it may also reveal the temporal aspects of design, of architecture being 'true to time' as opposed to necessarily just 'true to function'. Viewed in design terms, while buildings may be made to fit in by reflecting familiar elements in their construction, this can produce buildings which are less representative of their own time. To some extent this illustrates a regressive rather than progressive cultural attitude to time. However, it has been noted that the diversity of the temporal collage in the built environment, which represents a wealth of connections to different periods in time, is being consciously flattened by pursuing conservation policies concentrating on the aesthetic to the exclusion of the temporal. If one of the benefits of 'heritage' is the realisation that conservation value is created rather than discovered, then it demonstrates that the statutory framework for conservation is presently allowing little contribution to the debate.

Concluding remarks

In practice there appears to be a hierarchy of legitimacy in the interpretation of conservation value. The general pattern would appear to place greatest reliance on intrinsic, physical characteristics in aesthetic and artistic terms, followed by a feature's structural integrity and technical aspects of construction. These are perceived as self-evident values to the professionally trained eye. Historical factors, beyond supporting the above two aspects, constitute the lower rungs of the hierarchy, contributing far less to justify decision-making. Historical association tends to support the 'official' history associated with specific events and people, and although listing is consciously moving towards reflecting social and economic themes, these could well prove to be difficult to defend in the present system. Certainly the factors contributing to the 'unofficial' history of social and personal experience through time are barely explored at the local level, where their contributions may be most felt. Issues of attachment and identification with place, and people's orientation within an environment through the symbols and meaning carried by established features, are rarely cited in these local planning authorities' practice even though these ideas are used to justify national policy in PPG15. Perversely, perhaps the most neglected interpretation of value is in terms of temporal relations in the environment – the 'connection with history'. The hierarchy reflects the decreasing professional interest away from intrinsic to extrinsic interest, while a lay interpretation of value appears to invert this ordering of priorities. Indeed, the lower rungs of the hierarchy, while professionally neglected, may provide the areas in which public support for conservation is most deeply rooted.

However, the broadening of value interpretation sets an unresolvable conflict with the parameters of planning law. In accommodating broader social and cultural interpretations of value, the scope is being extended further away from the physical basis of land-use planning. The benefits that can be drawn from this process illustrate the wider social and economic contribution that conservation can make to develop an intelligible and enjoyable urban environment.

The influence of external pressures: threats or opportunities?

Much of the existing literature fails to address the effects of economic and political issues on conservation. This is partly the result of two inter-related suppositions: that conservation operates in an economic climate over which it has minimal influence, and that the profession's concern to protect buildings is far removed from being a political activity. Initially these statements appear incontrovertible, but the study highlights fundamental tensions which force a re-examination of these premises. Though presented as two separate sections throughout the study, the economic and political considerations can be surmised as one central consideration: that conservation involves the political balancing of priorities in the distribution and protection of finite resources. This is not simply a decision for politicians but occurs at all levels through conservation decision-making, penetrating even the 'objectivity' of allocating listing grades.

Economic regeneration

This agenda has caused significant tensions within the conservation profession. Some respondents were convinced that an emphasis on regeneration offered *carte blanche* to local authorities to accept inappropriate development. Others believed that without embracing this particular agenda, conservation would become politically irrelevant. Certainly national funding for conservation schemes is based on encouraging the regeneration of areas to a far greater extent than ever before. Conservation is now having to address a question often asked of planning: is the purpose of conservation to regulate or to facilitate land development? With planning increasingly having to operate in a framework of the public sector building partnerships with the private sector, conservation practice has arguably found it difficult to maintain a regulatory line, courting marginalisation in planning decision-making as a result.

In the local authorities studied, when conservation was perceived to regulate and restrict necessary economic development, it was often slapped down, eroding its future persuasiveness. Notably, though, considerations of economic viability often had a more subtle effect in determining planning applications. In the development cases studied, the conservation officers' interpretation of a feature's value was affected by what level of protection was realistic in the economic circumstances. Their appraisal of value was actually heavily influenced by the economics as well as the architecture of the building in question.

A further problem highlighted by the development cases is that measurement of economic against conservation benefits involves a balancing act heavily weighted in favour of economic interests. The economic benefits of development form harder-edged arguments, quantifiable in definite financial terms against which conservation often struggles to demonstrate its benefits in similar terms. This creates an inherent bias towards economic benefits over the wider social and community benefits which conservation may foster but which are difficult to present as quantifiable figures. This bias is not only prevalent in development control decisions; if the benefits of conservation are seen in particularly narrow terms, this has an effect at all levels through the authority, particularly illustrated by the allocation of resources within the council. Thus conservation faces a major challenge in promoting endemic conservation awareness in several respects:

penetrating the development process earlier, highlighting the 'added value' which a conservation approach generates, and ensuring that in political decision-making, conservation benefits are not seen as intangible in contrast with development schemes providing jobs and investment.

Political choices and transparency

Perhaps a central difficulty in exposing the added value of conservation is scrutinising the justifications and effects of conservation principles, policies and practice in a political forum. As noted above, this would necessarily involve conservation emerging from its neutral guise. The main reason for its apolitical persuasion has been the assumption of support across the political spectrum. However, the treatment of conservation and heritage issues by the current government questions whether the underlying political consensus supporting conservation is more accurately described as a passive interest in conservation or, more fatally, a reflection of apathy and it being 'taken for granted'. Thirty-five years ago, conservation enjoyed greater political prominence, the Civic Amenities Act was passed and the weight of popular opinion was reportedly stirring local authorities to implement conservation policies. The pressure to respond to the conservation imperative is arguably no longer felt in national or local politics. Despite relying on a 'latent' consensus, it is conceivable that unless conservation finds a new expression or contribution, it is in danger of finding that this lack of consensus tolerates its marginalisation by competing agendas. Urban regeneration has taken centre stage in terms of government interest, and the whole modernising planning agenda makes little reference to 'modernising conservation'. Perhaps this is simply an oxymoron.

The case studies show that this process has taken effect locally as well. Conservation in the metropolitan council studied in chapter 5, despite the council's having had a previous reputation for good practice, has been politically eclipsed by the drive to encourage regeneration. Although revitalising historic buildings has been pursued through the Implementation section, conservation's contribution to regeneration has been limited by a narrow political perception of conservation's benefits. In the borough (chapter 6), where conservation could be expected to number among local political priorities, external strategists considered the conservation approach a little outdated in contrast with the need for holistic and sustainable environmental management. This reflects Strange's (1996, 1997) work on policy issues in historic towns, which shows that a traditional conservation model has run its course. Similarly, conservation is not apparently benefiting from the introduction of new structures of public participation arising through LA21, though these initiatives may provide a way in which a two-way exchange of value could be encouraged. As political interest grows in these areas, without conscious redress conservation will be forced to the margins, concerned with little more than overseeing a minority of buildings' physical appearance.

Concluding remarks

Essentially, conservation must address the challenges faced by economic and political considerations outside the 'traditional' scope of conservation activity. In responding to these threats or opportunities, the balancing of priorities ought to be informed by as instructive an assessment as possible of the wider benefits which conservation can provide. Only naïve optimism would obviate the need for conservation controls in the face of development pressures. Conservation should not and cannot express its value solely by financial criteria. Rather it must present the benefits of conservation in measurable socio-economic terms to prove more persuasive in political decision-making. This may also involve greater political transparency, realising the undesirable side effects of conservation as well as the positive ones. It is over-simplistic to cast conservation and economic arguments as opposites. The more useful approach is to demonstrate how the outputs of conservation add their own economic value. The time may be ripe for the agencies of conservation to perform this makeover as the current (Blair) government is actively interested in addressing and improving people's 'quality of life'. It is to be hoped that this emphasis recaptures the political support which conservation previously enjoyed.

Summary and implications for research and practice

Conservation has enjoyed remarkable success within the planning system, to the extent that there has been a shift in attitudes, illustrated by the practice of developing rather than demolishing a listed building. Conservation has continued to expand its spatial coverage, with more buildings and areas being subject to controls, but latterly the processes have been criticised, particularly in relation to area-based protection. Given such a broad remit, it is difficult to conclude with recommendations devised to evaluate a particular policy brief. The study raises a number of observations which, in relating back to the original research issues, pose a further set of questions for research and practice in this field.

How does conservation relate to planning in principle and practice?

• Conservation has a genuine moral weight, recognised by all parties. However, in practice the emphasis on a separate conservation mind-set and consent system does not in itself highlight the special quality of conservation. The resultant separateness can be counterproductive, characterising conservation as an exclusive design consideration and not necessarily central to planning's aims.

- Planning officers are being given more responsibility to determine minor changes to listed buildings and developments in conservation areas despite questions over their design competence in this field. These minor changes cumulatively pose the greatest threat to character (as defined by planning policy) but conservation professionals do not necessarily deal with them.

- This questions the current status of the conservation officer, whose personal priorities and opinions are highly influential in the authority's implementation of PPG15. The scale of the task facing those who carry out this role could be made explicit in the creation of a clearer strategic brief for conservation professionals; certainly a proactive and quasi-evangelical role to boost wider support and understanding for environmental conservation is essential for longer-term success.

- A single planning permission has been suggested as a way of achieving greater integration. Given some local planning authorities' current working practices, perhaps integrating a conservation officer into the development control section would ensure a parity of status and continual involvement in a wider range of cases, thereby easing objections to this potential simplification in procedures.

- Through resource constraints and a consequent lack of policy/strategic development, these local authorities' conservation practices can create and reinforce a perception of conservation as concentrating on the specifics of listed building consents rather than having the scope to focus on area-based protection.

- It would appear that concepts supporting definitions of area-based value are under-developed, locally and also nationally. The way conservation operates and is implemented within the planning system creates inherent barriers to realising that this is so. While many conservation professionals consider that conservation involves much more than urban design, this discipline has much to offer to tie in conservation to wider planning strategies.

- As the lead body, EH could concentrate attention in this area, perhaps shifting the emphasis for its advisers to assisting local authorities to evaluate character at strategic and policy levels. Though statutory planning limits a 'material consideration', this ought not to restrict local authorities' use of the variety of available sources outside planning to develop area-based conceptions of value.

How is value in the built environment perceived and interpreted for conservation purposes?

- Though value is recognised in PPG15, there is a distinct hierarchy in its interpretation. Physical, tangible evidence is the paramount value, second is associational historic value and third are more open cultural and environmental perceptions which are notably undervalued despite their being used to justify policy statements.

- This hierarchy reflects the profession's paramount concern with intrinsic architectural value – it is considered a self-evident justification. The perceived legitimacy of conservation value decreases through the lower levels of this hierarchy in contrast to a corresponding increase in the value attached to the lower levels from the layperson's viewpoint. The public's broader scale of appreciation is not necessarily well represented by the professional interpretation and contribution to planning decisions.

- In line with other recent research recommendations, exploring and understanding the non-professional interpretation of value in the built environment is imperative. There is a distinct lack of evidence currently to guide the development of practice to appreciate this sphere.

- Similarly, the symbolism and cultural significance of features in the built environment may not necessarily relate to architectural quality. These sentiments can be more emotive yet remain largely under-represented in conservation not only through professional architectural preferences but also through a lack of recognition in empirical studies. Research to bridge perceptions of conservation and environmental and cultural qualities is of equal importance to architectural research into specific buildings.

- There is a distinct lay preference to blend in new development, creating 'national vernacular' architecture. This is a relevant issue for modern architecture as well as conservation since many people still see the two as being in opposition. This 'national vernacular' architecture is flattening the essential temporal collage of the urban environment. Relationships of time and space are as important as architectural detailing, though these are restricted by planning's limits.

- Contrast in the built environment is as important as harmony. However, a misplaced understanding or even a fear of new design among officers and elected members can lead to the inadvertent creation of a homogeneous environment. Better design training is essential, but also consideration ought to be given to respecting the temporal dimension of the built environment in managing place identity as well as the purely aesthetic.

- Issues of locality, place and the historical or temporal aspects of conservation may be more strongly felt at a local level but these lie towards the bottom of the value hierarchy. However, these value interpretations are closely associated with area-based protection, which itself is very weak in the UK.

- Local authorities have the autonomy but neither the resources nor the perceived creative will to explore and raise the profile of these lower rungs of the hierarchy. Heritage interpretation and extrinsic value are issues which conservation cannot wholly disregard, despite the constraints of planning law.

- There is still professional confusion over the public's contribution to conservation, and it hampers the extension of the scope of value interpretation beyond a one-way process of legitimation. However, many standards relating to intrinsic interest have been revealed as less defensible and objective than assumed. In this case, surely extrinsic interest cannot continue to be excluded on the grounds of its subjectivity and difficulty of quantification.

- Conservation requires a two-way exchange of information about value interpretation to gain the acceptance and support of local communities. The imposition of abstract valuations may not always be suitable; the recognitions of values outside orthodox professional interpretations ought to be used as a basis for ensuring that conservation action, rather than considering these wider interpretations, can dismiss them for their unorthodox perspective. Local Agenda 21 participation initiatives may provide a means to access the lay interpretations and provide a lead for more community-led character appraisals.

How do economic and political pressures contribute to or undermine conservation?

- Conservation has slipped down the political agenda at national and local levels, possibly on the assumption that it has accomplished its task by successfully deflecting the significant threats to the urban fabric. Pigeonholing it as an exclusive control for a minority of exclusive buildings has obscured its wider contribution to, and allowed its displacement by, the regeneration and sustainability agendas.

- One obstacle has been the measurement of conservation's wider socioeconomic benefits to the community in comparison with tangible economic benefits of permitting land development. While some research has addressed this concern, further work is required to provide a substantive framework for practical application.

- A further problem has been a professional reluctance to address the political nature of conservation activity. Making explicit political choices about resource allocation is necessary to highlight its benefits, though it also reveals losers as well as winners.

- It is necessary to build on the gravity of the moral responsibility towards conservation, encouraging more endemic conservation thinking and thereby reducing the need to coerce and enforce controls. The conservation profession faces a choice in response to this slippage in priorities. Either it must consolidate its success and recognise the limits of current practice by concentrating on the technical control of physical fabric for its didactic value, or alternatively, it must orient conservation to providing a means, a framework, in which the diversity of interpretations of cultural value can reinforce the wider economic and social benefits of conservation, potentially to reinvigorate conservation's flagging political profile.

Conclusion

The issues raised in the study recall a poignant observation by an interviewee at English Heritage. He distinguished between 'conservation in the small sense' – protecting historic buildings through specific consent procedures and technical knowledge – and 'conservation in the large sense' – forming a set of philosophical drivers which ought to underpin 'all of what local planning authorities and central government are doing'. Although the former was taken care of by an accomplished system, the latter still fell significantly short of realising this aspiration. That these conclusions should echo his remarks is perhaps unremarkable. The revealing aspect of the study is that the practical application of 'conservation in the small sense' in local planning authorities may actually inhibit the promotion and wider application of 'conservation in the large sense' as a principal goal.

The separate consent systems, the general preoccupation with buildings rather than area-based conservation and the particular focus on intrinsic interest provide a strong regime for those features falling within this orientation. The strength of these factors reinforces 'the small sense' as definitive of conservation, inhibiting and excluding the wider interpretations and contribution of conservation. This is unfortunate, given that conservation no longer occupies the political limelight it previously enjoyed, either nationally or locally. Conservation has much to contribute to urban renaissance: creating sustainable cities, making liveable and intelligible urban forms based on scales which relate to human cognition and perception. Where conservation is treated as a traditional form of exclusive design control, it is difficult to promote and re-unite the relationship and contribution of progressive conservation to emerging political agendas.

There is a case to answer that conservation ought to remain firm in its principles and approach, rapidly changing political fashions with caution. There is no certainty that these agendas will enjoy continuity in government policy or indeed that the ideas and aspirations driving them are sound and guarantee success. But the degree to which conservation has been politically eclipsed by them, despite its general moral support, is surely the most persuasive argument for re-examining the fundamental issues highlighted. Virtually all national respondents considered that PPG15 represented a high-water mark in conservation policy, yet conservation is losing ground in its relationship with planning and politics. If indeed there is a process of marginalisation, then revising the system becomes vital.

While inevitably there will always be a place for protecting the integrity of masterpieces of British architecture, the fundamental concern is to emancipate conservation from being perceived as just 'conservation in the small sense'. Its wider application and appeal need restating in terms which connect with broader public and political appreciation of its contribution. To this end, the scope of value interpretation could be broadened, opening a less exclusive framework to develop environmental and extrinsic values, thus allowing a more positive identification of the range of conservation effects benefiting the community.

A revision of such breadth can progress only if those involved in conservation embrace these tenets and there is sufficient political will to surmount the structural inertia to commence the process. Unfortunately, the political will is likely to be generated only by one of two means: the demonstration *a priori* of conservation's wider benefits (which may be realised only at the end of a review process); or an external threat. However, the opportunity to broaden conservation is perceived as the prime threat by many sectors of the profession; the regeneration and sustainability agendas are viewed with some cynicism as encroaching on the purity of the conservation mantel.

Conservation planning faces a choice; not a new decision, but one which has been avoided for far too long. Either it must consolidate conservation as the management of the country's buildings, or, in pursuing conservation as environmental and cultural management, it must realise that the concepts of the former approach require dramatic revision to address these aspirations. Re-examining the relationship with planning and value interpretation may mean losing aspects of exclusivity and 'separateness' in practice but the benefits of exploring such avenues are significant if the goal of 'conservation in the large sense' is ever to be achieved.

Postscript

It is somewhat ironic, although strangely appropriate, that at the time of this book's publication, a period of relative stability in the world of conservation appears to be ending. The culmination of several issues has recently given cause to believe that the landscape of conservation policy could be changing significantly. They have occurred relatively quickly, certainly during the process of producing this book, and now present the potential for a significant revision of existing standards and practices.

The first is the major revision to the planning system through the Planning and Compulsory Purchase Bill. Though introduced in to the House in November 2002, the Bill continues to wind its way through Parliament and so the introduction of local development frameworks is tangible but not yet enshrined in law.

Accompanying the Bill is the Government's desire to revise Planning Policy Guidance notes into more streamlined Planning Policy Statements (PPS) accompanied by more illustrative practice guidance. The Government's response to the consultation following the Green Paper noted that PPG15 and PPG16 were amongst the first Guidance Notes earmarked for early revision under the new system.

In anticipation of the introduction of PPS, those revisions are underway with the added interest of potentially combining the current PPG15 and PPG16 into one coherent policy statement reflecting the breadth of the historic environment, above and below ground. How far these documents will change the orientation of heritage protection is debatable but it is an unprecedented move.

The combination of these revised statements is all the more prescient given the publication in July 2003 of a DCMS consultation document, *Protecting our historic environment: Making the system work better*. A relatively short document, it comprises a series of proposals to overhaul the complexity of the current plethora of conservation regimes.

Despite flowing from statements in *A Force for Our Future* to undertake this review, it is not easy to point to any recent political moment or imperative which has catalysed this change. One can throw conjecture and caution to the wind and attribute it to the arrival of Simon Thurley at the helm of English Heritage, or perhaps it is merely to keep DCMS occupied, but there is no denying that this review does represent a significant opportunity for changing the whole system. The suggestions for change may be too radical for some and in no way far reaching enough for others, but it is clear that there is an appetite for a fresh look at conservation mechanisms.

Perhaps the most significant proposal is the creation of a single conservation consent which would replace the former regimes relating to scheduled ancient monuments, listed buildings and also some conservation areas. While a unified national inventory would simplify matters, the difficult relationship between national, regional and local interest is somewhat overlooked. Conservation areas, except those of truly national status, would appear under a local section of the list as could, over time, the majority of Grade II listed buildings. The move towards a more holistic approach to identifying and protecting the heritage must be welcomed, though first there must be a revision of what is actually of national interest, which will involve many tough choices. The proposed statement of significance for a feature on the list and possibly identifying any tolerable changes to a listed feature at the point of listing may assist this. However, the latter in particular may be seen to unduly fetter the discretion of conservation officers over the longer term as values are reappraised.

If greater responsibility is to be encouraged at the local or even regional level, clearly there are resource issues to be addressed as well. The capacity of local authorities is stretched and with the best will in the world, even those authorities who care passionately about their historic assets will find additional strains on staff time, budgets and conservation skills. A common theme throughout this study has been the rhetoric of local control and appreciation of the historic environment but, if it is to succeed, then the necessary framework and resources must be there in support.

Encouraging greater ownership and control over conservation assets at the local level is a very positive move, but this cannot be imposed from above mechanistically. There must be the culture and competency at the local level to ensure this is undertaken effectively. It has been seen that, despite the best intentions, this may be difficult to achieve. For instance, one proposal in the paper to promote greater local involvement in the appraisal of conservation areas is, in effect, acknowledging the deficiencies of the present system to not engage with local value and broad public sentiment. The introduction of conservation areas in 1967 was intended to do this but, patently, it fell short of this aspiration.

It is noteworthy that while there is a great deal about revising the internal mechanics of conservation, there is some brief discussion regarding the relationship with the revised planning framework, no discussion of the strength of a single conservation consent, and little consideration of the long-term status of the local section of the list (which would cover the majority of heritage assets in the UK) in planning deliberations. These are key issues which no doubt will emerge from the consultation process following this document.

But ultimately it ought to be asked whether these revisions address the core of the dilemma facing conservation? Processes may be streamlined, procedures simplified and made more accountable, but there remains one fundamental that perhaps the tenor of these proposals does not address explicitly: how will conservation contribute to, and be seen to contribute to, the wider social, economic and environmental imperatives of urban renaissance? This question has persisted throughout this study; it will continue to exercise conservation policy makers and, until it is resolved, conservation will remain the poor cousin amongst built environment disciplines.

References

Aldous, T. (1975) *Goodbye Britain?*, London: Sidgwick and Jackson.

Aldous, T. (1997) 'Call to simplify planning and listed controls', *Architects' Journal*, 206 (1) (24 July): 16.

Allison, G. *et al.* (1996) *The Value of Conservation*, London: Department of National Heritage, English Heritage, Royal Institute of Chartered Surveyors.

Allmendinger, P. and Thomas, H. (eds) (1998) *Urban Planning and the British New Right*, London: Routledge.

Amery, C. and Cruickshank, D. (1975) *The Rape of Britain*, London: Paul Elek.

Andreae, S. (1996) 'From comprehensive development to conservation areas', in Hunter, M. (ed.) *Preserving the Past: The Rise of Heritage in Modern Britain*, Stroud: Allan Sutton Publishing.

Antram, N. (1999) 'Heritage Economic Regeneration Scheme (HERS)', *Context*, 61 (March): 35.

Ascherson, N. (1987) 'Why heritage is right-wing', *Observer*, 8 November.

Ashworth, G. J. (1991) *Heritage Planning*, Groningen: Geo Pers.

Ashworth, G. J. (1994) 'From history to heritage – from heritage to identity', in Ashworth, G. J. and Larkham, P. J. (eds) *Building a New Heritage*, London: Routledge.

Ashworth, G. J. (1997) 'Conservation as preservation or as heritage: two paradigms and two answers', *Built Environment*, 23 (2): 92–102.

Ayers, J. (1977) 'The historical and architectural criteria' in *A Future for Old Buildings? Listed Buildings: The Law and the Practice*, Journal of Planning and Environmental Law Occasional Papers, p. 53–65.

Baker, D. and Chitty, G. (2002) 'Heritage under pressure', unpublished report commissioned by English Heritage.

Barrett, H. (1993) 'Investigating townscape change and management in urban conservation areas', *Town Planning Review*, 64 (4): 435–456.

Bateson, K. (1998) 'Report attacks urban policies', *Building Design*, 20 November: 2.

Bateson, K. (1999) 'Anger at lack of EH architect', *Building Design*, 26 March: 5.

Beazley, E. (1981) 'Popularity: its benefits and risks', in Binney, M. and Lowenthal, D. (eds) *Our Past before Us*, London: Temple Smith.

Bevan, R. (1996) 'Papers mock post-war list', *Building Design*, 6 September: cover and p. 5.

Binney, M. (1981) 'Oppression to obsession', in Binney, M. and Lowenthal, D. (eds) *Our Past Before Us*, London: Temple Smith.

Binney, M. (1998) 'Plenty of room to park in town?', *The Times*, 25 November.

Boland, P. (1999) 'The role of local lists', *Context*, 61 March: 26–28.

References

Bold, J. and Guillery, P. (1998) 'Historical assessment of suburbs', *Urban Design Quarterly*, 66 (April): 24–27.

Boyer, C. M. (1994) *The City of Collective Memory*, Cambridge, Mass.: MIT Press.

Brainsby, M. and Carter, H. (1997), 'Shimizu: Part II – The implications for conservation area controls', *Journal of Planning and Environmental Law*, July: 603–610.

Brindley, T., Rydin, Y. and Stoker, G. (1996) *Remaking Planning: The Politics of Urban Change*, London: Routledge.

British Council of Shopping Centres (2001) *Briefing Guide for Shopping Centre Development*, London: BCSC.

Brolin, B. (1980) *Architecture in Context*, New York: Van Nostrand Reinhold.

Buchanan, C. & Partners (1968) *Bath: A Study in Conservation*, London: HMSO.

Built Environment (1975) 'Conservation for whom?', *Built Environment*, 13: 3.

Burrows, G. S. (1968) *Chichester: A Study in Conservation*, London: HMSO.

Cantell, T. (1975) 'Why conserve?', *The Planner*, 61 (7): 6–10.

Central Office of Information (1993) *Conservation (Aspects of Britain)*, London: HMSO.

Charles, Prince of Wales (1989) *A Vision of Britain: A Personal View of Architecture*, London: Doubleday.

Cherry, G. (1975) 'The conservation movement', *The Planner*, 61 (7): 3.

Cherry, M. (1995) 'How to protect our industrial heritage', *Conservation Bulletin*, July: 3.

Cherry, M. (1996) 'Taking the mystery out of listing', *Conservation Bulletin*, March: 9.

Chitty, G. (1998) 'John Ruskin and the historic environment', *Urban Design Quarterly*, 66 (April): 30–33.

Clark, K. (1998) 'Conservation plans: a guide for the perplexed', *Context*, 57 (March): 7–10.

Clark, R. (1999) 'When the planning police go too far', *Daily Telegraph*, 20 February.

Cocks, R. (1998) 'The mysterious origins of the law for conservation', *Journal of Planning and Environmental Law*, March: 203–209.

Commission for Architecture and the Built Environment (2000) *The Value of Design*, London: CABE.

Construction Industry Council (2002) *Design Quality Indicators*, London: CIC.

Corner, J. and Harvey, S. (eds) (1991) *Enterprise and Heritage*, London: Routledge.

Corval, A. (1995) 'When original is far from a sin', *Daily Telegraph*, 28 October.

Council for British Archaeology (1966) *Historic Towns and the Planning Process*, London: CBA.

Cullen, G. (1971) *The Concise Townscape*, London: Butterworth.

Cullingworth, J. B. and Nadin, V. (1994) *Town and Country Planning in Britain*, London: Routledge.

Cunningham, A. (1998) *Modern Movement Heritage*, London: E. & F. N. Spon.

Datel, R. E. and Dingemans, D. J. (1984) 'Environmental perception, historic preservation and sense of place', in Saarinen, T., Seamen, D. and Sell, J. (eds) *Environmental Perception and Behaviour*, Department of Geography Research Paper 209, Chicago: University of Chicago.

Davis, F. (1979) *Yearning for Yesterday: A Sociology of Nostalgia*, New York: Macmillan/ Free Press.

Dean, J. (1992) 'Viewpoint – Conservation: a wider perspective', *Town Planning Review*, 63 (3): iii–iv.

Delafons, J. (1994) 'Planning & conservation 1909–1932', *Journal of Planning and Environmental Law*, 509–514.

Delafons, J. (1997a) *Politics and Preservation*, London: E. & F. N. Spon.

Delafons, J. (1997b) 'Sustainable conservation', *Built Environment*, 23 (2): 111–120.

Department of Culture, Media and Sport (2001) *The Historic Environment: A Force for Our Future*, London: DCMS.

Department of Culture, Media and Sport (2002) *EH Quinquennial Review – Stage 1 Report*, London: DCMS.

Department of the Environment (1972) *Town and Country Planning Act 1971*, Circular 52/72, London: HMSO.

Department of the Environment (1973) *Conservation and Preservation, Local Government Act 1972*, Circular 46/73, London: HMSO.

Department of the Environment (1974) *Town and Country Amenities Act 1974*, Circular 147/74, London: HMSO.

Department of the Environment (1987a) *Historic Buildings & Conservation Areas*, Circular 8/87, London: HMSO.

Department of the Environment (1987b) *Planning: General Policies and Principles*, PPG 1, London: HMSO.

Department of the Environment (1990) *Archaeology and Planning*, PPG16, London: HMSO.

Department of the Environment/Department of National Heritage (1994) *Planning and the Historic Environment*, Planning Policy Guidance Note 15, London: HMSO.

Department of the Environment, Transport and the Regions (1997) *General Policies and Principles*, Planning Policy Guidance Note 1, London: The Stationery Office.

Department of the Environment, Transport and the Regions (1998) *Modernising Planning: A Policy Statement by the Minister for the Regions, Regeneration and Planning*, London: DETR.

Department of the Environment, Transport and the Regions (1999) *Development Plans*, Planning Policy Guidance Note 12, London: The Stationery Office.

Department of the Environment, Transport and the Regions (2000a) *Housing*, Planning Policy Guidance Note 3, London: The Stationery Office.

Department of the Environment, Transport and the Regions (2000b) *'Our Towns and Cities: The Future. Delivering an Urban Renaissance*, London: DETR.

Department of the Environment, Transport and the Regions/Commission for Architecture and the Built Environment (2000) *By Design: Urban Design in the Planning System – Towards Better Practice*, London: DETR/CABE.

Department of the Environment, Transport and the Regions/Department of Culture, Media and Sport (1997) *Planning and the Historic Environment: Notification and Directions by the Secretary of State*, Circular 14/97, London: The Stationery Office.

Department of the Environment, Transport and the Regions/Department of Culture, Media and Sport (2001) *Arrangements for Handling Heritage Applications: Notification and Directions by the Secretary of State*, Circular 01/2001, London: The Stationery Office.

Department of Transport, Local Government and the Regions (2001) *Planning: Delivering a Fundamental Change*, Planning Green Paper, London: DTLR.

Department of Transport, Local Government and the Regions/Commission for Architecture and the Built Environment (2001) *Better Places to Live: A Companion Guide to PPG3*, London: DTLR/CABE.

References

Dobby, A. (1975) 'Conservation and planning', *The Planner*, 61 (7): 11.

Earl, J. (1997) *Building Conservation Philosophy*, Reading: College of Estate Management, University of Reading.

English Heritage (1992) *Managing England's Heritage: Setting Our Priorities for the 1990s*, London: English Heritage.

English Heritage (1993) *Conservation Issues in Strategic Plans*, London: English Heritage, the Countryside Commission and English Nature.

English Heritage (1995a) *Conservation Area Practice: Guidance Note*, London: English Heritage.

English Heritage (1995b) *Developing Guidelines for the Management of Listed Buildings*, London: English Heritage.

English Heritage (1996a) *Something Worth Keeping? Post-war Architecture in England*, London: English Heritage.

English Heritage (1996b) *Conservation Issues in Local Plans*, London: English Heritage, Countryside Commission and English Nature.

English Heritage (1997) *Sustaining the Historic Environment: New Perspectives on the Future*, London: English Heritage.

English Heritage (1998) *Conservation-Led Regeneration*, London: English Heritage.

English Heritage (1999) *The Heritage Dividend*, London: English Heritage.

English Heritage (2000) *Power of Place: The Future of the Historic Environment*, London: English Heritage.

English Heritage/Commission for Architecture and the Built Environment (2001) *Building in Context*, London: English Heritage/CABE.

English Historic Towns Forum (1992) *Townscape in Trouble: Conservation Areas – The Case for Change*, Bath: English Historic Towns Forum.

English Historic Towns Forum (1996) 'State of the heritage', unpublished internal survey of local authority members and report, Bristol: English Historic Towns Forum.

English Historic Towns Forum (1997) 'State of the heritage', unpublished internal survey of local authority members and report, Bristol: English Historic Towns Forum.

English Historic Towns Forum (1998) *Conservation Area Management: A Practical Guide*, Report 38, Bristol: English Historic Towns Forum.

English Partnerships/The Housing Corporation (2000) *The Urban Design Compendium*, London: English Partnerships.

English Tourist Council/English Heritage (2001) *The Heritage Monitor*, London: English Tourist Board.

Esher, L. B. (1968) *York: A Study in Conservation*, London: HMSO.

Eversley, D. (1975) 'Conservation for the minority', *Built Environment*, 3 January: 1.

Fairs, M. (1998) 'Three Richards attack needless conservation', *Building Design*, 1369 (16 October): 4.

Falk, P. (1988) 'The past to come', *Economy and Society*, 17: 2.

Fawcett, J. (1976) *Attitudes to Conservation, 1174–1974*, London: Thames and Hudson.

Fergusson, A. (1973) *The Sack of Bath: A Record and Indictment*, Salisbury: Compton Russell.

Foley, D. (1973) 'British town planning: one ideology or three?', in Faludi, A. (ed.) *A Reader in Planning Theory*, Oxford: Pergamon Press.

Fowler, P. J. (1981) 'Archaeology, the public and the sense of the past', in Binney, M. and Lowenthal, D. (eds) *Our Past before Us*, London: Temple Smith.

Fowler, P. J. (1992) *The Past in Contemporary Society: Then, Now*, London: Routledge.

Gamston, D. (1975) *The Designation of Conservation Areas*, York: Institute of Advanced Architectural Studies, University of York.

Garrod, G. D., Willis, K. G., Bjarnadottir, H, and Cockbain, P. (1996) 'The non-priced benefits of renovating historic buildings', *Cities*, 13 (6): 423–430.

Glass, R. (1973) 'The evaluation of planning: some sociological considerations', in Faludi, A. (ed.) *A Reader in Planning Theory*, Oxford: Pergamon Press.

Graves, P. and Ross, S. (1991) 'Conservation areas: a presumption to conserve?', *Estates Gazette*, 299 (9137): 108–110.

Griffith, R. (1989) 'Listed buildings and listed building control', *The Planner*, 75 (19): 16.

Grover, P., Thomas, M., and Smith, P. (2000) 'Local authority practice and PPG15: information and effectiveness', unpublished report commissioned by English Heritage, the Institute of Historic Building Conservation and the Association of Local Government Archaeological Officers.

Hall, P. (1988) *Cities of Tomorrow*, London: Routledge.

Hall, P. (1992) *Urban and Regional Planning*, London: Routledge.

Hanna, M. and Binney, M. (1983) *Preserve and Prosper*, London: SAVE Britain's Heritage.

Harding-Roots, S. (1997) 'Could this be next?', *Planning*, 28: February 24.

Hareven, T. and Langenbach, R. (1981) 'Living places, work places and historical identity', in Binney, M. and Lowenthal, D. (eds) *Our Past before Us*, London: Temple Smith.

Hayden, D. (1995) *The Power of Place: Urban Landscapes as Public History*, Cambridge, Mass.: MIT Press.

Heap (1975) details to follow

Hewison, R. (1987) *The Heritage Industry*, London: Methuen.

Hubbard, P. (1993) 'The value of conservation: a critical review of behavioural research', *Town Planning Review*, 64 (4): 359–373.

Hubbard, P. (1994) 'Professional vs lay tastes in design control: an empirical investigation', *Planning Practice and Research*, 9 (3): 271–287.

Hughes, D. J. (1995) 'Planning and conservation areas: where do we stand following PPG15, and whatever happened to Steinberg?', *Journal of Planning and Environmental Law*, 679–691.

Hunter, M. (1981) 'The preconditions of preservation: a historical perspective', in Binney, M. and Lowenthal, D. (eds) *Our Past Before Us*, London: Temple Smith.

Hunter, M. (1996) *The Preservation of the Past: The Rise of Heritage in Modern Britain*, Stroud: Alan Sutton Publishing.

Insall, D. W. and Associates (1968) *Chester: A Study in Conservation*, London: HMSO.

James, D. (1994) 'Every home needs its moat', *Independent*, 8 April.

Jencks, C. A. (1991) *The Language of Post-modern Architecture*, London: Academy Editions.

Jewkes, P. (1993) 'Protecting the historic environment', *Journal of Planning and Environmental Law*, 417–422.

Johnson, R. J. (1991) *A Question of Place*, Oxford: Blackwell.

Johnston, B. (1998) 'Holding the keys to the heritage chest', *Planning*, 29 May: 16.

Jones, A. N. and Larkham, P. J. (1993) *The Character of Conservation Areas*, London: RTPI.

References

Jones, M. (1993) 'The elusive reality of landscape: concepts and approaches in research', in Fladmark, J. M. (ed.) *Heritage: Conservation, Interpretation and Enterprise*, London: Donhead Publishing.

Journal of Planning and Environmental Law (1989) *'Making the most of our Heritage'* Journal of Planning and Environmental Law Occasional Papers No. 15, London: Sweet & Maxwell.

Kain, R. (ed.) (1981) *Planning and Conservation*, London: Mansell.

Kennet, W. (1972) *Preservation*, London: Temple Smith.

Kirk, G. (1980) *Urban Planning in a Capitalist Society*, London: Croom Helm.

Larkham, P. J. (1992) 'Conservation and the changing urban landscape', *Progress in Planning*, 37: 83–181.

Larkham, P. J. (1993) 'Conservation in action: evaluating policy and practice in the UK', *Town Planning Review*, 64 (4): 351–355.

Larkham, P. J. (1994) 'Conservation areas and plan-led planning: how far can we go?', *Journal of Planning and Environmental Law*, 9–12.

Larkham, P. J. (1996) *Conservation and the City*, London: Routledge.

Larkham, P. J. (2000) 'Residents' attitudes to conservation', *Journal of Architectural Conservation*, 6 (1): 73–89.

Larkham, P. J. and Barrett, H. (1998) 'Conservation of the built environment under the Conservatives', in Allmendinger, P. and Thomas, H. (eds) *Urban Planning and the British New Right*, London: Routledge.

Larkham, P. J. and Chapman, D. W. (1996) 'Article 4 directions and development control: planning myths, present uses and future possibilities', *Journal of Environmental Planning and Management*, 39 (1): 5–19.

Larkham, P. J. and Jones, A. (1993) 'Conservation and conservation areas in the UK: a growing problem', *Planning Practice and Research*, 8 (2): 19–29.

Latham, D. (1999) 'The concept of significance in the development of our historic cities, towns and villages', *Context*, 63 (September): 33–35.

Lewis, J. (1999) 'CABE role spelt out', *Building Design*, 1393 (30 April): 1.

Lichfield, N. (1988) *The Economics of Conservation*, Cambridge: Cambridge University Press.

Lichfield, N. (1997) 'Achieving the benefits of conservation', *Built Environment*, 23 (2): 103–110.

Lowenthal, D. (1981) 'Dilemmas of preservation', in Binney, M. and Lowenthal, D. (eds) *Our Past Before Us*, London: Temple Smith.

Lowenthal, D. (1985) *The Past Is a Foreign Country*, Cambridge: Cambridge University Press.

Lynch, K. (1972) *What Time Is This Place?*, Cambridge, Mass.: MIT Press.

McGuigan, J. (1996) *Culture and the Public Sphere*, London: Routledge.

Macinnes, L. (1993) 'Towards a common language: the unifying perceptions of an integrated approach', in Fladmark, J. M. (ed.) *Heritage: Conservation, Interpretation and Enterprise*, London: Donhead Publishing.

Macmillan, D. (1993) 'Not just an armchair at the fireside of history', in Fladmark, J. M. (ed.) *Heritage: Conservation, Interpretation and Enterprise*, London: Donhead Publishing.

Mageean, A. (1999) 'Assessing the impact of urban conservation policy and practice: the Chester experience 1955–96', *Planning Perspectives*, 14: 69–97.

Maguire, R. (1998) 'Conservation and divergent philosophies', *Journal of Architectural Conservation*, 3 (1): 7–18.

Marris, P. (1993) *Loss and Change*, London: Routledge.

Megarry, R. E. (1949) *Lectures on the Town and Country Planning Act 1947*, London: Stevens.

Mellis, H. (1998) 'Finding fault with the listing process', *Planning*, 29 May: 20.

Merriman, N. (1991) *Beyond the Glass Cage*, Leicester: Leicester University Press.

Miele, C. (1996) 'The first conservation militants: William Morris and the Society for the Protection of Ancient Buildings', in Hunter, M. (ed.) *Preserving the Past: The Rise of Heritage in Modern Britain*, Stroud: Allan Sutton Publishing.

Millichap, D. (1993) 'Sustainability: a long established concern of planning', *Journal of Planning and Environmental Law*, 1111–1119.

Ministry of Housing and Local Government (1967a) *Historic Towns: Preservation and Change*, London: HMSO.

Ministry of Housing and Local Government (1967b) *Civic Amenities Act 1967 – Parts I and II*, Circular 53/67, London: HMSO.

Ministry of Housing and Local Government (1968) *Town & Country Planning Act 1968 – Part V: Historic Buildings and Conservation*, Circular 61/68, London: HMSO.

Ministry of Town and Country Planning (1951) *Town and Country Planning 1943–1951: Progress Report*, London: HMSO.

Morris, C. (1981) 'Townscape images: a study in meaning', in Kain, R. (ed.) *Planning for Conservation*, London: Mansell.

Morton, D. (1991) 'Conservation areas: has saturation point been reached?', *The Planner*, 77 (17): 5–8.

Morton, D. (1997) 'What is making the grade?', *Planning*, 28 February: 18–19.

Morton, D. (1998) 'Good modern design in conservation areas', *Context*, 57 (March): 34–35.

Morton, D. M. and Ayers, J. H. (1993) 'Conservation areas in an era of plan led planning', *Journal of Planning and Environmental Law*, 211–213.

Mynors, C. (1984) 'Conservation areas: protecting the familiar and cherished local scene', *Journal of Planning and Environmental Law*, March: 144–157.

Mynors, C. (1995) *Listed Buildings and Conservation Areas*, London: FT Law and Tax.

Mynors, C. (1998) 'Do we need listed building consent?', *Journal of Planning and Environment & Law*, March: 101–115.

Nairn, I. (1955) *Outrage*, London: Architectural Press.

O'Rourke, T. (1987) 'Conservation, preservation and planning', *The Planner*, 73 (2): 13–19.

Orwell, G. (1989) *Nineteen Eighty-Four*, London: Penguin.

Owen, S. (1976) 'Change and conservation in settlements', *Planning Outlook*, 18: 35–41.

Page, J. (1990) 'The historic heritage', *Journal of Planning and Environmental Law* Occasional Papers 17: 52–65.

Pearce, P. *et al.* (1990) *The Conservation Areas of England*, London: English Heritage.

Pendlebury, J. and Townshend, T. (1999) 'The conservation of historic areas and public participation', *Journal of Architectural Conservation*, 5 (2) (July): 72–87.

Pickard, R. (1996) *Conservation in the Built Environment*, Harlow: Longman.

Planning (1998) 'Conservation: a special report', *Planning*, 29 May: 15.

Plumb, J. H. (1969) *The Death of the Past*, London: Macmillan.

References

Policy Studies Institute (1995) *Cultural Trends 1995: Cultural Trends in the 90s, Part 2*, Issue 26, London: PSI.

Powell, K. (1992) 'Have we all gone conservation crazy?', *Daily Telegraph*, 29 September.

Powell, K. (1999) *Architecture Reborn*, London: Lawrence King.

Prince, H. (1981) 'Revival, restoration, preservation: changing views about antique landscape features', in Binney, M. and Lowenthal, D. (eds) *Our Past Before Us*, London: Temple Smith.

Punter, J. V. (1986a) 'The contradictions of aesthetic control under Thatcherism', *Planning Practice and Research*, 1: 8–13.

Punter, J. V. (1986b) 'A history of aesthetic control: part 1', *Town Planning Review*, 57 (4): 351–381.

Punter, J. V. (1987) 'A history of aesthetic control: part 2', *Town Planning Review*, 58 (1): 29–62.

Punter, J. V. (1994) 'Aesthetics in planning', in Thomas, H. (ed.) *Values in Planning*, Aldershot: Avebury Press.

Punter, J. V. and Carmona, M. (1997) 'Design policies in local plans', *Town Planning Review*, 68 (2): 165–193.

Reade, E. (1987) *British Town and Country Planning*, Milton Keynes: Open University Press.

Reade, E. (1991) 'The little world of Upper Bangor', *Town and Country Planning*, 60 (12): 340–343.

Rees, P. (2002) Presentation to 'Property in the City', conference held at Merrill Lynch Financial Centre, London, May.

Relph, E. (1976) *Place and Placelessness*, London: Pion.

Relph, E. (1987) *The Modern Urban Landscape*, Baltimore: Johns Hopkins University Press.

Richards, H. (2000) 'Economic forces', *Guardian* Education, 6 June.

Rock, D. (1974) 'Conservation: a confusion of ideas', *Built Environment*, 3: 363–365.

Rogers, L. (1997) 'English Heritage seeks radical role change', *Building Design*, 22 August: 3.

Ross, M. (1995) *Planning and the Heritage*, London: E. & F. N. Spon.

Rowland, T. (1997) 'Property myths', *Daily Telegraph*, 21 May.

Royal Town Planning Institute (1990) 'Caring for the environment through conservation and change: an RTPI position statement', *The Planner*, 60 (40): 11.

Royal Town Planning Institute (1993) *Conservation in the Built Environment: A Discussion Paper*, London: RTPI.

Ruskin, J. (1865) *Sesame and Lilies*, new edition D. E. Nord (ed.), 'Of King's Treasures', (2002), Newhaven: Yale University Press

Saint, A. (1996) 'How listing happened', in Hunter, M. (ed.) *Preserving the Past: The Rise of Heritage in Modern Britain*, Stroud: Allan Sutton Publishing.

Samuel, R. (1994) *Theatres of Memory*, London: Verso.

Saunders, M. (1998) 'Dealing with a new definition of "demolition"', *Planning*, 29 May: 21.

SAVE Britain's Heritage (1979) *Preservation Pays*, London: SAVE Britain's Heritage.

SAVE Britain's Heritage (1998) *Catalytic Conversion*, London: SAVE Britain's Heritage.

Scanlon, K., Edge. A., Wilmott, T., *et al.* (1994) *The Economics of Listed Buildings*, Discussion Paper 43, Department of Land Economy, Cambridge: University of Cambridge.

Shankland, G. (1975) *The Conservation of Cities*, Paris: UNESCO.

Shelbourn, C. (1996) 'Protecting the "familiar and cherished local scene"', *Journal of Planning and Environmental Law*, 463–469.

Skea, R. (1996) 'The strengths and weaknesses of conservation areas', *Journal of Urban Design*, 1 (2): 215–228.

Smith, D. (1969) 'The Civic Amenities Act', *Town Planning Review*, 40: 149.

Smith, D. (1974) *Amenity and Urban Planning*, London: Crosby Lockwood Staples.

Smith, P. F. (1974) 'Familiarity breeds contentment', *The Planner*, 60: 901.

Society for the Protection of Ancient Buildings (1877) *Manifesto*, London: SPAB.

Stamp, G. (1996) 'The art of keeping one jump ahead: conservation societies in the twentieth century', in Hunter, M. (ed.) *Preserving the Past: The Rise of Heritage in Modern Britain*, Stroud: Allan Sutton Publishing.

Stones, A. (1998) 'Conservation: an inspiration', *Urban Design Quarterly*, 66 (April): 28–30.

Strange, I. (1996) 'Local politics, new agendas and strategies for change in English historic cities', *Cities*, 13 (6): 431–437.

Strange, I. (1997) 'Planning for change, conserving the past: towards sustainable development policy in historic cities?', *Cities*, 14 (6): 227–233.

Suddards, R. (1996) *Listed Buildings: The Law and Practice of Historic Buildings, Ancient Monuments, and Conservation Areas*, London: Sweet and Maxwell.

Suddards, R. and Morton, D. (1991) 'The character of conservation areas', *Journal of Planning and Environmental Law*, 1011–1013.

Tarn, J. N. (1985) 'Urban regeneration: the conservation dimension', *Town Planning Review*, 56 (2): 245–268.

Taylor, D. (1998) 'Battle to boost new design in conservation areas', *Architects' Journal*, 208 (October 29): 12.

Thomas, M. J. (1994) 'Values in the past', in Thomas, H. (ed.) *Values and Planning* Aldershot: Avebury Press.

Thornley, A. (1993) *Urban Planning Under Thatcherism: The Challenge of the Market*, London: Routledge.

Toffler, A. (1970) *Future Shock*, London: Bodley Head.

Townshend, T. and Pendlebury, J. (1999) 'Public participation in the conservation of historic areas: case-studies from north-east England', *Journal of Urban Design*, 4 (3): 313–331.

Tuan, Y.-F. (1974) *Topophilia*, Englewood Cliffs, NJ: Prentice-Hall.

Tuan, Y.-F. (1977) *Space and Place*, London: Edward Arnold.

Urban Design Skills Working Group (2001) *Final Report*, London: CABE.

Urban Green Spaces Task Force (2002) *Green Spaces, Better Places*, London: DTLR.

Urban Task Force (1999) *Towards an Urban Renaissance*, London: E. & F. N. Spon.

Urry, J. (1990) *The Tourist Gaze*, London: Sage.

Urry, J. (1995) *Consuming Places*, London: Routledge.

Venning, P. (1998) The government turning its back on the historic environment, *Context*, 61 (March): 7.

Weiner, M. J. (1981) *English Culture and the Decline of the Industrial Spirit, 1850–1980*, Cambridge: Cambridge University Press.

Whitehand, J. W. R. and Whitehand, S. M. (1984) 'The physical fabric of town centres: the agents of change', *Transactions of the Institute of British Geographers*, NS 9 (2): 231–247.

References

Whitfield, C. J. (1996) 'Conservation and planning in Chester and Shrewsbury, 1967–1990', unpublished PhD thesis, Department of Geography, Birmingham: University of Birmingham.

Worskett, R. (1969) *The Character of Towns*, London: Architectural Press.

Worskett, R. (1975) 'Conservation and public opinion', *The Planner*, 61 (7): 268–269.

Worskett, R. (1982) 'Conservation: the missing ethic', *Monumentum*, 25 (2): 129–154.

Worthington, J., Warren, J. and Taylor, S. (1998) *'Context: New Buildings in Historic Settings*, Oxford: Architectural Press.

Wright, P. (1985) *On Living in an Old Country*, London: Verso.

Zanchetti, S. M. and Jokilehto, J. (1997) 'Values and urban conservation planning: some reflections on principles and definitions', *Journal of Architectural Conservation*, 3 (1) (March): 37–51.

Index

acceptable change; defined by whom
206–7; extent 222–5; market town
184; mill town 162–3; national survey
91–2, 96–7
Adelphi, London *56*, *57*
amenity 29–33, 35
Ancient Monuments Acts 31, 60, 61
The Annexe 179, 194–200
antiquarianism 29–33
architectural interest 66, 99
area-based conservation 38–41, 62, 96
authenticity 13, 53, 73, 74, 259
Avebury Stone Circle *2*, *3*

The Bank 179, 186–94
built environment conservation 8–9, 109

CABE (Commission for Architecture and
the Built Environment) 19–20
case studies 125–37; criteria for
identification 126; respondents
interviewed 126–7; sampling strategy
127
central–local relations 116–17
change *see* acceptable change
The Character of Conservation Areas
(RTPI) 45
clearance policies 36–7
Commission for Architecture and the
Built Environment (CABE) 19–20
commodification 14, 49
commodity value 74
conformity 204
consent 45–6, 62, 87, 253–4, 267
conservation; area-based 38–41, 62, 96;
attitudes; market town 184–6, 190–4,
198–200, 202–4; mill town 141–4,
148–51, 155–60; centrality to
planning 85–6; contemporary issues

41, 44–6; criticisms 11; development
28–54; legitimacy, basis for 225–7;
problems 13–14; scale 250–2;
separateness of processes 86–7;
tensions 58
conservation areas 10–11, 12, 36–41,
148–9
conservation bodies 82
conservation officers 88, 174–5, 264
conservation planning 7; integration or
marginalisation 248–54; market town
204–7; mill town 160–3, 168; national
survey 84–9, 120
conservationism 63–4
context 14–17, 62, 254–60
continuity 184, 259
contrast 189–90, 210
controls 45–6, 61–3, 95–7, 220–2
Cossons, Neil, Sir 45
Covent Garden *124*, 125
cultural collage 72–4, 100–1, 107–9

Delivering an Urban Renaissance (White
Paper, DETR 2000b) 16–17
deregulation 42–3
design training 176–7
development control 19
development plans 18–19
dumbing down 108–9

economic pressures; impact on
conservation 74–5, 238–40, 266–7;
market town 186, 193–4, 210–11; mill
town 157–8, 166–7; national survey
112–14, 117–18
economic regeneration 261–2
English Heritage; conservation philosophy
85; creation in 1983 43; lead body
46–8; listed building consent 87;

morphology of urban areas 100;
national interest 102; policy 6, 76, 77,
86; *Power of Place* 21, 22–3;
Quinquennial Review (DCMS 2002)
23–4
establishment protection 29–30
Euston Arch, London *80*, 81
experience 70–2, 232–5
expert opinion vs lay opinion 70–2
extrinsic value 109

familiarity 68, 70, 191–3, 259
features value 66–8, 109–12, 227–30;
market town 203–4, 207–10
Firestone factory *170*, 171
A Force for Our Future (DCMS 2001) 21,
22–3
funding 47, 102, 173

The Gardens 179, 201–4
General Permitted Development Order
(GPDO) 86–7
General Policies and Principles (PPG1,
DETR 2000a) 18, 20
geographical priorities 89–91
Georgian Group 34, 57
government departments 84

heritage 48–53, 65, 107–9, 112
Heritage Lottery Fund 47, 83
heritage planning 165–6
heritage valuation 72–4, 210, 235–7
high-quality urban design 19–22
historic buildings 16–17
historic interest 66–7, 99, 109
historic towns 37–8
historical knowledge 72
holistic attitude 35, 61
Housing (PPG3, DETR 2000a) 18, 20

informed opinion 70–2, 256–8
integration 248–54
intrinsic value 74, 109, 254–5

knowledge 70–2, 165, 232–5

land-use controls 95–7
lay opinion vs expert opinion 70–2
listed buildings 10, 11–12, 159–60
listed status 110

listing 60, 61, 96, 98, 101, 171, 255;
introduction of 33–6
local authorities 24–5, 77, 84, 114
Local Development Frameworks 18
local interest 68, 69, 103, 149–50, 208–9
locality 164–5
The Lodge 136, 137–44

Maclagan Committee 34
marginalisation 248–54
market town 170–213; accountability
177–9; conservation practice 171–3;
conservation section 173–5; design
training 176–7; development and
control section 175–6; regulation
176–7
mill town 124–68; Conservation and
Design section 131–2; Development
and Control section 132–4; Heritage,
Environment and Implementation
section 130–1; policy 134–5; politics
134–5; public interest, perceptions of
136
minor works 253
minority interest vs popular interest 64–6
Modernising Planning (DETR 1998) 253
monumentalism, early schemes 30–1
Morris, William 29, 30
The Mount 136, 158–60

national amenity societies (NAS) 85–6,
88, 91, 93
national interest 68, 101–3, 110, 164–5,
208–9
national survey 81–122
National Trust 36
new design 184–6, 188–9
nostalgia 100

objectivity 99
organisational structures 76
organisations 82

partnership 43–8
place management 63
planning; and conservation controls 95–6;
early schemes 31–3; high-quality
design 21–4; modern system 33–6;
responsive 17–18; vs conservation
155–6

Planning Green Paper (DTLR 2001) 18, 253
Planning and the Historic Environment see Planning Policy Guidance Note 15
planning officers 88, 264
planning permission 17, 19, 114, 151, 264
Planning Policy Guidance Note 15 (PPG15) 8–9, 18–19, 60
policy 76, 83
political agendas; effect on conservation 75–7, 114–18, 241–4, 266–7; market town 186, 193–4, 211; mill town 143–4, 167; transparency 262–3
popular interest vs minority interest 64–6
postmodern design 145–6
Poultry *216*, 217
Power of Place (EH 2000) 21, 22–3
PPG1 (*General Policies and Principles* DETR 2000a)18 20
PPG3 (*Housing* DETR 2000a) 18, 20
PPG15 *see* Planning Policy Guidance Note 15 (PPG15)
practice 83, 171–3
preservationism 63–4, 91–2
private property rights 61
professional culture 13, 104–6, 111, 209–10
professional expertise 87–9, 165
professional relations 87–9
professionalism 249–50
project works 253
public interest 35–6, 162–3, 165
public paradigms 104–6
public participation 71
public support 93–5, 97–8

regeneration 85, 198, 200, 261–2
regulation 176–7
replication 189–90, 191–3, 210
research issues 77–8, 263–7
Ruskin, John 29, 30

St. Albans Cathedral *26*, 27
sentiment 100

shifting landscapes 5–7
shopping centres 20
significance, hierarchy 68–70, 230–2
significant works 253
spatial focus 61–3, 220–2
spatial priorities 89–91
'special architectural, historic or artistic interest' 32, 38–9, 40, 66, 109
special interest 68, 69, 98–101
The Square 136, 152–8
standards 255–6
statutory planning 59–61, 217–19
Stevens, Jocelyn, Sir 46
subjectivity 99
support 93–5, 97–8, 225–7, 252–3
sustainability 43–6

Tate Modern *246*, 247
temporal collage 73, 100, 259, 260
The Terrace 179, 180–6
Thatcherism 41–3, 50
tourism 70
Towards an Urban Renaissance (UTF) 15
Town and Country Planning Acts 32, 33, 34
Townscape in Trouble (EHTF) 12
traditional design 146–7
transparency 262–3

urban design 6, 19–24, 190
Urban Task Force 19
Urban White Paper (DETR 2000b) 16–17

value 25; architectural vs historic 99–100; context 254–60; extrinsic 109; features 109–12, 254–60; interpretation 265–6; intrinsic 74, 109, 254–5; market town 199, 207–10; mill town 163; national survey 120–1; perception 265–6; reconceptualising 258–60
visibility 156–7

The Yard 136, 144–51, 220